Shakespeare's Anonymous Editors

Shakespeare's Anonymous Editors

Scribe and Compositor
in the Folio Text of
2 Henry IV

Eleanor Prosser

STANFORD UNIVERSITY PRESS
Stanford, California 1981

Stanford University Press
Stanford, California

© 1981 by the Board of Trustees of the
Leland Stanford Junior University

Printed in the United States of America

ISBN 0-8047-1033-3
LC 78-66179

This book is dedicated to the memory of
CHARLTON HINMAN

Preface

This book is, in part, an experiment. As a study in analytical bibliography and textual criticism, it is necessarily addressed to the specialist. However, I have attempted to write it in such a way as to make my findings clear to the average Shakespeare scholar and also to convey the excitement of discovery that such work can hold, even for those of us who are novices in the mystery.

My reasons for this approach arose during my journey into a fascinating new field. Trained primarily in literary criticism and theater arts, I embarked on the current project only by chance. During a Shakespeare seminar several years ago, some students of acting and directing paused to ask, "How do you scan Shakespeare?" The immediate result was an ad hoc tutorial, during which we shortly found ourselves comparing different readings, different lineation, and different punctuation of modern editions. Turning to the quartos and the First Folio, we often found clues to interpretation that have been obliterated by subsequent editing. In the ensuing summer, I began working on a handbook of scansion for actors but again and again found myself faced with textual problems. Does Richard II say "I'll hammer it out" (Q1) or "I'll hammer't out" (F)? Does Cordelia stress "I," as the actress must, given Pope's lineation—

> You have begot me, bred me, lov'd me: I
> Return those duties back as are right fit

—or does she slur "I" into the first syllable of "return," as the lineation of Q1 and the Folio indicates?

> You have begot me, bred me, lov'd me:
> I return those duties back as are right fit.

Stimulated by early discoveries, I presented a proposal for a new edition of Shakespeare's plays at the annual convention of the Shakespeare Association of America in 1974 and, because of the encouraging response, decided to tackle the project myself. The first step was to devote a sabbatical year solely to learning my craft. And I learned, of course, that a year was not enough. In that time, I had done little more than to survey the basic bibliography, to grasp the technical vocabulary, and to understand why perfectly sane men and women have devoted their lives to distinguishing between compositors A and B or to studying the distribution of blank space in the First Folio. My apprenticeship had barely begun. I became acutely aware of my presumption in assuming that I could establish "new" and "authoritative" texts of the plays during a telephone conversation with Charlton Hinman. "Ah yes," he said, "I envy you. I recall my own excitement as I began editing the plays thirteen years ago. I should finish in another two years." At that point, I suffered an epiphany of sorts and decided to leave editing to the qualified.

During that apprentice year, however, my study of Hinman's monumental contributions had led to some chance discoveries that gave rise to the present inquiry. Moreover, I had become totally engrossed by the kind of research that, in my ignorance, I had always assumed could interest only the Dryasdusts of this world. It is these two facts that have led to the experimental approach of this book. My primary aim has been to encourage specialists to reexamine the texts of several of Shakespeare's plays in light of Hinman's discoveries about the methods of printing the First Folio. At the same time, one of my major interests has been to make Hinman's findings accessible to the Shakespearean who is primarily a literary critic, the type of scholar who, though largely untrained in matters of bibliography, is nonetheless responsible for many of today's editions. Unfortunately, most work by specialists is largely unintelligible to the average scholar without considerable background study. For this reason, I have defined terms for the non-specialist and—recalling my own diffi-

PREFACE ix

culties in assimilating such highly technical material—have provided background and added explanations where I felt they would be helpful.

My profound debt to the late Charlton Hinman will be apparent throughout the following pages, but my debt extends far beyond his published work. In 1975, heady with excitement at what I thought might be significant discoveries, I telephoned him. Having no idea of the severity of his illness at the time, I bombarded him for an hour with questions, and he gently responded with such patience and grace that I did not realize until later how totally naive my questions had been. Had he not given me such generous encouragement, this book would never have been written. Although I never met him, I feel a real sense of loss.

I am particularly grateful to Myra Hinman, not only for making available to me the unpublished results of further research completed by her and her husband, but also for her continuing interest and support.

To John F. Andrews and Trevor Howard-Hill I also owe a major debt. Both of them read the manuscript in early stages and provided the kind of extensive and exacting criticism that I urgently needed.

All photographs are reproduced by permission of the Folger Shakespeare Library, to whose director and staff I am most grateful, both for their unfailing helpfulness and for a grant-in-aid to help defray the costs of photocopying. I also wish to thank the office of the Dean of the Graduate Division of Stanford University for funds that helped to cover the costs of preparing the manuscript.

E.P.

Stanford University
August 1979

Contents

I The Textual Problem 1

II Reflections of Stage Practice in the Folio 19

III Textual Changes by the Folio Compositors 51

IV Textual Changes by the Scribe 122

V Conclusion 163

Appendixes

A: The Nature of the Copy
    Underlying Folio Additions 181

B: The Placement of Stage Directions
    in Elizabethan Manuscripts 187

C: Recommended Adoptions 191

Notes 195

Index 211

Shakespeare's Anonymous Editors

CHAPTER I

The Textual Problem

The present study arose from a question that at first seemed only marginally related to the major textual problem of *2 Henry IV*. As the result of a study of Shakespeare's metrics, I had become increasingly uneasy over the lineation of modern editions as well as their adoption of certain Folio variants that regularize meter. To determine the authority of these variants, I undertook a close comparison of the "good quarto" plays and their Folio counterparts. Beginning with *Richard II*, I discovered considerable evidence of editing in the Folio to eliminate metrical "irregularities" and I worked through the remaining good quartos asking one limited question: is there substantial evidence in the Folio that someone consciously set out to make Shakespeare's verse conform to strict rules of prosody?

When I turned to *2 Henry IV*, it was immediately apparent that the Folio text presented a unique problem. Comparing the Quarto edition of 1600 with the Folio version of 1623, I first noted the many Folio changes that scholars have long recognized—including the addition of eight major passages, the radical revision of stage directions, several apparently valid corrections of readings, and many suspect sophistications. Few of these changes had any bearing on my original question about prosody, but the textual problem became progressively intriguing as my work progressed and I shortly gave it my full attention.

In the course of listing all the Folio additions over and above the eight major passages that require a source independent from the Quarto, I gradually became aware of a group of ten partial lines. Most of the words and brief phrases added throughout the text can be explained as the particular type of literary sophistication found only in the Folio text of *2 Henry IV*. This group of partial lines was different. Six were of particular interest: in each case the addition completed what might be considered an irregular short line in the Quarto. In the following six quotations from the Folio, the additions are italicized.[1]

> To speake a truth. If he be slaine, *say so*. . . .
> (1.1.96)
> Meet for Rebellion, *and such Acts as yours*.
> (4.2.117)
> And how accompanyed? *Canst thou tell that?*
> (4.4.52)
> So thinne, that Life lookes through, *and will breake out*.
> (4.4.120)
> Into some other Chamber: *softly pray*.
> (4.4.132)
> What would your Maiestie? *how fares your Grace?*
> (4.5.49)

Were these authoritative additions that reflect, as has been assumed, the Folio's reference to an independent manuscript superseding the one underlying the Quarto, or did they arise from an editor's attempt to regularize meter? Given the nature of the additions, the latter possibility seemed worth considering. On the other hand, three more additions, equally suspicious for reasons to be noted, either added an irregular short line—

> O my Sonne!
> (4.5.177)
> My gracious Liege. . . .
> (4.5.220)

—or dislocated the meter of a passage that is regular in the Quarto (4.5.74–76):

> Q: When like the bee toling from euery flower,
> Our thigh, packt with waxe our mouthes with hony. . . .

F: When, like the Bee, culling from euery flower
   The vertuous Sweetes, our Thighes packt with Wax,
   Our Mouthes with Honey....

(Not only did this Folio addition create a faulty line, it required realigning the four subsequent lines so that the fourth is another irregular short line. Editors normally follow the Quarto lineation, making a short line of "The vertuous Sweetes.") One addition at the end of a prose line had nothing to do with metrics. For the Quarto's

No more of that master Shallow.

the Folio substitutes

No more of that good Master *Shallow:* No more of that. (3.2.196–97)

Considered as a group, the ten additions puzzled me. They range from flat repetition to pedestrian amplification. All are unnecessary dramatically and several even destroy the dramatic impact of the Quarto lines. Only one, the last quoted, has a distinctly Shakespearean ring. All ten, however, have been universally adopted.

Why have these additions been so readily accepted as authoritative? First, the consensus of editors is that the Folio text in part derives from a manuscript of authority superior to that of the Quarto. Since the eight major additions in the Folio must be authoritative, editors have understandably assumed that all the other Folio additions deserve serious consideration. Second, Dover Wilson has defined a principle of editing that seems unquestionably valid: "Compositors . . . are apt both to omit and to insert letters or small insignificant words; but inasmuch as omission is commoner than addition, the longer variant [is to] be preferred when the merits are otherwise fairly evenly balanced."[2] As a result, editors have assumed that unless additions are demonstrably the result of compositor error or reflect the particular kind of non-Shakespearean sophistication found throughout the Folio text of *2 Henry IV*, they should be accepted.

4 THE TEXTUAL PROBLEM

As my comparison of the Quarto and the Folio texts progressed, my intuitive uneasiness with the ten partial lines became compounded by increasing uneasiness with the arguments for their authority. Charlton Hinman's significant discovery in 1955 that the Folio was set by two-page printing formes, not by successive pages, together with his subsequent discovery of the serious problems facing the Folio compositors when they set type for *2 Henry IV* and my own observations of their solutions to those problems, raised grave doubts about the validity of Wilson's principle in relation to the Folio variants. Moreover, my early study led me to doubt that, with the exception of the eight major additions, any revision in the Folio required a source other than the Quarto. It was thus that I was led from a study of metrics to a reconsideration of the major textual problem of *2 Henry IV*: the nature of the printer's copy for the Folio.

Any attempt to resolve this problem must begin with determining the nature of the printer's copy on which the Quarto version was based, for if the Quarto had no authority, we would have no measuring stick by which to evaluate the many Folio changes.[3] Fortunately, in *2 Henry IV* we are dealing with a "good quarto," a text that was entered for publication in the Stationers' Register in 1600 and legitimately published in the same year, one of a group of four texts that Shakespeare's company may have sold to raise money to build the Globe in 1599.

A curious fact about the 1600 Quarto of *2 Henry IV* is that it was the only edition published before the Folio in 1623. The tremendous popularity of *1 Henry IV* had already required three editions in 1598 and 1599, and demand was such that four more were published before the Folio, in 1604, 1608, 1613, and 1622. The failure to reprint its sequel, which is assumed to have been equally popular, is thus surprising and raises a question to which we shall return in the final chapter.[4]

Another curious fact is that the single quarto edition was published in two separate issues, distinguished as Qa and Qb. For some reason, the first issue, Qa, was printed without the first scene of act three. Several explanations for the error have been offered, but the best seems to be that a leaf of the manuscript had temporarily been mislaid.⁵ In the portion of the manuscript of *Sir Thomas More* thought to be in Shakespeare's hand, we find 45, 52, and 53 lines per page. The omitted scene in *2 Henry IV* contains 108 lines and thus may have occupied two sides of one sheet of foolscap. If the copy used to print the Quarto was also Shakespeare's autograph, this explanation for the omitted scene is plausible. Judging from the number of extant copies (ten of Qa and eleven of Qb), the error was not caught until about half the edition had been printed. At that point, presumably, presswork was stopped and the lost scene added, a process that required not merely adding two leaves to accommodate the three and a half pages of the new scene, 3.1, but also resetting the end of 2.4 and the beginning of 3.2 so that the new pages could be spliced into the Qa text without noticeable interruption. As a result, eight new pages in Qb replace four in Qa. In all other respects, the two issues are identical and will be referred to simply as "the Quarto."

What, then, was the nature of the copy for the Quarto? On the basis of the eight major passages omitted in the Quarto but replaced in the Folio, early scholars argued that the Quarto text was set from a theatrical promptbook, the omissions indicating that the bookkeeper had cut the play for performance. Indeed, four of the omitted passages—1.1.166–79, 1.3.21–24, 1.3.36–55, and 2.3.23–45—are either redundant amplification or poetic digression. Since all are unnecessary dramatically, their omission may represent a beginning attempt to shorten the long play. This type of cutting, however, stops in 2.3, and the total loss is a mere 61 lines. The other four omitted passages—1.1.189–209, 1.3.85–108, 4.1.55–79, and 4.1.101–37—are different. In losing them, the Quarto lost material that is absolutely essential to both the structure and the argument of the play. These cuts, totaling 106 lines, were undoubtedly made by the official censor, who deleted all material deemed politically inflammable in that particularly unstable period of Elizabeth's reign.⁶ The Archbishop's role in the rebellion and his detailed defense of it are ruthlessly cut, as are all references to Richard II, to whom even Elizabeth had compared herself. As a result, the Quarto is a seriously mutilated text. Such cuts cannot have originated in the playhouse.

Today opinion is unanimous that the Quarto was set from the most authoritative type of manuscript available: Shakespeare's autograph. Certain features of the text suggest that the Quarto copy was Shakespeare's final rough draft, but "rough" only in the sense that some traces of revision would need to be removed and some features peculiar to dramatic scripts would need to be completed and regularized before the manuscript could serve as efficient prompt copy backstage. The text thus reveals most of the signs that point to Shakespeare's "foul papers," his completed draft of the play: ready, if necessary, to be copied as "fair copy" or, if relatively clean, to be handed to the bookkeeper and prepared as the company's official promptbook.

Throughout *2 Henry IV*, the Quarto stage directions point to Shakespeare's foul papers. Many essential exits as well as some essential entrances are omitted when they are indicated in the dialogue. The company's bookkeeper could be trusted to supply them. Several stage directions are indefinite (*"Enter Bardolfe, and one with him,"* 3.2.54; *"Enter Iohn Westmerland, and the rest,"* 4.3.23) or permissive (*"Enter Hostesse of the Tauerne, and an Officer or two,"* 2.1.1; *"Enter Sinclo and three or foure officers,"* 5.4.1), leaving the bookkeeper to add the actors' names when casting was complete.[7] Sporadically, generic names are substituted in stage directions and speech prefixes: for example, Lady Northumberland is merely "*Wife*," but Hotspur's widow (who was probably still fresh in Shakespeare's memory from *1 Henry IV*) is "*Kate*"; similarly we find "*Enter Hostesse of the Tauerne*" at 2.1.1, but "*Enter mistris Quickly*" at 2.4.21.

At times the inconsistency in character names may indicate an author working at top speed, uninterested in minor details. Often, however, one can see Shakespeare's creative mind at work. Doll Tearsheet's prefixes seem to change with the mood of the moment.

In 2.4, her prefixes begin simply as "*Tere.*," but after Falstaff has called her "Doll" twice in one sentence, she becomes the more intimate "*Doll.*" Thereafter, it is "*Dorothy*," "*Dol*," "*Teresh.*," and "*Doro.*," until she finally settles down to being "*Dol*" for her last fifteen speeches in the scene. But in 5.4, Shakespeare sees her in a different aspect. As a shrieking harlot hauled off to jail for murder, she is simply "*Whoore.*" Prince Hal's speech prefixes also reflect a shift in Shakespeare's perspective. They are consistently "*Prince*" until, as a penitent son, Hal faces his father. When he is chastised as "Harry," it is "*Harry*," not "*Prince*," who responds.

Descriptive stage directions also point to foul papers: for example, "*Enter Rumour painted full of Tongues*" (Ind. 1) and "*Enter sir Iohn alone, with his page bearing his sword and buckler*" (1.2.1). Where a promptbook would state simply "*Knock*" for an offstage sound effect, we find "*Peyto knockes at doore*" (2.4.351). And probably no Elizabethan promptbook would include the theatrically irrelevant fact that the entrance of the rebels in 4.1 takes place "*within the forrest of Gaultree.*"

Another indication of foul papers is the presence of "ghost characters": characters who enter but are given no lines and are never referred to. It is possible that some of these were intended by Shakespeare as supernumeraries: for example, Fauconbridge (1.3.1), Bardolph (4.1.1), and Kent (4.4.1). Other ghost characters probably represent the playwright's false starts. At times Shakespeare seems to have given a character an entrance expecting to use him, but then found no need for him as the writing progressed. For example, at 2.2.1, we find "*Enter the Prince, Poynes, sir Iohn Russel, with other.*" The Prince and Poins are in private conversation for almost seventy lines before Bardolph and the Boy enter to deliver Falstaff's letter. The letter is read and the scene closes. Since Sir John Russell and that "other" serve no function whatever, they clearly should not be there. Shakespeare, it seems, had changed his mind.

A final indication of foul papers in *2 Henry IV* is seen in traces of incomplete revision. The two most notable examples are the one line still assigned to "*Vmfr.*" (1.1.161), although Shakespeare had already revised to give Umfrevile's part to Lord Bardolph, and the telltale speech prefix "*Old.*" (1.2.120), reminding us that Falstaff was originally Oldcastle.

In sum, the evidence in favor of foul papers as the copy for the Quarto is solid and convincing. The argument for Shakespeare's own hand is further strengthened by the occurrence of some idiosyncratic spellings known to be his: *mas* for *mass*, *on* for *one*, *yeere* for *ear*, and, most notably, *Scilens* for *Silence*. There is, then, no "textual problem" in regard to the Quarto.

The Folio text is quite another matter. It remains, in fact, one of the few seriously puzzling textual problems in Shakespeare. What was the nature of the copy transmitted to Jaggard's printing house? The question is urgent because of many superior readings in the Folio, and it has become even more urgent with our increasing awareness of the fallibility of the man in Valentine Simmes' printing-house who set the copy for several of the quartos. Simmes' Compositor A (as distinguished from Jaggard's Compositor A, who set much of the Folio) was responsible for setting the original quartos of *2 Henry IV*, *Much Ado About Nothing*, and *Hamlet*, as well as most of *Richard II* and part of *Richard III*. From the perspective of a Shakespearean scholar, it is unsettling to learn that he bordered on the incompetent. In addition to many obvious typographical errors, he made many errors not easily detected: omitting and adding words, transposing words, and substituting variants that, unfortunately, often make sense.[8]

In the past, logical and sometimes even preferable Folio variants in *2 Henry IV* have been rejected on the grounds of the Quarto's superior authority. In light of our growing distrust of Simmes' Compositor A, we should probably give more serious consideration to Folio variants—if, that is, we could be sure that the changes in the Folio rest on a manuscript of independent authority. Because eight major passages are added in the Folio and because, as we shall note, the Folio's version of 3.1 cannot have been based on the

Quarto, the preparation of the Folio copy manifestly required access to some authoritative source. At the same time, the many and distinctive kinds of revisions in the Folio text reflect such marked editorial interference that no one has suggested it be granted authority superior to that of the Quarto.

The Folio text differs so markedly from that of the Quarto that one major student of the play has argued that the two are totally independent.[9] We shall return to most of the differences, and hence a brief summary will suffice here. The Folio text restores the eight passages omitted in the Quarto but it also makes several deletions, most of them of one line or less. Some lines were probably expurgated as profane, some may have been deleted as indecent, some may be the result of compositor error; but no satisfying explanation has yet been offered for other omissions. The Folio also inserts act and scene divisions, regularizes speech prefixes, and overhauls stage directions—adding, deleting, and completely revising the directions so that only the simplest, such as "*Enter Falstaffe*," remain as they appear in the Quarto.

Most striking are the many changes in the Folio dialogue.[10] Some variants seem to be valid corrections of Quarto errors, but the vast majority reflect a surprising kind of literary sophistication found nowhere else in the Folio. Grammatical and syntactical errors are corrected, contractions are expanded, and colloquial and archaic expressions are revised. Somewhere behind the Folio text of *2 Henry IV* lies a conscientious and exacting editor with literary pretensions.

What, then, was the nature of the copy? Agreement has been general on only one point: it was not a promptbook. The text omits several essential entrances and all sound effects, both of which would be required of a promptbook. Moreover, in several stage directions at the openings of scenes the text includes characters who do not enter for several lines—or even, in the case of Colevile, who is included in the opening entrance to 4.1, for 350 lines. A promptbook with such stage directions would foster chaos backstage.

Until the second quarter of this century, most scholars assumed that the Folio text was set from an edited copy of the Quarto, but this view was effectively challenged in 1940 by M. A. Shaaber in his New Variorum edition of the play. He argued that the copy for the Folio was a transcript based on the official promptbook of Shakespeare's company, a transcript prepared by a scribe who incorporated some authoritative corrections and revisions found in the promptbook but who also revised the play to suit sophisticated literary tastes. In 1953 Shaaber was challenged in turn, and with equal effectiveness, by Alice Walker. Refining the older position, she argued that the Folio text was printed from a copy of the Quarto, but that the copy used by the Folio compositors had been collated with a "fair copy" of Shakespeare's foul papers and meticulously annotated. The issue was joined, and in the ensuing debate most readers probably found themselves at sixes and sevens. It seemed then—and does to this day—that both Shaaber and Walker were, in the main, right.

Walker's case for the Folio's dependence on the Quarto is strong. It is true, as Shaaber argued, that we do not find in the two texts the unmistakable similarities in spelling, punctuation, and typographical style that distinguish other Folio plays set from quarto copy.[11] Nonetheless, there are several common errors and anomalies that cannot be convincingly explained unless the Folio text somehow derived from the Quarto. We find the same questionable readings nine times in both texts, readings that almost all editors believe should be emended.[12] Three might be explained as coincidental misreadings by two different men of Shakespeare's *d* for an *e*: *hole* for *hold* (Ind. 35), *appeare* for *appeard* (4.1.36), and *imagine* for *imagind* (4.2.19). But no amount of coincidence can explain how two different men could both misread *And either end in peace* as *At either end in peace* (4.1.178) or *my friends* as *thy friends* (4.5.204).*

* Other common verbal errors frequently cited are *borrowed* for *borrower's* (2.2.115), *your ancient swaggrer* (F: *Swaggerer*) *comes* for *your ancient swagger, a comes* (2.4.83–84), *inuincible* for *inuisible* (3.2.313), and *rage* for *rags* (4.1.34).

Despite the general dissimilarities in spelling, a few curious spellings found in both texts seem persuasive. The texts' common use of *dowlny* (F: *dowlney*) and *dowlne* (4.5.32,33) for *downy* and *down* might be explained by a common source underlying both texts, but common shifts in spelling point to the Folio's dependence on the Quarto. Both texts read *Welch* at 1.3.79 but then shift to *Welsh* at line 83. Both read *breuitie* at 2.2.123, but *breuity* at line 124; *thin* at 5.4.18, but *thinne* at line 30.[13] These are familiar words, the kind that compositors and scribes were likely to spell consistently, according to their own preferences. Shaaber's argument that the Quarto and Folio are based on independent texts would thus require a remarkable series of coincidences: Shakespeare making the original shifts (in the foul papers serving as copy for the Quarto); two scribes consecutively repeating the shifts (in the promptbook and again in the transcript on which Shaaber argues the Folio is based); and both the Quarto and the Folio compositors independently repeating the shifts. The Folio's dependence on the Quarto is strongly indicated.[14]

In addition, there are many inept Folio variants that by their nature seem to be attempted corrections of errors found in the Quarto rather than readings from an independent source. For example, at 4.4.103-4, the Quarto's

> Will Fortune neuer come with both hands full,
> But wet her faire words stil in foulest termes?

is revised in the Folio to

> But write her faire words still in foulest Letters?

The Folio's version seems to be an attempt—and a thoroughly unsuccessful one—to make sense out of the Quarto's nonsense. Similarly, the Quarto's reading of 2.4.335-36

> for the boy there is a good angel about him, but the diuel blinds him too.

is revised in the Folio to

> but the Deuill outbids him too.

12   THE TEXTUAL PROBLEM

Both readings are certainly wrong, and the Folio substitution again looks like a stab in the dark.*

The case for the influence of the Quarto on the Folio is thus impressive. At the same time, it seems equally certain that, as Shaaber argued, the Folio compositors were setting not from a copy of the Quarto but from a manuscript. Three errors in the Folio cannot easily be explained other than by the fact that the compositor was misreading handwriting. The Quarto's *win* becomes a meaningless *ioyne* in the Folio (4.5.179), a likely misreading if the compositor found *winne* in his manuscript. The Quarto's *Amurath*, which appears twice in one line, twice becomes *Amurah* (5.2.48).[15] Typographical error could explain one instance but hardly two. The Quarto's *Couetua* (i.e., "*Cophetua*") becomes *Couitha* (5.3.102), an error that again can be easily explained as a misreading of Elizabethan hand, in this instance of *i* for *e* and of *th* for *tu*.

Because these three errors occur in the work of the Folio's Compositor B, notorious for his carelessness, perhaps more convincing evidence for the use of a manuscript is found in the treatment of stage directions.[16] The curious introduction of semi-massed entrances at the opening of a few scenes—entrances that include some characters who actually enter later—cannot be explained if we assume a compositor who had a copy of the Quarto open before him. Moreover, the changed position of some stage directions points directly to the use of a manuscript. Throughout the Folio, compositors normally centered internal entrances. Thus when they were setting from a quarto they would rarely have had reason to move directions that were already centered in their printed copy. Their treatment of some directions that are centered in the Quarto of *2 Henry IV* is, therefore, telling. For example, the Quarto places the entrance of Bardolph and the Page at 2.2.69, just after Poins announces

---

* For further evidence suggesting that the Folio was influenced by the Quarto, note the Folio's faulty revision of Quarto errors at 2.4.336 and 4.5.161 and its introduction of a new character, "Bardolph's boy." See below, pp. 166–67 and 49–50.

here comes Bardolfe.
>*Enter Bardolfe and boy.*

Prince   And the boy that I gaue Falstaffe, a had him from me Christian, and looke if the fat villaine haue not transformd him Ape.

Bard.   God saue your grace.

In contrast, the Folio centers the entrance just before Bardolph speaks—a delay that would be inexplicable if the compositor were setting from the Quarto. In play transcripts of the period, however, brief internal entrances were usually placed beside speeches, in the right or left margins. The Folio's placement of Bardolph's entrance thus suggests manuscript copy, with the entrance written laterally beside the Prince's speech or perhaps Bardolph's. The Folio's treatment of some entrances set laterally in the Quarto is also significant. For example, the Quarto places the entrance of Travers to the right of 1.1.25:

>**Bar.**   I spake with one, my lord, that came from thence,   *enter*
>A gentleman well bred, and of good name,   *Trauers.*
>That freely rendred me these newes for true.
>
>**Earle**   Here comes my seruant Trauers who I sent
>On tuesday last to listen after newes.

If the Folio compositor were setting from the Quarto, he would undoubtedly have centered Travers' entrance after Lord Bardolph's speech; instead he centered it after the Earl of Northumberland's. In all probability, Shakespeare's foul papers placed the entry to the right of Bardolph's speech, but the manuscript used as Folio copy placed it to the right of Northumberland's. In neither of the cases just discussed could the Folio compositor have been setting directly from the Quarto. (The placement of stage directions will be considered in detail in the next chapter.)

Two of the strongest arguments in favor of the use of a manuscript rather than an annotated copy of the Quarto are based on common sense. If Jaggard had access to both a copy of the Quarto and a corrected manuscript, why did not the compositors use the Quarto as their basic text and consult the manuscript only for the additions? Why would someone in Jaggard's shop undertake the arduous task of entering in the Quarto hundreds of revisions that are solely literary in nature, revisions that polish the text of *2 Henry IV* to a state of refined gentility found nowhere else in the Folio? No conceivable purpose would be served. Moreover, the type of meticulously annotated quarto envisaged by Alice Walker would be almost wholly indecipherable, particularly in the prose passages, where colloquialisms, archaisms, and grammatical errors are extensively revised.[17]

Thus we are faced with a paradoxical conclusion: both Shaaber and Walker were right. As Shaaber claimed, the Folio text was undoubtedly set from manuscript—and, as Walker argued, it undoubtedly reflects the influence of the Quarto. On the other hand, in the particular details of their theories, both Shaaber and Walker seem to have been wrong. Shaaber's conclusion that the manuscript in question was based on a promptbook, that it had no direct relation to the Quarto, is unsatisfactory, as is Walker's conclusion that the Folio text was set directly from an annotated copy of the Quarto.

The first attempt to resolve the contradiction was made by Fredson Bowers in 1953. Tentatively, he proposed that "for some reason an annotated quarto was transcribed to form a manuscript which was used as printer's copy for the Folio."[18] In his introduction to the New Arden edition of the play in 1966, A. R. Humphreys modified Bowers' theory, and his solution is probably the most satisfying to date:

> The ingredients of F's copy must, it would seem, have been a quarto and a virtually full MS showing some cognizance of stage practice. These ingredients appear to have been combined in a transcript made either from an elaborately annotated Q or (which seems more likely) from a Q and a MS concurrently, the scribe keeping his eye on both in varying degrees. The transcript, if made with 'literary' pretensions, would be responsible for F's gentility.[19]

It is easy to identify which issue of the Quarto was used by the scribe. When the lost leaf containing the text of 3.1 was belatedly discovered, Simmes' Compositor A had to reset one and a half pages of 2.4 and two and a half pages of 3.2 in order to accommodate the insertion of 3.1 in Qb. In so doing, he made many errors: once he reversed words; twice he omitted words; three times he added a word. None of these variants occurs in the Folio. In each case, the Folio text follows Qa.

Humphreys' thorough analysis leaves only one major question unresolved: what was the nature of this "virtually full MS" used to supplement Qa in preparing the transcript that served as the Folio's copy? The question is crucial, for all theories agree on one point: that such a manuscript was consulted. Given the fact that eight major passages and all of 3.1 are omitted in Qa but replaced in the Folio, that conclusion is undebatable. Further, almost all theories agree that the manuscript consulted was independent of the Quarto's copy, that it was both subsequent to, and in several respects superior to, Shakespeare's foul papers.* Three major arguments are offered First, the corrections of stage directions and speech prefixes reflect stage practice; thus the consulted manuscript in some way reflects the promptbook, or at least some undefined kind of manuscript corrected with an eye to production. Second, the Folio contains a few corrections and variants that are superior to readings in the Quarto, and these must derive from a source of some authority. Third, given Dover Wilson's principle that omission may be compositorial but that additions are probably authorial, the minor additions throughout the Folio text indicate that an independent manuscript was consulted throughout the preparation of the Folio copy. The present study has cast doubt on all three arguments and thus on the conclusion to which they lead.

In the discussion that follows, I shall often need to refer to my conclusions before the necessary proof has been established. For the purposes of clarity, I offer here a brief statement of my major conclusion about the nature of the Folio copy. At this point, the reader should consider it a working hypothesis.

* The exception is the theory of George Walton Williams. See below, pp. 176–77.

Analysis of stage directions and speech prefixes (Chapter II), of the problems faced by the Folio compositors and their solutions (Chapter III), and of the given scribe's distinctive cast of mind and working habits (Chapter IV)—all suggest that except for the eight major additions and the first scene of act three, no source beyond Qa was required to prepare the transcript serving as the Folio's copy. Given this probability, what manuscript did the scribe consult to provide the Folio's additions? Because errors either remain or are introduced in the Folio that could have been corrected had the scribe preparing the transcript consulted a corrected manuscript, the supplementary document may have been exactly the copy used by the Quarto compositor: Shakespeare's foul papers.

The possibility that Shakespeare's foul papers would have been preserved after the Quarto was printed is, I realize, rather slim. Nonetheless, the idea deserves consideration. In *Proof-Reading in the Sixteenth, Seventeenth, and Eighteenth Centuries*, Percy Simpson corrected an earlier assumption that "the printer invariably made a filthy mess of copy and burnt it when he had done with it." (On extant copy from the period, typically the only printers' marks are those marking off pages.) On the contrary, "copy would always be returned to the author, or to the friend acting for him, or, if the author were dead, to the person responsible for sending the work to the press."[20] Unfortunately, we cannot be sure of the evidence that led Simpson to such an absolute assertion, for the extant manuscripts serving as printers' copy that he discusses are all works of major consequence: part of Sir John Harington's translation of *Orlando Furioso*, the fifth book of Richard Hooker's *Laws of Ecclesiastical Politie*, and the like. Moreover, most of these manuscripts are by authors who closely followed the process of printing and proofing. Despite Simpson's assurance that copy was "always" returned, the printer of works so lightly regarded as plays may simply have destroyed the now-useless copy—especially in the case of Shakespeare's plays, since their author took no interest in their printing.

Granting, then, a legitimate area of doubt, I nominate Shakespeare's foul papers as the most logical candidate for the supplementary manuscript scholars have sought to identify. Folio errors of a certain type—errors that either remain from the Quarto or are introduced in the Folio—could have been corrected had the scribe consulted a corrected manuscript. Moreover, certain features of the Folio additions may reflect the direct influence of Shakespeare's autograph.* I thus propose that the copy for the Folio text of *2 Henry IV* consisted of a transcript based solely on Qa and Shakespeare's foul papers. For some reason, the transcript was prepared for a reader of exclusively literary tastes. It was not prepared to serve as copy for the Folio, an inference that seems self-evident in light of the unique sophistication of the text. The scribe, who was obviously experienced in the preparation of literary manuscripts, carefully edited the play line by line as he copied, correcting and—as he thought—"improving" the text according to his own logical bent and literary training.[21] By making educated guesses, he added some necessary stage directions and moved others, but he reduced the theatrical apparatus to a minimum, abbreviating and regularizing stage directions and speech prefixes and omitting details essential for production but of little concern to a reader. Solely on his own authority, he extensively revised the dialogue, making emendations dictated by his sense of logic and propriety. He probably shifted his eyes from his printed copy to his supplementary manuscript only to add 3.1 and the eight passages that had been omitted in Qa. In very rare instances, facing especially difficult problems in his Quarto copy, he may have made spot checks in the manuscript, but there is no evidence that he kept his eye on Qa and the manuscript concurrently. The resulting copy used by the Folio compositors thus incorporated several intelligent corrections that, given the inaccuracy of the Quarto compositor, are undoubtedly valid; but none of the scribe's revisions of material found in Qa has any

---

* For a discussion of this point, see Appendix A, "The Nature of the Copy Underlying Folio Additions."

demonstrable authority, and his emendations should be treated as are the emendations of any other editor.

For many readers, even considering such a hypothesis may seem pointless because of one major objection: the widespread agreement that the Folio in some way derives from an authoritative manuscript that was subsequent to Shakespeare's foul papers. This belief is based primarily on the assumption that certain revisions in the Folio reflect stage practice and thus that the Folio reflects authoritative revisions made when the play actually went into production. Before turning to the work of the compositors and the scribe, let us consider this crucial assumption. Do any of the Folio revisions indicate that the scribe consulted an independent manuscript in some way deriving from the theater?

CHAPTER II

Reflections of Stage Practice in the Folio

It is agreed by all modern scholars that the Folio copy was prepared by a man of purely literary interests.[1] Four kinds of changes in the Folio stage directions make this fact self-evident. (1) All supernumeraries are eliminated, even when they would be essential in production. At the opening of 4.2, for example, the Quarto's "*Enter Prince Iohn and his armie*" becomes "*Enter Prince Iohn*" in the Folio. (2) All mutes are eliminated, even when they are referred to and thus indisputably required in a given scene. In 2.1, the entry of Falstaff's boy is eliminated as is that of the men who accompany the Chief Justice. (3) All references to offstage sound effects are eliminated, such as Peto's knocking in 2.4 and the alarum and excursions at the opening of 4.3. (4) All descriptive material is deleted from stage directions. At the opening of 1.2, "*Enter sir Iohn alone, with his page bearing his sword and buckler*" is reduced to the bare "*Enter Falstaffe, and Page.*"

A manuscript prepared to serve as a promptbook would require all but the fourth type of stage direction, but the transcriber-editor who prepared the Folio copy was interested only in the lines themselves. He was preparing a work of literature, not a script for an acting company. To be sure, he made speech prefixes uniform, reduced character names to the bare essentials (*sir Iohn* becomes *Falstaffe*, *antient Pistol* becomes *Pistol*, *Thomas duke of Clarence* becomes *Clarence*), and made indefinite stage directions precise ("*Enter a Drawer or two*" becomes "*Enter two Drawers*")— all revisions of the type that would be made in preparing a promptbook. However, his radical excision of much material that would be essential in a promptbook suggests that his aim was to reduce non-literary material to the barest of essentials and to make his transcript tidy, a desire reflected in changes throughout the Folio text.

Even while granting the scribe's literary aim, scholars have nonetheless held that the Folio reflects stage practice and thus that the scribe must have consulted an independent manuscript in some way deriving from the theater. The argument is four-fold: (1) many essential stage directions omitted in the Quarto are added in the Folio; (2) the placement of stage directions in the Folio often accords better with the action; (3) some speech prefix errors in the Quarto have been corrected in the Folio; and (4) a few changes in the action show that the Folio reflects adaptation for the stage. Each of these assertions must be considered in detail.

Many essential stage directions are, indeed, omitted in the Quarto, but we must remember that it is based on Shakespeare's rough draft.[2] In all cases, the company bookkeeper could be trusted to supply the missing action. For example, Shakespeare did not always bother to clear the stage at the end of each scene. Why waste words over the obvious? Following the induction, the stage is cleared seventeen times; of these, the Quarto gives the necessary *exit* or *exeunt* only six times. The Folio supplies all but one of the missing eleven.

Throughout the play, the Quarto omits many other essential stage directions. When exits are unmistakable in the lines, the Folio usually supplies them: when, for example, the line indicating an exit is as clear as "hie thee captaine" (4.2.71), "Go, good Lord Hastings" (4.2.95), "Blunt leade him hence" (4.3.75), "set on" (5.5.72), or "Fare you wel" (4.3.84).[3] Similarly, when omitted entrances are unmistakable, the Folio usually supplies them: when, for example, the Quarto has the Chief Justice enter without his servant, although the servant has the fourth speech following the Chief Justice's entry (1.2.54); when the Quarto omits Peto's entrance although Peto is addressed as he enters (2.4.353); or when the Quarto gives a directed entry for Sincklo and the officers but not for the Hostess and Doll, although the Hostess has the first speech in the scene and Doll the third (5.4.1). All of these entrances could easily have been supplied by any reader who glanced no more than a few lines ahead.

Several times, however, an omitted entrance would be obvious to anyone involved in a production of the play but not immediately apparent to a reader. At 2.4.207 and 211, for example, Bardolph's exit pursuing Pistol and his subsequent reentry can be easily overlooked by a reader, though not by actors. The same is true of Davy's exit at 5.3.71 in response to Pistol's knocking and his subsequent reentry at 79. A manuscript revised for stage production would add these essential stage directions, but the Folio does not.

More significant are the several errors introduced by the scribe in his attempt to supply missing stage directions. Five instances are closely related. In each case, an onstage character calls an offstage character who immediately enters, often responding with a line such as "Here sir" or answering a question. The required entrance is so obvious to a theater man that Shakespeare's omission of the stage direction would present no problem. In all five instances, however, the scribe supplied the missing entry in the wrong place. Though not a serious error, his first stage direction is typical. At the opening of 1.1, the Quarto reads "*Enter the Lord Bardolfe at one doore.*" He calls "Who keepes the gate here ho?"—a sign that the Porter does not enter simultaneously but responds to a call. A quick glance at the ensuing dialogue showed the scribe that an entrance was missing, and he supplied it—but too early. Thus in the Folio we find "*Enter Lord Bardolfe, and the Porter.*" A more serious error occurs in 4.5. At line 225, the Quarto reads "*enter Lancaster*" and the King responds with "Looke, looke, here comes my Iohn of Lancaster." Six lines later, the King asks, "Where is my lord of Warwicke?" and Prince Hal calls out, "My Lord of Warwicke." Immediately, although there is no entrance in the Quarto, Warwick enters, as is indicated by the King's subsequent question to him. Seeing that Warwick needs an entrance, the scribe supplied it—but seven lines too early, so that Warwick enters with Lancaster rather than in response to the Prince's summons. That the Folio entrance is wrong is indicated by the fact that the King has seen Lancaster on his entry but not Warwick. A similar error is found in 5.1. In the entrance at the opening of the scene, the Quarto lists only Shallow, Falstaff, and Bardolph. In his first speech, Shallow calls "what Dauy I say?" but there is no response. Again, at line 7, he calls "why Dauy," and this time Davy responds "Here, sir." Clearly Davy enters at this point. Had the energetic and efficient Davy entered with his master, he certainly would have responded to the first call. The Folio supplies the missing entrance but again at the wrong place: seven lines earlier, at the opening of the scene.[4]

It might be argued that all three of the misplaced entrances described so far are not technically errors but merely reflect a tendency in the Folio to use "massed entries"—entries at the beginning of a scene that name all the characters who appear in the entire scene, both those who enter at the opening and those who enter subsequently. Too much attention has been given, I believe, to the assumed fact of massed entries in this text without close analysis of the entries in question. In point of fact there are only two massed entries in the Folio text of *2 Henry IV*. One is unquestionable. At the opening of 2.2, the Quarto reads "*Enter the Prince, Poynes, sir Iohn Russel, with other.*" The Folio reads "*Enter Prince Henry, Pointz, Bardolfe, and Page.*" The scribe eliminated what he may have assumed to be two mutes (but editors now believe to represent an error by Shakespeare) and then for some reason added Bardolph and the Page, although their entrance is not indicated in the Quarto until line 69. (Curiously, when the scribe arrived at that stage direction, he gave Bardolph a second entry but reverted to his habit of eliminating mutes by cutting the Page.)

The second massed entry was not, I believe, so intended. At the opening of 5.1, the Folio reads "*Enter Shallow, Silence, Falstaffe, Bardolfe, / Page, and Dauy,*" whereas the Quarto reads merely

"*Enter Shallow, Falstaffe, and Bardolfe.*" As noted above, the inclusion of Davy in this opening stage direction is undoubtedly an error. The scribe saw lines for him but no entrance and too easily assumed that Davy enters with his master. The other two characters added in the Folio entry, Silence and the Page, have no lines in the scene, and their inclusion is curious in light of the scribe's usual deletion of mutes. Silence may have been added because of the scribe's memory of a stage performance. For anyone who has seen the play, Shallow and Silence are inseparable. (In fact, Silence should probably be in the scene: at the end of 5.1 all exit to dinner and he is in 5.3, which takes place immediately after dinner.) The addition of the mute Page may represent the culmination of a rather comic series of errors by the scribe, to be detailed below. Whatever the reasons for the addition of the mutes, the inclusion of Davy in the opening stage direction seems to stem from the scribe's misunderstanding rather than his intention to write a neoclassical massed entry.

No other Folio entrance is truly massed, although two more have been frequently cited. The entrance to 4.1 includes the Archbishop, Mowbray, Hastings, Westmoreland (who enters later), and Colevile (a puzzling addition to be considered below), but it does not include the Messenger, Prince John, Falstaff, and Bardolph. The entrance to 5.3 might be thought of as a massed entrance because it includes Pistol, who enters eighty-two lines later, but it omits Davy, who not only enters at the opening but also pops out and returns twice during the scene.

Few scholars have suggested that the presence of massed entries is, in itself evidence of stage practice.[5] I have paused here to question the assumption that massed entries of the type encountered in the work of Ralph Crane were a conscious feature of the scribe's work because two more stage directions that I take to be scribal errors might be dismissed as merely two more massed entries. More commonly these two have been cited as evidence of stage practice. Both, I believe, result from the scribe's misunderstanding of the type of omission I have just discussed: instances in which Shakespeare omitted a stage direction when a character is called and immediately enters in response.

At the opening of 3.2, the scene in which the recruits are "pricked," the Quarto reads "*Enter Iustice Shallow, and Iustice Silence.*" Following their quiet chat over country matters, Falstaff enters and the recruiting begins. Shallow calls for Rafe Mouldy, and Mouldy responds "Here and it please you" (101). Thereafter Shallow calls the recruits in succession and each responds with "Here sir." For none does the Quarto provide an entrance. Again the scribe misunderstood the action inherent in a call and response, as he did in the case of the Porter, Warwick, and Davy. Thus the Folio provides entrance for all of the recruits at the opening of the scene, together with the justices. Editors have almost unanimously adopted the Folio "correction," some modifying the direction slightly to indicate that the recruits enter "behind."*

The evidence of the lines I find to be unequivocal: the recruits do not enter with Shallow and Silence. The justices give no hint in their quiet colloquy that they are not alone. It is early morning. Falstaff is coming today, but they do not know when. When he does arrive, he asks if they have provided "halfe a dozen sufficient men." Assured that they have, Falstaff asks "Let me see them I beseech you." Obviously Falstaff does not see a line-up of recruits as he enters. If he did, his question would be "are these men sufficient?" and his response, "let me question them." After a bit of dither, Shallow finds the roll and announces "let them appeere as I call." One by one he calls the names, and one by one the recruits appear. As they are called, we find recurrent phrases like "let me see him" and "where's he?" If the recruits were already lined up, the logic of the situation would require "let him stand forth" and "which one is he?" When stage productions follow the Folio, action and dialogue are at cross-purposes.

It has been argued that in production "the effect is probably better if, as in the Folio, the scarecrows are visible from the start."[6] I doubt it. Each of the recruits is a marvelously comic Shake-

---

* The sole exception is Peter Davison. See his note to the stage direction in his New Penguin edition of the play (Harmondsworth, 1977), pp. 228–29.

spearean grotesque, each strikingly different from the others, each probably played originally by an accomplished comedian. According to the action implied in the Quarto, each gets his own comic entrance. Shallow's calling of each name thus arouses the anticipation of the audience. What will a "Mouldy" be? And what a "Shadow"? Perhaps the role was played by that string bean Sincklo, the actor for whom Shakespeare wrote the part of the officer in 5.4, a "thin man in a censor," a "filthy famisht correctioner" (18, 20). In a repertory company, each actor is familiar to the audience, and their delight is increased by the anticipated matching of a comic name with a familiar face—and body. Thus each entrance gets its own whoop of laughter. Imagine, for example, the richly comic effect of juxtaposing the sturdy little "reverend" Feeble's quiet determination to do his duty against the bellow of the entering Bullcalf. Would Shakespeare or his company have missed such an opportunity? According to the action implied by the Folio, the recruits tag along after Shallow and Silence, unrecognized, unexplained. They just stand there—a motley crew who can serve no purpose but to distract from the dialogue of the justices.

Only one explanation for the Folio's misplaced entry seems plausible. The scribe was a literary man, wholly unprepared to do the necessary translation that a script, and especially the rough draft of a script, requires and for which a bookkeeper was trained. From his treatment of the entry of the recruits, as well as that of the Porter, Warwick, and Davy, I believe we can detect his procedure. Apparently he quickly skimmed each scene before he started copying the opening entrance. Perhaps he had been warned that the Quarto was often incomplete in its stage directions. Perhaps he had been alerted by the omission of an entrance for the Porter at the opening of 1.1. Whatever the reason, he tried to account for all speakers and to delete all mutes. If he detected a speaking character for whom there was no entrance in the Quarto, he added the required entrance, often, as in the case of the recruits, in the scene's opening stage direction.

This procedure of the scribe accounts, I believe, for a similar

Folio change at the opening of 2.1. In the Quarto we find one of the permissive stage directions characteristic of Shakespearean foul papers: "*Enter Hostesse of the Tauerne, and an Officer or two.*" The Hostess addresses "Master Phang" and asks where his yeoman is. At this, Fang calls "Sirra, wheres Snare?" and Snare answers "Here, here." According to the pattern we have noted elsewhere in the play, this sequence of lines suggests that Snare enters when he hears his name, although the Quarto gives no stage direction. Following his usual procedure, the scribe supplied the missing direction in the opening entry and eliminated mutes. The result is plausible—"*Enter Hostesse, with two Officers, Fang and Snare*"— and it has been widely adopted. Several considerations make it doubtful, however, that the change rests on any authoritative theatrical manuscript. In the Quarto, Snare's entry is delayed— undoubtedly for some comic reason. Is he, perhaps, a foot-dragging dolt? The Hostess asks where he is. He has not entered with Fang. To whom, then, does Fang address "Sirra, wheres Snare?" Explanations have been many and ingenious, but the most obvious would seem to be that Fang suddenly becomes aware that his second-in-command is absent and asks an underling where he is. Note the form of the stage direction in the Quarto: "*Enter Hostesse of the Tauerne, and an Officer or two.*" It may say, in effect, "Enter Hostess and Fang, and, if possible, give Fang a mute." "*An Officer or two*" suggests that one officer alone, Fang, would suffice at the opening of the scene. If, however, Fang could be given a mute attendant who—by costume, expression, or bearing—was manifestly unequal to the fray that the Hostess expects, the urgency of her questions about Snare would be doubly comic. "Wheres your yeoman? ist a lusty yeoman? wil a stand too't?" One look at the totally worthless mute attendant would understandably make the Hostess uneasy about the law's determination in the face of Falstaff's expected resistance.

Thus far we have considered only those instances in which the Folio adds exits or entrances that are omitted in the Quarto, and thus far there is no evidence to suggest that the scribe needed to have access to anything other than the Quarto and his own logical, albeit theatrically inept, mind.

Let us next consider the placement of stage directions. Do certain changes in the Folio accord better with the action and thus indicate that the scribe consulted an independent manuscript deriving from the theater? On this question, the evidence is particularly difficult to evaluate, for the placement of a stage direction in a printed text is no sure guide to its placement in the manuscript that served as the printer's copy. In manuscripts of the period, authors and scribes normally centered entrances at the opening of scenes, but they usually—space permitting—placed internal directions laterally, to the right (or sometimes left) of the dialogue.[7] They could often accommodate a brief direction such as "*Enter Morton*" on one line, but they might stagger a long direction laterally on two or more lines. In such a case, it is impossible to determine from the printed text where the stage direction began in the printer's copy. A quarto compositor might also stagger the direction to the right but, as a result of space limitations or arbitrary choice, he might begin and end the direction beside lines other than those by which it appeared in the manuscript. If the direction was very long, he would need to center it after the speech beside which it appeared in the manuscript. Practice in placing internal entrances varies in the Shakespearean quartos, but in the Folio almost all entrances are centered in plays set after *The Tempest*, making it even more difficult to determine their placement in manuscript copy. Moreover, the placement of stage directions in the quartos and the Folio often depended far more upon the specific setting problems a given compositor faced at a given moment than on any attempt to reflect dramatic action accurately, and the problems faced by the compositors of the Folio *2 Henry IV* were, as we shall see in the next chapter, far more demanding than those faced by the Quarto compositor.

In short, compositors often had little or no choice. For example, the entrance of Falstaff, Bardolph, and the Page at 2.1.38 is placed as follows in the Quarto (the Hostess is speaking):

> no honesty in such dealing, vnlesse a woman should be made an asse, and a beast, to beare euery knaues wrong: yonder he comes, and that arrant malmsie-nose knaue Bardolfe with him, do your offices, do your offices master Phãg, & master Snare, do me, do me, do me your offices.
> *Enter sir Iohn, and Bardolfe, and the boy.*

Since the Hostess cannot be shrieking to officers to arrest Falstaff before he appears, the Folio placement would seem far closer to stage practice:

> a woman should be made an Asse and a Beast, to beare e-
> uery Knaues wrong. *Enter Falstaffe and Bardolfe.*
> Yonder he comes, and that arrant Malmesey-Nose *Bar-*
> *dolfe* with him. Do your Offices. . . .

Should we then conclude that the copy used for the Folio reflected stage practice? Not at all. The Quarto stage direction is longer than the abbreviated Folio version. In Shakespeare's foul papers it may have been centered as it is in the Quarto or it may have been staggered on three or four lines to the right of the Hostess's speech, beginning at or even before "yonder he comes."[8] The Quarto compositor had no choice but to center the long direction after the Hostess's speech. The Folio compositor, on the other hand, did have a choice. His manuscript probably had the stage direction in the right margin, but it was much shorter (omitting, according to the scribe's practice, characters' titles and mutes). As we shall see in the next chapter, Compositor B was compressing copy at this point and could not afford the luxury of a centered stage direction. He had to fit the direction in to the right of a short line. He could have placed it at the end of the speech (which, if uninterrupted by the stage direction, would end with a line of two or three words), but wouldn't it be more logical to interrupt the speech at the proper point? The number of lines would remain the same.

Comparisons between the two texts are significant only when both the Quarto and the Folio compositors had a choice. Such instances are rare, but they are instructive. In a few cases, the Folio placement of entrances is slightly better, but in far more cases the Quarto placement is markedly better for the purposes of production. In order to determine whether or not certain Folio changes do, in fact, reflect stage practice, we must bear in mind the distinctive configuration of the Elizabethan stage. There are three ways by which a reader can detect an entry from the dialogue alone: an onstage character says "But who comes here?" or "Here comes so-and-so"; an entering character is addressed; or an entering character speaks. Elizabethan stage practice suggests that a character should be given a directed entrance before—or, at the very latest, on—any one of these three signs of entry. On a modern proscenium stage, a character can look into the wings and say "Here comes so-and-so" before the entering character actually appears, but an entrance on the Elizabethan stage is made from one of the doors to the rear of the platform. A character on stage cannot easily see an approaching character before the audience does. The entering actor must begin his movement in the tiring-house, come through the door, and move forward onto the platform before his entrance is detected by a character onstage. Thus in promptbooks, authorial manuscripts, and printed texts of the period, we often find anticipatory entrances: that is, entrances noted one or even several lines before the fact of entrance is recognized in the dialogue.[9]

In light of this production requirement, we find that the Folio placement of stage directions is slightly better in a few cases: for example, the entry of Bardolph at 3.2.54 and the entry of Westmoreland at 4.1.25 are both centered after the "Here comes" line in the Quarto but centered before it in the Folio. In far more cases, however, the Quarto placement reflects the conventions of Elizabethan staging. At 1.1.29, Travers' entry in the Quarto begins in the right margin three lines before Northumberland's "Here comes" line.

> *Bar.* I spake with one, my lord, that came from thence. *enter*
> A gentleman well bred, and of good name, *Trauers.*
> That freely rendred me these newes for true.

>   *Earle* Here comes my seruant Trauers who I sent
> On tuesday last to listen after newes.

In the Folio, the entrance is centered two lines after Northumberland's "Here comes" signal.

> *L. Bar.* I spake with one (my L.) that came frõ thence,
> A Gentleman well bred, and of good name,
> That freely render'd me these newes for true.
>   *Nor.* Heere comes my Seruant *Trauers*, whom I sent
> On Tuesday last, to listen after Newes.
>   *Enter Trauers.*

The Quarto placement gives the actor time to enter from an upstage door and join the actors on the forestage.

Similar evidence suggesting that the Quarto is closer than the Folio to stage practice is found in the placement of several other entrances. At the opening of 4.2 (a modern division of what is a continuous scene in both the Quarto and the Folio), the Quarto centers the entrance of Prince John just after Westmoreland announces that the Prince is at hand, two full lines before John speaks; the Folio centers the entrance just before John speaks, at the last possible moment. At 4.2.96, the Quarto places the entry for Westmoreland two lines before he is addressed by John; the Folio centers the entrance—again, at the last possible moment—just before John speaks to him. At 4.5.87, the Quarto places the entry of Prince Hal to the right of Warwick's assurance to the King that his son is coming, two lines before the King's "Loe where he comes"; the Folio centers the entry just before the King's line. At 5.2.42, the Quarto staggers the entrance of the Prince and Blunt on two lines, the second of which is placed to the right of Warwick's "Here comes the Prince"; the Folio centers the stage direction after Warwick's signalling line, one line too late. In the five cases just considered, the Quarto allows from one to three lines for the actor to enter and take his position on the forestage, whereas the Folio three times places the entry at the last possible moment and twice places it one line late.

One final example of better placement in the Quarto may illuminate both the difficulty in determining the kind of copy underlying a text by studying the placement of printed stage directions and the difficulty in determining the influence of stage practice. At 5.3.81, the Quarto places Pistol's entrance as follows:

> *Dauy* And't please your worship, theres one Pistoll come from the court with newes.   *enter Pistol.*
> *Falst.* From the Court? let him come in, how now Pistol?
> *Pistol* Sir Iohn, God saue you.

Is this logical? Davy announces Pistol, Pistol enters, and then Davy is told to admit him. From the point of view of a reader, the Folio surely makes more sense:

> *Dau.* If it please your Worshippe, there's one *Pistoll* come from the Court with newes.
> *Fal.* From the Court? Let him come in.
>
>   *Enter Pistoll.*
>
> How now Pistoll?

Where did the stage direction appear in the manuscripts used by the Quarto and Folio compositors? Shakespeare's foul papers may have placed the entrance to the right of Davy's words announcing Pistol's arrival, exactly where it appears in the Quarto. To be sure, the Quarto column width did not leave room at the end of Falstaff's "let him come in" line, but if the direction appeared there in Shakespeare's manuscript, it could easily have been accommodated below, to the right of Pistol's entering speech. According to the Folio setting, however, we can be fairly sure that the scribe wrote the direction to the right of Falstaff's speech. For reasons that will be discussed in the next chapter, Compositor B was doing everything possible to waste space at this point. Had his copy placed the direction to the right of Davy's speech, B would have centered it immediately thereafter, taking the opportunity to add blank lines both before and after the stage direction. Instead, he inserted Pistol's entrance in the middle of Falstaff's speech. Throughout the Folio, entrances that interrupt a continuing speech are normally not set off by blank lines, but B here varied from his usual practice to add one blank line. The fact that by placing Pistol's entrance in the middle of Falstaff's speech B felt he could add only one blank line, when at this point, he would probably have welcomed the opportunity to add two, points to the placement of the direction in the scribe's manuscript: to the right of Falstaff's speech.

But which version accords better with the probable stage action? The Quarto's far better suits Pistol's character and his mood at this moment in the play. He has rushed from London, bursting with the glorious news of Hal's accession. Is Pistol the man to wait for a formal invitation to enter? He roars in, hot on the heels of Davy, probably beginning his entrance with Davy's last words announcing his arrival. The Quarto punctuation of Falstaff's speech may provide a clue: "let him come in, how now Pistol?" Falstaff is startled by the unexpected entrance and perhaps taken aback by the appearance of Pistol—who has probably struck an appropriately theatrical "Aha, victory is ours!" pose. Note that Falstaff says "how now Pistol?" not "how now, what news?" Compare this action with that implied by the Folio. The scribe, as we shall see, was a man of rigid logic and an acute sense of decorum. According to the rules of both sense and civility, if Falstaff feels the situation such that permission must be granted Pistol to enter, Pistol surely should not enter before "let him come in." If Pistol were a Westmoreland, the scribe's logic would be impeccable. But Pistol is Pistol. The Quarto placement far better conveys the dramatic movement of the scene.

In the preceding analysis of the Folio's additions to and different placement of stage directions, we have found no evidence to support the argument that the Folio reflects stage practice more closely than does the Quarto. But what of the Folio's corrections of speech prefixes? Do they not show the hand of the bookkeeper? Five corrections in the Folio are unquestionably valid. However, given the scribe's logical mind, and his probable method of skimming ahead before he began work on a scene, three of the corrections can be attributed solely to him, rather than to some authoritative revised source. At 3.2.300, the Quarto gives Falstaff's soliloquy to Shallow. Examination of the Quarto text shows the probable reason not only for the compositor's error but also for the Folio change.

> *Shal.* Go to, I haue spoke at a word, God keep you.
> *Fal.* Fare you well gentle gentlemen. *exit*
> *Shal.* On Bardolfe, leade the men away, as I returne I will fetch off these iustices. ...

I would conjecture that the passage in Shakespeare's manuscript stood just as it is printed in the Quarto—with one exception, the attribution of the final speech to Shallow. Shakespeare probably gave an entire line to Falstaff's farewell and the *exit* for the justices. (He often used the singular verb for plural exits.) Then he continued Falstaff's speech, but on a new line. When the Quarto compositor reached the continuation, he had just finished setting seven speeches shifting from *Fal.* to *Shal.* to *Fal.* to *Shal.* Now he saw what looked like an exit for Falstaff and, apparently, the line of a new speaker, but one that had no prefix. Since Falstaff was the last speaker, he remedied the assumed omission by prefixing *Shal.* All perfectly sensible—unless you are thinking of the meaning of what you are copying. The scribe preparing the Folio copy was, indeed, thinking, and he made what is really a simple correction by giving "On Bardolfe ... " to Falstaff.

Equally reasonable for a scribe who is thinking carefully are the corrections at 4.2.67 and 69 and at 5.5.24. For the first, the Quarto reads

> *Bishop* I take your princely word for these redresses,
> I giue it you, and will maintaine my word,
> And therevpon I drinke vnto your grace.
> *Prince* Go Captaine, and deliuer to the armie
> This newes of peace, let them haue pay, and part.
> I know it will well please them, hie thee captaine.

Even if one has read no further in the scene, something is clearly wrong in the assignment of the second line to the Archbishop. It is Prince John who has given his word and pledges to maintain it. To reassign these two lines to John is an easy matter. But who orders the captain to discharge the army, and which army? To answer this question, the scribe would have had to read to the end of the scene, which, as I have suggested above, was his probable procedure. At lines 91–92, John sends Westmoreland ostensibly to dismiss the royal army. Here, then, it must be Hastings, the rebel commander, who gives the order to the nameless captain. Even easier to solve is the Quarto's faulty continuation to Shallow of Falstaff's "but to stand stained" speech at 5.5.24. It is Falstaff who has been excitedly anticipating the effect of his appearance on the newly crowned king; Shallow functions as but a supporting echo. Any alert editor should be able to make the correction.

None of the three corrections just noted required any source other than the Quarto and the scribe's thoughtful method of working. Two valid corrections of speech prefixes, however, may have required a source other than the Quarto: Shakespeare's foul papers, as I have conjectured. At the close of 1.3, the Quarto gives the penultimate line to the Archbishop, a weak line that is totally out of character for him: "Shall we go draw our numbers, and set on?" The line is certainly Mowbray's, and it is so assigned in the Folio. The faulty assignment of the speech in the Quarto no doubt resulted from the extensive expurgation of the Archbishop's role. Immediately preceding the line in question, the Archbishop originally had a strong speech of twenty-four lines defending the rebellion. When the speech was cut, what remained at the end of the scene was a sequence of five speeches by secondary characters (Hastings, Bardolph, and Mowbray). The Archbishop, however, is the dominant character in the scene. Thus in the Quarto he was assigned Mowbray's line in a feeble attempt to give him some final word. For the scribe, there was no problem if, as I have proposed, he had before him Shakespeare's manuscript with the canceled passages he was to add. As he finished copying the

REFLECTIONS OF STAGE PRACTICE 35

Archbishop's speech, he returned to his printed copy of the Quarto and saw that the next speech was also assigned to the Archbishop. If he had not already noticed that the speech was originally Mowbray's, all he needed to do was to take a quick glance back at the sheet of foolscap before him to find the correct prefix.

Although I doubt that the scribe regularly consulted his supplementary manuscript while copying from the Quarto, he may have referred to it sporadically when he hit a particular problem and when checking was relatively easy. Beginning at 3.2.104, the Quarto prints a sequence that would perplex any reader who was even half-awake. After Falstaff has questioned Mouldy, and Shallow has gurgled appreciatively over his friend's witticisms, we find "*Iohn prickes him*" set as a stage direction to the right of Shallow's last line. But Mouldy's next speech—beginning "I was prickt wel enough before"—indicates that the words "prick him" were actually spoken by someone. Encountering such a puzzle, the scribe may indeed have turned to his supplementary manuscript. He had just finished copying from it all of 3.1 (omitted in Qa, with which he was working), and this particular problem occurs on line 109 of 3.2. Since Shakespeare may have written about fifty lines to a page and thus perhaps a hundred or so lines to a leaf, the scribe would have needed to flip only one leaf of foolscap for a quick check. In the foul papers, Shakespeare probably wrote "Iohn pricke him" to the right of Shallow's last words, as the line appears in the Quarto, or added a marginal insertion.[10] Whatever the case, the Quarto compositor was confused and, making a common misreading of Shakespeare's final *e* for an *s* in *pricke*, assumed the line to be a stage direction. The scribe, being a more highly trained reader, could easily solve the dilemma. On the other hand, the scribe may have solved this problem by logic alone. Someone must say "Prick him." Shallow has the roll, but if the scribe had read the scene he would have known that it is Falstaff who decides which men should be pricked. For a really alert editor, even this correction would not have required consultation of any source other than the Quarto.

In addition to the five correct changes in speech prefixes in the Folio, there are two revisions that may or may not be valid; neither would require consultation of a source other than the Quarto. At 1.1.161, the Quarto gives one line to an otherwise nonexistent "Vmfr.": "This strained passion doth you wrong my lord." Next, Lord Bardolph chastises Northumberland with "Sweet earle, diuorce not wisedome from your honor," and Morton joins in with "The liues of all your louing complices, / Leane on your health. . . ." Shakespeare's error in assigning a speech to Umfrevile is apparent, though the probable causes need not concern us here. The scribe's solution was simple: he merely cut the line, a frequent strategy when he hit an insoluble problem. However, the line is important, and the entire sequence is typically Shakespearean. A man rages and one by one a series of counselors warn him of the hazards of his passion. Modern editors usually give Umfrevile's speech to Bardolph and then attach Bardolph's line to Morton's longer speech. To me, the rhythm suggests that three speakers urgently warn Northumberland in turn, but I face the same problem faced by the scribe. Who is the first? The only available character onstage is Travers, who, after delivering his bad news, has been cowed into silence by Bardolph and has not been heard from since. He scarcely seems strong enough to be the first to admonish his lord. Moreover, the scribe had a finely developed sense of decorum that would probably not allow the man to whom Northumberland refers as "my seruant Trauers" to be so insolent. In short, something is certainly wrong, but the scribe's solution is open to question and almost all editors have rejected it.

The other Folio change that is open to question presents a more complicated problem. In some copies, Qa reads as follows for 3.2.52–56:

> *Sha.* And is olde Dooble dead?
> *Si.* Here come two of sir Iohn Falstaffes men, as I thinke.
> *Enter Bardolfe, and one with him*
> Good morrow honest gentlemen.
> *Bardolfe* I beseech you, which is iustice Shallow?

For this, the Folio reads

> *Shal.* And is olde *Double* dead?
> *Enter Bardolph and his Boy.*
> *Sil.* Heere come two of Sir *Iohn Falstaffes* Men (as I thinke.)
> *Shal.* Good-morrow, honest Gentlemen.
> *Bard.* I beseech you, which is Iustice *Shallow*?

The scribe made a logical correction by assigning "Good morrow, honest Gentlemen" to Shallow rather than continuing it to Silence, though Walker makes an interesting case for assigning it to Bardolph.[11] We cannot be positive that the Folio's change is authoritative but we can, I believe, be sure that the scribe could have made the change solely on the basis of the Quarto and his own sense of decorum. Silence is a guest. He should not greet the newcomers. The scribe's correction is even more easily understood if his copy of Qa had an uncorrected page at this point. There "Good morrow honest gentlemen" is assigned to Bardolph, thus giving him two speeches in a row. "Good morrow" would then need to be reassigned, and the obvious candidate is Shallow. Moreover, we can be certain that the scribe did not consult an authoritative, corrected manuscript at this point. In a comedy of errors to be detailed below, he early became confused by Falstaff's page and began assuming that the page was Bardolph's. Here he rejected the Quarto's indeterminate "*and one with him*" in favor of the mythical "Bardolph's boy."

In one Folio change of a speech prefix, the scribe attempted a correction by logic but only made a more serious error. In the Quarto version of 2.2.118–136, a sequence in which Hal reads a letter from Falstaff while Poins intersperses comments, we find an unmistakable error, but only one. After some preliminary joking about Falstaff's flaunting of his knighthood, Hal begins reading the letter. For clarification, I include quotation marks to distinguish between read portions of the letter and side comments. Hal begins:

> but the letter, "Sir Iohn Falstaffe knight, to the sonne of the king, nearest his father, Harry prince of Wales, greeting."

> *Poynes* Why this is a certificate.
> *Prince* Peace.
> "I will imitate the honourable Romanes in breuitie."
> *Poynes* He sure meanes breuity in breath, short winded,
> "I commend mee to thee, I commend thee, and, I leaue thee, be not too familiar with Poynes...."

Following the completion of the letter, in which Falstaff casts further aspersions on Poins's motives but on which Poins makes no side-comment, we find the next speech.

> *Poynes* My Lord, Ile steep this letter in sacke and make him eate it.

The single error in the Quarto is at line 126: "I commend mee to thee...," which is continued to Poins, but which clearly marks Hal's return to his reading of the letter. In the foul papers, these words probably began a new line, just as they do in the Quarto. Either Shakespeare forgot to add the prefix *Prince* or the Quarto compositor overlooked it. As Walker notes, "Prince Henry should presumably have the privilege of reading his own letter."[12] If there were any doubt, it is erased by Poins's response. Since the response has its own prefix in the Quarto, Poins is incorrectly given two speeches in a row. Thus the continuation of the letter (beginning with "I commend mee to thee") should be assigned to the Prince. The Folio compounds the error by removing the apparently redundant speech prefix before Poins's announcement of his determination to steep the letter in sack, thereby making explicit the faulty inference that Poins reads the Prince's letter. Here the scribe's logic operated, but his dramatic sense failed. There is no possibility at this point that he collated the Quarto with an independent manuscript.

Common speech prefix anomalies may indicate the Folio's reliance on the Quarto, but they deserve only brief mention because they are not undebatable errors. Perhaps Falstaff should ask Feeble his trade (3.2.149), but the speech is assigned to Shallow in both the Quarto and the Folio. Probably all of the panting repetitions of "It doth so.... It doth so.... It doth, it doth, it doth" (5.5.15, 17, 19) should be assigned to Shallow. All three speeches are assigned to Pistol in the Quarto. In the Folio, the first speech is reassigned to Shallow, probably on the logical grounds that Falstaff has just been addressing Shallow, referring to his debt of a thousand pounds, but the second two remain assigned to Pistol. In both cases, the scribe's reliance on the Quarto alone seems probable.

Thus far, nothing in our consideration of the Folio's treatment of stage directions—its addition of necessary entrances and exits, its placement of directions, its changes in speech prefixes— indicates any changes that cannot be accounted for by the procedures of a thoughtful scribe copying from the Quarto and consulting his supplementary manuscript only at or near those points where passages were to be added. Three major changes remain to be discussed, changes of the kind that have led to the widespread assumption that the transcript serving as copy for the Folio derives from some independent manuscript reflecting adaptation of the play for the stage.

First, why does the Folio include Colevile in the entrance at the beginning of 4.1? According to the Quarto, Colevile does not enter until he encounters Falstaff at the opening of what is designated as 4.3 in modern texts. Does the Folio change thus indicate that in production Colevile was included as a mute at Gaultree Forest? The stage direction at the beginning of 4.1 reads as follows in the Quarto:

> Enter the Archbishop, Mowbray, Bardolfe, Hastings, within the forrest of Gaultree.

In contrast, the Folio reads,

> Enter the Arch-bishop, Mowbray, Hastings, Westmerland, Coleuile.

Characteristically, the scribe has cut a mute (Lord Bardolph, who probably should be present) and the descriptive material. The addition of Westmoreland, who enters at line 25, can be explained by the scribe's tendency to include in the opening stage direction characters who enter shortly. (The messenger who enters at line 18 is omitted; messengers do not seem to count.) But why the addition of Colevile, who, according to the Quarto, does not encounter Falstaff for some 350 lines? Only one thing is certain. The scribe is not writing a massed entry. According to the Folio's division, Colevile's meeting with Falstaff occurs in 4.1, the scene beginning at Gaultree Forest, but neither Prince John nor Falstaff, both too important to be overlooked, is included in the opening stage direction. Colevile is.

The division of act four is faulty in both the Folio and modern editions. Editors assign scene 1 to the conference of the rebels with Westmoreland at Gaultree, scene 2 to John's trick, and scene 3 to Falstaff's capture of Colevile. The Folio comprehends all three of these scenes under 4.1. To the extent that act and scene divisions have any validity at all in the play, both divisions are wrong. Scenes 1 and 2 are continuous. At the end of what is designated as scene 1 in modern editions, we find the following Quarto setting:

> *West.*   The prince is here at hand, pleaseth your Lordship
> To meet his grace iust distance tweene our armies.
> *Enter Prince Iohn and his armie.*
> *Mow.*   Your grace of York, in Gods name then set forward.
> *Bishop.*   Before, and greete his grace (my lord) we come.
> *Iohn*   You are well incountred here, my cousen Mowbray....

The Folio moves John's entrance two lines later, immediately before he speaks, and this placement is followed by modern editors. The delay in John's entry led Capell to insert the scene 2 division, and that too is maintained today (although most editors indicate that the stage is not cleared).

The continuous action indicated by the Quarto is, however, correct. As John enters with his forces, the Archbishop's army—which has remained onstage—advances to meet him. The action is continuous in the Folio as well, although we again see the scribe's tendency to delay entrances until the last possible moment. Following the parley, John orders the traitors to execution and exits with his army. At that point, the stage is cleared, though the Folio indicates no scene division. If the scribe was responsible for dividing the play into acts and scenes, his confusion at this point is understandable, for the Quarto gives no exit for John and his army following the arrest of the traitors. Thus a quick glance at the Quarto might have suggested to the scribe that the Falstaff-Colevile meeting continues "scene 1." Then, when he began transcribing the Gaultree sequence, he made another faulty assumption. Following his likely procedure, he had probably skimmed the scene before beginning to transcribe, assuring himself that all speakers were accounted for. But in the Quarto, Colevile is not accounted for. Following John's unmarked exit, the Quarto reads

Alarum   *Enter Falstaffe*   *excursions*

but it gives no entrance for Colevile. In adding Colevile to the entering stage direction at the beginning of 4.1, the scribe may merely have been following his habit of including in the opening entrance any speaking characters for whom the Quarto does not provide directed entries. Of course, he may have assumed that Colevile, as a "famous rebel," should be present at Gaultree Forest. Whatever the case, by the time he completed copying the first continuous scene (through the exit of John) he realized that something was wrong. At this point, he now saw, the stage is cleared. The sure sign is his direction *Exeunt*. Throughout the play, he used *Exit* for all exits within scenes, no matter how many characters the direction refers to, reserving *Exeunt* for exits clearing the stage. (See, for example, 2.4.366, 4.3.85, 4.5.90, and 5.5.72.) And, having cleared the stage, he now realized that he must give Colevile an entrance. Omitting the offstage sound effects, he thus provided "*Enter Falstaffe and Colleuile.*"

Is there any reason, however, why the Folio could not be right in including Colevile at Gaultree? I believe there is. If he accompanies the doomed rebels, how does he escape John's grasp to meet Falstaff on the open field? Colevile, moreover, is undoubtedly a comic character. Any man who gives himself "gratis" to Falstaff must be a cowering fool. (One wonders how he attained the fame to which Prince John later refers.) If he was played as comic, his very presence and appearance in the Colevile stance would tend to distract from the serious affairs that take place at Gaultree. In sum, the inclusion of Colevile in the opening stage direction to 4.1 is probably the result not of theatrical practice but of scribal confusion.

A second Folio change that has been cited as suggesting adaptation to the stage is in the Drawers' scene at the opening of 2.4. The problem is sufficiently complicated to require full quotation of the Quarto passage, with speeches numbered for purposes of discussion.

Enter a Drawer or two.

[1]   *Francis* What the diuel hast thou brought there apple Iohns? thou knowest sir Iohn cannot indure an apple Iohn.

[2]   *Draw.* Mas thou saist true, the prince once set a dish of apple Iohns before him, and tolde him there were fiue more sir Iohns, and putting off his hat, said, I will now take my leaue of these six drie, round, old, withered Knights, it angred him to the heart, but he hath forgot that.

[3]   *Fran.* Why then couer and set them downe, and see if thou canst find out Sneakes Noise, mistris Tere-sheet would faine heare some musique.

[4]   *Dra.* Dispatch, the roome where they supt is too hot, theile come in straight.

[5]   *Francis* Sirra, here wil be the prince and master Poynes anon, and they will put on two of our ierkins and aprons, and sir Iohn must not know of it, Bardolfe hath brought word.

Enter Will.

[6]   *Dra.* By the mas here will be old vtis, it wil be an excellent stratagem.

[7]   *Francis* Ile see if I can find out Sneake.   *exit*

Before attempting to resolve the many problems in the scene as it is set in the Quarto, let us speculate on the questions that may have occurred to the scribe. He would have been stopped immediately by the indefinite stage direction. How many speakers are there? Apparently only two. And why name one but not the other? Very well, he will call them simply "1 Drawer" and "2 Drawer." And who is "Will"? He serves no function. Very well, cut his entrance. And speech 4 makes no sense. The two drawers have been making leisurely preparations; then the first has told the second to go find the music. Now—for no reason—the second drawer suddenly announces a fact not known before: that Falstaff and the women will soon enter. The drawers must finish their preparations with "dispatch." Why the sudden urgency? There is no apparent reason. Very well, cut speech 4 also. Now the sequence makes sense, except for one problem. With the cutting of speech 4, the first drawer (Francis) now has two consecutive speeches, ordering the music (speech 3) and then explaining the stratagem (speech 5). That can be easily fixed. Simply alternate the speakers throughout the scene: have the first drawer order the music (speech 3), the second explain the trick (speech 5), the first be delighted by the plan (speech 6), and the second announce that he will go seek the music (speech 7).

The Folio version does indeed solve three of the problems in the Quarto. The seemingly illogical "Dispatch" speech and the pointless entry of Will are solved by the simple expedient of cutting. By good luck, another problem is also solved. In the Quarto, Francis orders his underling to go find the music but at speech 7 he exits to carry out his own order. By alternating prefixes, the Folio fittingly gives speech 7 to the second drawer. Only incidentally does the revision cut the number of actors required from three to two.

Primarily because of the last improvement, it is widely assumed that the Folio reflects adaptation of the scene for the stage. On the contrary, I find that the scribe has solved logical, not dramatic problems, and in such a way as to reveal no understanding of the dramatic situation. In fact, his version creates a new dramatic problem and weakens the comic possibilities of the scene. Francis is obviously first in command: it is he who orders the removal of the apple-johns, he who orders his underling to go find the music.

It is surely he who knows about the trick described in speech 5. Moreover, that speech is prefaced by "Sirra," a form of address no underling would use with his superior. In the Folio, however, by his cuts and his reassignment of speeches, the scribe has given speech 5 to the second drawer. The roles of the two men suddenly reverse. Because of the scribe's changes the comic opportunities suggested by the Quarto scene—when, that is, its problems are resolved—are largely lost. Gone is the sudden intrusion of a sense of urgency, the type of situation that has rich potential for a group of comic servants. (One has only to recall a good production of *The Taming of the Shrew*.) I cannot believe that Shakespeare's company would sacrifice a good comic scene solely to save an actor when the tiring-house was at the moment full of skilled men ready to double.

The many errors in the Quarto suggest that Shakespeare's foul papers were very confusing at this point, but the problems can all be resolved, I believe, if we bear in mind both Shakespeare's known methods of preparing rough drafts and the dramatic movement of the scene. The permissive stage direction—"*Enter a Drawer or two*"—is curious here, for the dialogue requires a minimum of two speakers. The second drawer is not optional. May this be another instance in which Shakespeare omits an obvious entrant (as, for example, he omits Peto at 2.4.353, Colevile at 4.3.1, Davy at 5.1.7, and the Hostess and Doll at 5.4.1)? Following *1 Henry IV*, the comic Francis of "Anon, anon, sir" would still be vivid in Shakespeare's mind. By the indefinite stage direction, he may mean "Enter Francis with at least one drawer, but if possible add one mute; the scene will be funnier." Then still one more drawer will be needed to burst in at speech 4 and warn that the supper party is breaking up. Why "Will"? Perhaps for the same reason that we find "Sincklo," an actor's name. Shakespeare may have thought of Will Kempe (if he was not to play Falstaff) or of another "Will" in the company who was especially good at harried entrances.[13] But why the faulty placement of Will's entry in the Quarto? In Shakespeare's manuscript, the stage direction may have been in the right margin and, given the long lines of prose, the two words "*Enter Will*" were probably staggered on two lines. "*Enter*" may have been written beside speech 4, Will's "Dispatch" speech, with "*Will*" beside the first line of Francis's speech. It would then have been a simple matter for the Quarto compositor to misplace the entry.

The only other problem in the Quarto is the assignment of speech 7 to Francis, making him carry out his own order to find Sneak. It is quite possible that both of the last two speeches were headed only "*Dra.*" in the foul papers, with Shakespeare intending the "old vtis" line for the entering Will and the final exit line ("Ile see if I can find out Sneake") for the original drawer who had been given the order. If so, an error by the Quarto compositor in assigning the two speeches would be understandable, especially because he was confused as to Will's entry and thus as to his function in the scene.

When we compare the potential stage action underlying the Quarto—the sudden injection of urgency and the frantic scurry as last-minute preparations are completed and the three or four drawers scuttle out of sight—with the sedate colloquy of the Folio's two drawers who are unclear as to their respective roles, I think there can be little doubt that the Folio's version derives from the narrowly logical mind of the scribe, not from the backstage knowledge of the Globe bookkeeper.*

A third series of changes that have been thought to suggest

---

* Editors have unanimously agreed that one of the drawers, usually Francis, must remain on stage to heed Falstaff's order to "empty the iourdan" and then exit. There is, however, neither textual authority nor dramatic need for such a delayed exit. Following the drawers' scene, the Quarto stage direction of "*exit*" probably refers to all three, who hurriedly clear the stage so that the Prince's "play" can take place. (Not only must they meet the Prince and Poins to prepare the disguises; the regular staff must be out of sight if the trick is to work.) Was it an eighteenth-century sense of delicacy that led Capell to keep a drawer on stage so that Falstaff could make his request privately? Dover Wilson is doubly discreet by prefacing Falstaff's order with the direction "*to the drawer, aside.*" Falstaff is not noted for his gentility. He enters singing lustily "When Arthur first in court"— and then probably bellows "empty the iourdan" offstage at full voice before continuing the song.

stage practice presents a far more difficult problem. In the Folio version of the final scene of the play, the Quarto's three "Strewers of rushes" become two "Groomes," the third strewer's speech is reassigned to the first groom, and his final "Dispatch, dispatch" is omitted. Also omitted is the first procession of the King and his train, passing over the stage on the way to the coronation. Toward the end of the play at 5.5.90, there is a third omission, that of the Quarto's stage direction marking the reentry of John and the Chief Justice. The implication is that as the King exits they stand aside, together with some officers, and remain on stage for eighteen lines before stepping forward to order Falstaff and his followers to Fleet Prison.

This is the first, and only, scene in which I find a possibility that revisions could reflect adaptation for the stage, though I believe the possibility to be remote. Too much significance should not be placed on an omitted reentrance for Prince John and the Chief Justice in a text in which so many essential stage directions have been omitted. Furthermore, their exit with the coronation procession and their reentry shortly thereafter with officers, as provided in the Quarto, is far better dramatically. Visualize the change in dramatic effect if Prince John, who would be second only to the new King in the procession, and the Chief Justice, who would also be near the King, were to peel off from the formal procession and draw aside some officers. The impact of the procession would be radically disturbed. Moreover, the threatening presence of the Prince, the Chief Justice, and the officers would raise an uneasy question in the audience's mind and would seriously distract from Falstaff's subdued colloquy with Shallow. Thus both the focus on the procession and the focus on Falstaff's reaction to the King's rejection would be greatly diffused.

It would be easy to dismiss the Folio deletion of the first procession on the grounds that the scribe was preparing a literary document and thus omitted matters of spectacle, but it seems more probable that he was confused by the scene, as, frankly, am I. In the Quarto, the strewers speak with a strong sense of urgency.

Apparently they are strewing the streets with rushes and haste is essential:

    1 More rushes, more rushes.
    2 The trumpets haue sounded twice.
    3 Twill be two a clocke ere they come from the coronation, dispatch, dispatch.

At this moment the trumpets sound for the expected third time (one assumes) and the King enters—but passing on his way to, not "from," the coronation. In addition, the third strewer speaks as if they have ample time, as if the strewing need be completed only before the King's return from the Abbey. Surely either the Quarto compositor or Shakespeare made an error, though no simple change of a word or two can make sense out of the third strewer's statement.

The Folio revisions make a certain amount of sense, though one cannot be at all sure that the sense is that of Shakespeare. If one takes the third strewer's words at their face value, the men are to strew rushes on a street over which the King will pass after the coronation has taken place. Except for the contradictory words "dispatch, dispatch," he also seems to be saying that there is more than ample time to complete the job. Very well, the scribe cuts the contradictory words and lessens the sense of urgency. Next he adds an exit for his two grooms. All quite logical. After their three lines in the Quarto they serve no function, and the scribe may think that they are on their way to strew rushes in some other street over which the King will pass after the ceremony. Finally, he cuts the first procession—as he must, once he believes that the awaited procession will be coming from the coronation, rather than going to it. This explanation is highly speculative, but it is the only one I can offer to account for the three interrelated changes: the cutting of "dispatch, dispatch," the adding of an exit for the grooms, and the omitting of the first procession.

What, then, points to the possible influence of adaptation for the stage? Only the Folio's reduction of three strewers to two grooms, and I doubt that much significance should be placed on that change. The scribe has revealed throughout the play that he was uninterested in minor characters. In addition to eliminating mutes, he eliminated one drawer and even deprived Francis of his name. That three rather than two minor characters speak in the Quarto simply would not, I believe, have mattered to him, and there is a certain neatness to 1 *Groo.*, 2 *Groo.*, as there is to 1 *Draw.*, 2 *Draw*. The Folio's omission of the first procession most certainly does not reflect adaptation for the stage. That an Elizabethan acting company would miss the opportunity for spectacle provided by two royal processions I find inconceivable. A maxim of the Elizabethan stage seemed to be "If it is good once, it is better twice." Note, for example, the double triumphal procession of the victorious army in 1.2 of *The Spanish Tragedy*, repeated for no better reason than the delight of the audience. There is far better reason for repeating the procession in *2 Henry IV*. On the way to the Abbey, Prince Henry is in proper coronation dress, but on his return he is wearing the royal crown of state and other coronation regalia and possibly even carrying the orb and sceptre. The audience sees the transformation from prince to king in what amounts to two contrasting emblems, and the shock of Falstaff's effrontery is heightened. A company that would cut such a theatrical and dramatically essential bit of pageantry would not be the type of company to inspire Shakespeare's allegiance.

In all of the evidence considered, I find nothing to indicate that the scribe consulted an independent manuscript deriving from stage practice. Moreover, many outright errors on matters relating to production suggest that he did not. Several errors, such as misplaced entrances and the compounding of the Quarto's error in assigning to Poins the reading of the Prince's letter, have already been discussed. In addition, the Folio omits stage directions that are both essential and unambiguous in the Quarto. It is one thing to eliminate supernumeraries who are required in a good production; it is quite another to eliminate silent characters who are absolutely essential to the action: for example, the Chief Justice's men at 2.1.60, to whom Falstaff specifically refers, and poor Blunt, whose solid presence is important in three scenes but who is never given an entrance in the Folio. Other essential Quarto stage directions that are omitted in the Folio include the exit of the Hostess and the sergeant at 2.1.165 (set prematurely in the Quarto), the exit of Westmoreland at 4.1.180, and the exit of Falstaff and the justices to dinner at 3.2.219, together with their reentrance at line 240.

Of particular interest is the scribe's total confusion about Falstaff's page. The case of "Bardolph's boy" becomes increasingly comic as one moves through the script, seeing the scribe flounder periodically and then—as he thinks—begin to understand and make a necessary "correction." The Boy first enters at 2.1.38 with Falstaff and Bardolph. This time the scribe's skimming of a scene has been a little careless. Overlooking the Boy's one line at 59–60, the scribe assumes that he is a mute and deletes him from the opening stage direction. After copying the scene and belatedly noting the Boy's line, he is not caught off guard at the opening of 2.2. Here, for some reason, he decides to use a massed entry and, seeing in the Quarto that Bardolph enters with the Boy at line 69, he includes both Bardolph and the Boy in the opening stage direction. That gesture seems to be quite enough for such a minor character because, again for some unexplained reason, he omits the Boy from the actual entry with Bardolph at line 69. By the end of the scene, the Boy at last really enters the dialogue. The scribe will not overlook him again. At 2.4.109, he finds "*Enter antient Pistol, and Bardolfes boy.*" How curious. That Boy who was with Bardolph before is now with Pistol? The usual summary check of the scene ahead shows that Bardolph is an important speaker and that the Boy (who, now, is not to be ignored) has two lines. Obviously the stage direction is faulty, and the scribe "corrects" it: "*Enter Pistol, and Bardolph and his Boy.*" Thus has Falstaff's page been transferred to Bardolph.* By now, one

---

* Shakespeare could not have written "Bardolfes boy." The Quarto compositor may have misread "Bardolfe, boy" or "Bardolfe & boy." On the other hand, the internal entry of Hand D in *Sir Thomas More* reads "Enter the L maier

gathers, the scribe feels quite proud of himself for having solved a difficult problem and he is prepared to handle Shakespeare's vague entry at 3.2.54: "*Enter Bardolfe, and one with him.*" And who should be with him? Of course! It was probably with a great feeling of satisfaction that the scribe substituted "*Enter Bardolph and his Boy.*" No matter that the "one" with Bardolph is a mute, whom normally the scribe would omit. At last he has that slippery character pinned down.

It is impossible that the scribe could have been consistently collating the Quarto with some manuscript corrected with an eye to production and still omit so many important entries, place so many directions incorrectly, solve so many problems inadequately, and make so many serious errors. Assuming that the company bookkeeper would supply the stage directions that Shakespeare omitted, I think there is little doubt that the Quarto brings us much closer to a Shakespearean production of the play than does the Folio. In short, the extremely sketchy and doubtful evidence suggesting that the Folio copy derived from a manuscript reflecting stage practice is more than outweighed by the evidence that it did not.

Surrey / Shrewsbury," with no commas (ll. 24–25). Shakespeare may have omitted commas in stage directions: witness the Quarto setting at 4.3.23 of *2 Henry IV*: "*Enter Iohn Westmerland, and the rest.*" If Simmes' Compositor A saw before him "Enter antient Pistol / Bardolfe boy," he may have been confused and made an assumed correction.

CHAPTER III

Textual Changes by the Folio Compositors

In 1953, Alice Walker noted that "for some reason" Compositor B apparently deleted words on certain pages of *2 Henry IV* in an attempt to save space. "The trouble," she added, "may not have been local."[1] With Charlton Hinman's important discovery in 1955 that the Folio compositors normally worked from the inside of a quire outward, rather than proceeding by successive pages, and with his subsequent analysis of the order of setting the Folio plays and the individual problems faced in setting specific plays, Compositor B's reason for deleting words became clear, as did the fact that the "trouble" was far more extensive than Walker could realize.[2] Hinman's work marks a breakthrough for editors of Shakespeare's plays, but to my knowledge they have applied his findings only occasionally. For the editor of *2 Henry IV*, his conclusions are crucial.

In setting *2 Henry IV*, Jaggard's compositors faced a familiar problem, but shortly found it compounded by a far more serious one. The first problem was encountered in setting all of the Folio texts: many of its pages were not set in normal reading order. Following a detailed study of certain typographical features of the Folio—primarily the recurrence of individually distinctive types, such as an imperfect *A* or a damaged *b*, and the recurrence of irregular rules—Hinman discovered that the Folio had not been set in the manner long assumed. Rather than beginning with the first page of a given play and then working through to the end, page by page in normal succession, the compositors often had to set pages in the reverse of reading order, in effect setting page 6, then page 5, and so on back to page 1.

52 TEXTUAL CHANGES BY THE COMPOSITORS

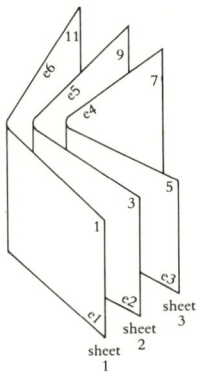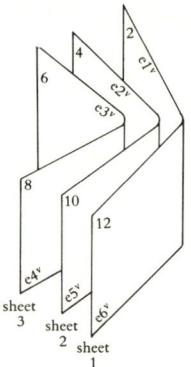

The Folio is made up of a series of quires: gatherings of sheets stitched together. Each quire is identified by a "signature," or identifying letter. For almost all of the Folio quires, three sheets of paper were each folded in half and interleaved; thus a typical quire consists of six leaves, or twelve pages. When the two pages comprising one side of a sheet were set in type, they were laid out so that the pages would be printed in the proper order, locked up in a metal frame, and sent to the press.[3] This unit of two pages, called a "forme," was the work unit for all Folio typesetting and presswork. The accompanying figure represents two views of a typical Folio quire, quire e of *1 Henry IV*. The outer forme of the outermost sheet (sheet 1) thus consists of signatures e1 and e6^v, the first and the twelfth pages in reading order. Similarly, the inner forme of the innermost sheet (sheet 3) consists of signatures e3^v and e4, the sixth and the seventh pages.

Hinman's discovery was that the normal procedure in setting the Folio was for compositors to begin setting type at the inside of a quire and to work outward. They began work on quire e, for example, with the forme composed of 3e^v and e4, pages 6 and 7. When they finished that forme and sent it to the press to be "machined," they began working on the second forme, e3:e4^v. When the press had completed printing the first forme and had begun working on the second, compositors distributed the type of the first forme (returning it letter by letter to the appropriate

TEXTUAL CHANGES BY THE COMPOSITORS 53

divisions of the cases propped on stands before them) and began work on the third: e2^v:e5. The normal work order was thus to set pages as follows: 6:7, 5:8, 4:9, 3:10, 2:11, and, finally, 1:12. Moreover, normal procedure was for two compositors to work simultaneously as a team. In setting quire e, Compositor B began with e3^v and worked back to e1 while his colleague, Compositor A, began with e4 and worked ahead to complete the quire with e6.[4] There were many variations during the almost two years of work on the Folio: sometimes pages were set in an order slightly different from the normal one here described; sometimes one compositor set an entire play by himself; sometimes another compositor stepped in while one member of the original team was pulled aside to work on another job. But despite the variations in this basic pattern, not one play in the Folio was set by successive pages.

How was this possible? If a compositor was to commence setting type with page 6, how did he know exactly where in his copy page 6 would begin? Moreover, when two compositors were working simultaneously, as Hinman's study indicates was normal procedure, how did his co-worker, who was to begin his stint with page 7, know exactly where page 6 would end? The answer is that the first half of every quire had to be "cast off" before composition could begin. Starting with the first page of the quire, the compositor, or someone else assigned to the task, had to count the lines, and determine exactly how much copy would fit on each of the first six pages. A rough guess would not do. When working with cast-off copy, compositors had to know the exact line with which to begin a page, or, if the page break occurred in the middle of a prose passage, the exact word. For plays, the line count also had to take into consideration the number of blank lines to be used in setting off scene boxes and certain types of stage directions.

The difficulty of casting off copy for the Folio, as well as the difficulties faced by compositors, has, I believe, been underestimated. Joseph Moxon, a master printer of the later seventeenth century, describes in detail his method of casting off, or "counting," handwritten copy. After first studying the characteristics of the given hand—noting whether the hand was fairly consistent or erratic, whether letters were large or small, whether they were close together or spaced out—he would set a typical manuscript line to determine how its length corresponded to the established measure of the line of type. Thereafter, he would count off lines by rotating a pair of compasses. Moxon's discussion makes the process sound relatively simple for an experienced craftsman.* Nevertheless, in the words of Hinman, "there is abundant evidence that the amount of copy that could be got neatly into a given Folio page was frequently misjudged." Indeed, "so numerous and so striking ... are various phenomena that can be satisfactorily explained only as the products of miscalculation in casting off that it seems incredible—now that we know what to look for—that they could have escaped attention for so long."[5] The conclusions of the present study amply confirm Hinman's study. In fact, I will argue that several readings in *2 Henry IV*, long assumed to be authoritative, are the result of serious miscalculation. Before turning to the play, however, it is first necessary to establish not only the difficulty in casting off copy for the Folio but also the pressures under which compositors were often forced to work and some of the less obvious methods by which they responded to those pressures.[6]

Moxon's method of casting off written lines by means of a pair of compasses would probably work very well if the copy were written throughout by one hand and if it were a manuscript of solid verse to be set in wide columns or a manuscript of solid prose. The copy used for the Folio, however, presented several distinctive problems. In the first place, copy varied from play to play. Compositors had to deal now with an unmarked printed

* *Mechanick Exercises*, (1683–84), ed. Herbert Davis and Harry Carter (London, 1958), pp. 239–44. We should note, however, that casting off by formes had been abandoned by Moxon's day. Moxon cast off merely to determine the total number of sheets that a given piece of copy would require, not to determine the exact allotment of words to a given page.

quarto, now with one that was heavily edited by hand; now with a manuscript by Ralph Crane, now with one by a scribe whose characteristics were unfamiliar. They also had to deal with Shakespeare's foul papers—probably written in an uneven hand, with line-counting further complicated by deletions and by insertions between the lines and in the margins.* For each new kind of copy encountered, the caster-off would have to begin all over, making the type of analysis that Moxon defines. Moreover, a systematic analysis would be almost impossible with certain kinds of copy, such as an extensively annotated quarto or Shakespeare's foul papers marked up for production by the playhouse bookkeeper.

The width of the Folio column created an additional problem. Counting verse lines in any kind of copy would seem simple, but even an exact count (and it was not always exact) was no guarantee that the same number of lines would be needed in the Folio. Most lines of Shakespearean verse fall well short of the maximum length permitted by the Folio column, but some are one or more words too long. Because of the space required by the speech prefix, compositors faced this problem most often in the first line of a speech. In such cases they normally "overran" the extra words, setting them on a new line, or they divided one regular line of verse into two short ones. Certain pages in the Folio suggest that the workmen responsible for casting off anticipated this problem and counted extra lines where required, but others show that compositors had to compensate for unexpected overruns by compressing elsewhere on the page.[7]

Casting off verse accurately was thus difficult enough, but casting off prose must often have presented a frustrating challenge. Consider what was probably the easiest kind of prose copy to cast off: a printed quarto. Here predictable type replaced the erratic human hand, and counting prose lines might seem fairly routine.

* "Probably uneven" because written over a period of time. The writing of most of us varies considerably from day to day and hour to hour, depending on many variables: mood, pressures, a playful dog, and the like.

The quarto line, however, is slightly longer than the Folio line and—depending on such variables as the quarto compositor's spacing, spelling, and use of abbreviations, as well as on the Folio compositor's heavier punctuation and more frequent use of capital letters—it may accommodate anywhere from one to five or even more letters. How many Folio lines would be required for the following speech in Q1 of *Much Ado About Nothing*?

> *Conſt.* Come you ſir, if iuſtice cannot tame you, ſhe ſhall here weigh more reaſons in her ballance, nay, and you be a curſing hypocrite once, you muſt be lookt to.

Given the unused space at the end of the third line, one assumes that the speech should take only three Folio lines, and such is the case at 2291–93.[8]

> *Conſt.* Come you ſir, if iuſtice cannot tame you, ſhee ſhall nere weigh more reaſons in her ballance, nay, and you be a curſing hypocrite once, you muſt be lookt to.

Consider, then, the following speech as set in Q1.

> *Claud.* I faith I thanke him he hath bid me to a calues head & a capon, the which if I doe not carue moſt curiouſly, ſay my kniffe's naught, ſhall I not find a woodcocke too?

Would not an eye moving swiftly, counting lines, gauge that these three lines would again take three Folio lines? But they do not.

> *Clau.* I faith I thanke him, he hath bid me to a calues head and a Capon, the which if I doe not carue moſt curiouſly, ſay my knife's naught, ſhall I not finde a woodcocke too?

The Folio requires four lines (2242–45), partly because in this instance the quarto compositor omitted spaces and used the ampersand, partly because the Folio compositor added a capital letter, and partly because of sheer coincidence. In the first example, the Constable's speech, the last word in the first quarto line—the word that had to be set on the second Folio line (*shall*)—includes three thin letters (one long *s* and two *l*'s). In the second example,

Claudio's speech, all four letters of the last word in the first quarto line, *head*, are relatively thick. The result of all these differences is that twelve characters accommodated by the first two quarto lines had to be thrown into the third Folio line—requiring a fourth line for two words. Even with printed copy, then, it is doubtful that the most trained eye could have taken into consideration the many variables in each line.

Casting off was further complicated by the demands of Folio page layout and the particular kind of material being set. Each column was to be sixty-six type-lines, no more, no less. The modern printer often allows deviations of one line from the established page length, provided that the facing page matches. The Folio compositors did not have this option; they violated the sixty-six-line rule very rarely, and then only when faced with a special problem. On seven pages, we find a sixty-seventh line, and on four of the pages the circumstances suggest that the compositors were following a specific aesthetic policy, rather than finding a way to accommodate an additional line on the page. Later in the seventeenth century, Joseph Moxon would specify that "good *Compositors* [do not] account it good Workmanship to begin a *Page* with a *Break-line*...."[9] The "break-line"—or what modern English and American printers call a "widow" (and Dutch printers a "whore's son")—is the last line of a paragraph, or, in the case of a play, the last line of a speech. Just as some modern printers establish strict rules against the use of widows less than a full line long at the beginning of a page, so Jaggard's compositors may have attempted to avoid short break-lines at the head of a column. The rule could not be absolute in setting the text of a play with its many short prose speeches, but the circumstances surrounding four of the long columns suggest that compositors at least tried to follow it. In three cases, they were setting pages in the second half of a quire, pages that had not been cast off, and thus they could use as many lines as they needed. On $X5^v$, setting the one word *further* on the sixty-seventh line removed the need to begin the next page with a one-word break-line, as did the setting of *Pockets* on the sixty-seventh line in the right column of e5.[10] In the left column of H6ᵛ, the stage direction "*Runne all out*" is set to the right on the sixty-seventh line, probably because it would have looked awkward at the head of the right column. Although V3 occurs in the first half of its quire and was thus cast off, pressures of space cannot account for the long left column, because in the right column the compositor added a superfluous blank line before the stage direction. Apparently he was avoiding a one-word break-line of *you* at the top of the right column.[11]

The problems in casting off copy for the Folio were further compounded by the fact that Jaggard's staff was working with plays, most of which were divided into acts and scenes for printing in the Folio. As sixty-six lines were counted, by sheer bad luck the middle of a scene heading might fall at the bottom of a column. Although scene boxes could be compressed—even, in an emergency, to the equivalent of two lines—they could not, of course, be divided. Moreover, a policy of the Jaggard shop apparently forbade ending a column with a scene box alone. Before the column break, compositors were also to set the scene's opening stage direction and at least one line of dialogue.[12] (Again note a related modern policy: the requirement that a subhead near the bottom of a page be followed by at least two lines of text before the page break.) Thus in the first third of the Folio, bad luck compounded with the compositors' inexperience in dealing with such matters to create nine short columns, each prior to a scene box at the top of the next column. As Jaggard's compositors became more experienced and more adventurous, they apparently learned how to solve such problems. In the plays set after *The Winter's Tale*, I have noted only one short column.[13]

Another problem met in casting off plays for the Folio was the fact that in some printed copy and in much manuscript copy, internal stage directions were often placed to the right of the dialogue; similarly, when the lines of two speakers were short, their speeches were often placed on one line. Following the setting of *The Tempest*, compositors usually centered all entrances

TEXTUAL CHANGES BY THE COMPOSITORS 59

occurring between speeches and began a new line for all speakers. In *The Tempest*, entrances are placed to the right ten times, whereas in the twenty plays composed between *The Tempest* and *2 Henry IV*, there are a total of only twenty instances. In *The Tempest*, two speakers are placed on the same line eight times; in contrast, there are only eight instances in all the other plays set before *2 Henry IV*.[14] Searching the Folio for examples, one becomes aware of how difficult it is to spot such anomalies even in a printed text. How often were they overlooked in both printed and manuscript copy as lines were being counted?

I have been this detailed about specific difficulties in casting off Folio copy because it is important to grasp the severity of the problems that often faced compositors if one is to be alert to, and understand the reasons for, many of their previously inexplicable settings—and, as we shall see, some of their previously overlooked revisions. Often they were, quite simply, compelled to tamper with their copy.[15]

Signs that compositors often had to compensate for miscalculation in casting off are widespread in the Folio, though many of them are not noticeable without close study. The most easily detected are scene headings that have been either expanded or compressed. Scene headings usually take six or seven type-lines: a scene box four or five lines deep, framed with one blank line above it and another below. Compare, then, the three boxes on Plate I. The setting of the fourth act division of i4^v of *Henry V* is normal. The box is four lines deep and framed by blank lines. In addition, the opening entrance is separated from the dialogue by another blank line. Given this normal setting, even a quick glance reveals that the act divisions of O1 of *A Midsummer Night's Dream* and on l1 of *1 Henry VI* are abnormal. On O1, Compositor C used four lines more than usual by setting the stage direction at the close of the preceding scene on a new line, creating two "white lines" before the box, and enlarging the box to use six type-lines.[16] Equally obvious is the crowding on l1. Although the page is solid verse and lines should have been simple to count off

Giue the word through. *Exit*

Actus Quartus.

Enter Fluellen and Gower.

Flu. Kill the poyes and the luggage, 'Tis expressely

Sig. i4ᵛ

The man shall haue his Mare againe, and all shall bee well.
They sleepe all the Act.

Actus Quartus.

Enter Queene of Fairies, and Clowne, and Fairies, and the King behinde them.

Tita. Come, sit thee downe vpon this flowry bed,

Sig. O1

Or make my will th'aduantage of my good. *Exit.*

Actus Tertius. Scena Prima.

Flourish. Enter King, Exeter, Gloster, Winchester, Warwick, Somerset, Suffolk, Richard Plantagenet. Gloster offers to put vp a Bill: Winchester snatches it, teares it.
Winch. Com'st thou with deepe premeditated Lines?

Sig. l1

PLATE I

TEXTUAL CHANGES BY THE COMPOSITORS 61

accurately, the act box is telescoped to two lines, and the customary blank lines before and after the opening entry are omitted. The compositor was not compensating for unexpected overruns in the text. Only one line is too long for the Folio column (1212), and he held it to one type-line by using three abbreviations. Apparently three or four lines too many were allotted to the page in the castoff.

Because abnormal scene headings are often signs of miscalculation, they warn us to look for less noticeable signs of adjustment. On F1^v (Plate II), the shallow scene box in the lower right column and the abbreviations in the subsequent stage direction show the pressure under which the compositor was working. Without that obvious clue, however, we might not notice two more signs of miscalculation: the setting of two internal entrances to the right of short lines (at 137 and 175) and the use of a "turn-up" rather than the preferred overrun or line division at 214.

Even when there are no anomalous scene headings to provide clues, some pages on which crowding is unmistakable are also easily detected. For example, the last half of the right column of Bb3 is jammed (Plate III). Following the setting of *The Tempest*, compositors normally framed songs with blank space when possible and often centered the word *Song* or a similar heading on its own line. On Bb3, compare the normal setting of Autolycus' song in the left column with that of the two songs in the right. As the end of the page approached, Compositor B sacrificed any concern for aesthetics, omitting blank lines and twice setting *Song* to the left of the song's first line. The pressure caused by miscalculation is also reflected in the setting of the Clown's speech. B used abbreviations in 2135 so that the Clown's final line runs short, thus leaving space to set a second speaker on 2138. At least six lines too many were allotted to this page.

Serious misjudgment is even more apparent in the setting of L1, the final page of *Much Ado About Nothing* (Plate IV). We first notice the setting of *FINIS* on the sixty-seventh line of the right column. Once alerted, we also note the substitutions of y^u and y^t

Scena Secunda.

Enter Lucio, and two other Gentlemen.

Luc. If the *Duke*, with the other Dukes, come not to composition with the King of *Hungary*, why then all the Dukes fall vpon the King.

1.Gent. Heauen grant vs its peace, but not the King of *Hungaries*.

2.Gent. Amen.

Luc. Thou conclud'st like the Sanctimonious Pirat, that went to sea with the ten Commandements, but scrap'd one out of the Table.

2.Gent. Thou shalt not Steale?

Luc. I, that he raz'd.

1.Gent. Why? 'twas a commandement, to command the Captaine and all the rest from their functions: they put forth to steale: There's not a Souldier of vs all, that in the thanks-giuing before meate, do rallish the petition well, that praies for peace.

2.Gent. I neuer heard any Souldier dislike it.

Luc. I beleeue thee: for I thinke thou neuer was't where Grace was said.

2.Gent. No? a dozen times at least.

1.Gent. What? In meeter?

Luc. In any proportion, or in any language.

1.Gent. I thinke, or in any Religion.

Luc. I, why not? Grace, is Grace, despight of all controuersie: as for example; Thou thy selfe art a wicked villaine, despight of all Grace.

1.Gent. Well: there went but a paire of sheeres betweene vs.

Luc. I grant: as there may betweene the Lists, and the Veluet. Thou art the List.

1.Gent. And thou the Veluet; thou art good veluet; thou'rt a three pild-peece I warrant thee: I had as liefe be a Lyst of an English Kersey, as be pil'd, as thou art pil'd, for a French Veluet. Do I speake feelingly now?

Luc. I thinke thou do'st: and indeed with most painfull feeling of thy speech: I will, out of thine owne confession, learne to begin thy health; but, whilst I liue forget to drinke after thee.

1.Gen. I think I haue done my selfe wrong, haue I not?

2.Gent. Yes, that thou hast; whether thou art tainted, or free. *Enter Bawde.*

Luc. Behold, behold, where Madam *Mitigation* comes. I haue purchas'd as many diseases vnder her Roofe, As come to

2.Gent. To what, I pray?

Luc. Iudge.

2.Gent. To three thousand Dollours a yeare.

1.Gent. I, and more.

Luc. A French crowne more.

1.Gent. Thou art alwayes figuring diseases in me; but thou art full of error, I am sound.

Luc. Nay, not (as one would say) healthy: but so sound, as things that are hollow; thy bones are hollow; Impiety has made a feast of thee.

1.Gent. How now, which of your hips has the most profound Ciatica?

Bawd. Well, well: there's one yonder arrested, and carried to prison, was worth fiue thousand of you all.

2.Gent. Who's that I pray'thee?

Bawd. Marry Sir, that's *Claudio*, Signior *Claudio*.

1.Gent. Claudio to prison? 'tis not so.

Bawd. Nay, but I know 'tis so: I saw him arrested: saw him carried away: and which is more, within these three daies his head to be chop'd off.

Luc. But, after all this fooling, I would not haue it so: Art thou sure of this?

Bawd. I am too sure of it: and it is for getting Madam *Iulietta* with childe.

Luc. Beleeue me this may be: he promis'd to meete me two howres since, and he was euer precise in promise keeping.

2.Gent. Besides you know, it drawes somthing neere to the speech we had to such a purpose.

1.Gent. But most of all agreeing with the proclamatiō.

Luc. Away: let's goe learne the truth of it. *Exit.*

Bawd. Thus, what with the war; what with the sweat, what with the gallowes, and what with pouerty, I am Custom-shrunke. How now? what's the newes with you? *Enter Clowne.*

Clo. Yonder man is carried to prison.

Baw. Well: what has he done?

Clo. A Woman.

Baw. But what's his offence?

Clo. Groping for Trowts, in a peculiar Riuer.

Baw. What? is there a maid with child by him?

Clo. No: but there's a woman with maid by him: you haue not heard of the proclamation, haue you?

Baw. What proclamation, man?

Clow. All howses in the Suburbs of *Vienna* must bee pluck'd downe.

Bawd. And what shall become of those in the Citie?

Clow. They shall stand for seed: they had gon downe to, but that a wise Burger put in for them.

Bawd. But shall all our houses of resort in the Suburbs be puld downe?

Clow. To the ground, Mistris.

Bawd. Why heere's a change indeed in the Commonwealth: what shall become of me?

Clow. Come: feare not you: good Counsellors lacke no Clients: though you change your place, you neede not change your Trade: Ile bee your Tapster still; courage, there will bee pitty taken on you; you that haue worne your eyes almost out in the seruice, you will bee considered.

Bawd. What's to doe heere, *Thomas* Tapster? let's withdraw?

Clo. Here comes Signior *Claudio*, led by the Prouost to prison: and there's Madam *Iuliet*. *Exeunt.*

Scena Tertia.

Enter Prouost, Claudio, Iuliet, Officers, Lucio, & 2.Gent.

Cla. Fellow, why do'st thou show me thus to th' world? Beare me to prison, where I am committed.

Pro. I do it not in euill disposition,
But from Lord *Angelo* by speciall charge.

Clau. Thus can the demy-god (Authority)
Make vs pay downe, for our offence, by waight
The words of heauen; on whom it will, it will,
On whom it will not (foe) yet still 'tis iust. (straint.

Luc. Why how now *Claudio*? whence comes this re-

Cla. From too much liberty, (my *Lucio*) Liberty
As surfet is the father of much fast,
So euery Scope by the immoderate vse
Turnes to restraint: Our Natures doe pursue

Like

The Winters Tale.

Ser. He hath songs for man, or woman, of all sizes: No Milliner can so fit his customers with Gloues: he has the prettiest Loue-songs for Maids, so without bawdrie (which is strange,) with such delicate burthens of Dildo's and Fadings: Iump-her, and thump-her; and where some stretch-mouth'd Rascall, would (as it were) meane mischeefe, and breake a fowle gap into the Matter, hee makes the maid to answere, *Whoop, doe me no harme good man:* put's him off, slights him, with *Whoop, doe mee no harme good man.*

Pol. This is a braue fellow.

Clo. Beleeue mee, thou talkest of an admirable conceited fellow, has he any vnbraided Wares?

Ser. Hee hath Ribbons of all the colours i'th Rainebow; Points, more then all the Lawyers in *Bohemia*, can learnedly handle, though they come to him by th'grosse: Inckles, Caddysses, Cambrickes, Lawnes: why he sings em ouer, as they were Gods, or Goddesses: you would thinke a Smocke were a shee-Angell, he so chauntes to the sleeue-hand, and the worke about the square on't.

Clo. Pre'thee bring him in, and let him approach singing.

Perd. Forewarne him, that he vse no scurrilous words in's tunes.

Clow. You haue of these Pedlers, that haue more in them, then you'd think (Sister.)

Perd. I, good brother, or go about to thinke.

Enter Autolicus singing.
Lawne as white as driuen Snow,
Cypresse blacke as ere was Crow,
Gloues as sweete as Damaske Roses,
Maskes for faces, and for noses:
Bugle-bracelet, Necke-lace Amber,
Perfume for a Ladies Chamber:
Golden Quoifes, and Stomachers
For my Lads, to giue their deers:
Pins, and poaking-stickes of steele.
What Maids lacke from head to heele:
Come buy of me, come: come buy, come buy,
Buy Lads, or else your Lasses cry: Come buy.

Clo. If I were not in loue with *Mopsa,* thou shouldst take no money of me, but being enthrall'd as I am, it will also be the bondage of certaine Ribbons and Gloues.

Mop. I was promis'd them against the Feast, but they come not too late now.

Dor. He hath promis'd you more then that, or there be lyars.

Mop. He hath paid you all he promis'd you: May be he has paid you more, which will shame you to giue him againe.

Clo. Is there no manners left among maids? Will they weare their plackets, where they should bear their faces? Is there not milking-time? When you are going to bed? Or kill-hole? To whistle of these secrets, but you must be tittle-tatling before all our guests? 'Tis well they are whispring: clamor your tongues, and not a word more.

Mop. I haue done; Come you promis'd me a tawdry-lace, and a paire of sweet Gloues.

Clo. Haue I not told thee how I was cozen'd by the way, and lost all my money.

Aut. And indeed Sir, there are Cozeners abroad, therefore it behooues men to be wary.

Aut. I hope so sir, for I haue about me many parcels of charge.

Clo. What hast heere? Ballads?

Mop. Pray now buy some: I loue a ballet in print, a life, for then we are sure they are true.

Aut. Here's one, to a very dolefull tune, how a Vsurers wife was brought to bed of twenty a oney baggs at a burthen, and how she long'd to eate Adders heads, and Toads carbonado'd.

Mop. Is it true, thinke you?

Aut. Very true, and but a moneth old.

Dor. Blesse me from marrying a Vsurer.

Aut. Here's the Midwiues name to't: one Mist. *Tale-Porter,* and fiue or six honest Wiues, that were present. Why should I carry lyes abroad?

Mop. 'Pray you now buy it.

Clo. Come-on, lay it by: and let's first see moe Ballads: Wee'l buy the other things anon.

Aut. Here's another ballad of a Fish, that appeared vpon the coast, on wensday the fourescore of April, fortie thousand fadom aboue water, & sung this ballad against the hard hearts of maids: it was thought she was a Woman, and was turn'd into a cold fish, for she wold not exchange flesh with one that lou'd her: The Ballad is very pittifull, and as true.

Dor. Is it true too, thinke you.

Autol. Fiue Iustices hands at it, and witnesses more then my packe will hold.

Clo. Lay it by too; another.

Aut. This is a merry ballad, but a very pretty one.

Mop. Let's haue some merry ones.

Aut. Why this is a passing merry one, and goes to the tune of two maids wooing a man: there's scarse a Maide westward but she sings it: 'tis in request, I can tell you.

Mop. We can both sing it: if thou'lt beare a part, thou shalt heare, 'tis in three parts.

Dor. We had the tune on't, a month agoe.

Aut. I can beare my part, you must know 'tis my occupation: Haue at it with you;

Song	Get you hence, for I must goe
Aut.	Where it fits not you to know.
Dor.	Whether?
Mop	O whether?
Dor.	Whether?
Mop.	It becomes thy oath full well, Thou to me thy secrets tell.
Dor:	Me too: Let me go thether:
Mop	Or thou goest to th' Grange, or Mill,
Dor:	If to either thou dost ill,
Aut:	Neither.
Dor:	What neither?
Aut:	Neither:
Dor:	Thou hast sworne my Loue to be,
Mop	Thou hast sworne it more to mee. Then whether goest? Say whether?

Clo. Wee'l haue this song out anon by our selues: My Father, and the Gent. are in sad talke, & wee'll not trouble them: Come bring away thy pack after me, Wenches Ile buy for you both: Pedler let's haue the first choice; folow me girles.   *Aut:* And you shall pay well for 'em.

Song. *Will you buy any Tape, or Lace for your Crpe?*
My dainty Ducke, my deere-a?
Any Silke, any Thred, any Toyes for your head
Of the new'st, and fins't, fins't weare-a.
Come to the Pedler, Money's a medler,
That doth vtter all mens ware-a.   *Exit*

Seruant. Mayster, there is three Carters, three Shepherds, three Neat-herds, three Swine-herds ȳ haue made them

Much adoe aboat Nothing.

Then this for whom we rendred vp this woe.	*Exeunt.*
Enter Leonato, Bene. Marg. Vrsula, old man, Frier, Hero.
Frier. Did I not tell you she was innocent?
Leo. So are the *Prince* and *Claudio* who accus'd her,
Vpõn the errour that you heard debated:
But *Margaret* was in some fault for this,
Although against her will as it appeares,
In the true course of all the question.
Old. Well, I am glad that all things sort so well.
Bene. And so am I, being else by faith enforc'd
To call young *Claudio* to a reckoning for it.
Leo. Well daughter, and you gentlewomen all,
Withdraw into a chamber by your selues,
And when I send for you, come hither mask'd:
The *Prince* and *Claudio* promis'd by this howre
To visit me, you know your office Brother,
You must be father to your brothers daughter,
And giue her to young *Claudio.* *Exeunt Ladies.*
Old. Which I will doe with confirm'd countenance.
Bene. Frier, I must intreat your paines, I thinke.
Frier. To doe what Signior?
Bene. To binde me, or vndoe me, one of them:
Signior *Leonato,* truth it is good Signior,
Your neece regards me with an eye of fauour.
Leo. That eye my daughter lent her, 'tis most true.
Bene. And I doe with an eye of loue requite her.
Leo. The sight whereof I thinke you had from me,
From *Claudio,* and the *Prince,* but what's your will?
Bened. Your answer sir is Enigmaticall,
But for my will, my will is, your good will
May stand with ours, this day to be conioyn'd,
In the state of honourable marriage,
In which (good Frier) I shall desire your helpe.
Leon. My heart is with your liking.
Frier. And my helpe.
Enter Prince and Claudio, with attendants.
Prin. Good morrow to this faire assembly.
Leo. Good morrow Prince, good morrow *Claudio:*
We heere attend you, are you yet determin'd,
To day to marry with my brothers daughter?
Claud. Ile hold my minde were she an Ethiope.
Leo. Call her forth brother, heres the Frier ready.
Prin. Good morrow *Benedicke,* why what's the matter?
That you haue such a Februarie face,
So full of frost, of storme, and clowdinesse.
Claud. I thinke he thinkes vpon the sauage bull:
Tush, feare not man, wee'll tip thy hornes with gold,
And all *Europa* shall reioyce at thee,
As once *Europa* did at lusty *Ioue,*
When he would play the noble beast in loue.
Ben. Bull *Ioue* sir, had an amiable low,
And some such strange bull leapt your fathers Cow,
A got a Calfe in that same noble feat,
Much like to you, for you haue iust his bleat.
Enter brother, Hero, Beatrice, Margaret, Vrsula.
Cla. For this I owe you: here comes other reckings.
Which is the Lady I must seize vpon?
Leo. This same is she, and I doe giue you her.
Cla. Why then she's mine, sweet let me see your face.
Leon. No that you shal not, till you take her hand,
Before this Frier, and sweare to marry her.
Clau. Giue me your hand before this holy Frier,
I am your husband if you like of me.
Hero. And when I liu'd I was your other wife,
And when you lou'd, you were my other husband.
Clau. Another *Hero*?

Hero. Nothing certainer.
One *Hero* died, but I doe liue,
And surely as I liue, I am a maid.
Prin. The former *Hero, Hero* that is dead.
Leon. Shee died my Lord, but whiles her slander liu'd.
Frier. All this amazement can I qualifie,
When after that the holy rites are ended,
Ile tell you largely of faire *Heroes* death:
Meane time let wonder seeme familiar,
And to the chappell let vs presently.
Ben. Soft and faire Frier, which is *Beatrice*?
Beat. I answer to that name, what is your will?
Bene. Doe not you loue me?
Beat. Why no, no more then reason.
Bene. Why then your Vncle, and the Prince, & *Claudio,* haue beene deceiued, they swore you did.
Beat. Doe not you loue mee?
Bene. Troth no, no more then reason.
Beat. Why then my Cosin *Margaret* and *Vrsula*
Are much deceiu'd, for they did sweare you did.
Bene. They swore you were almost sicke for me.
Beat. They swore you were wel-nye dead for me.
Bene. 'Tis no matter, then you doe not loue me?
Beat. No truly, but in friendly recompence.
Leon. Come Cosin, I am sure you loue the gentlemã.
Clau. And Ile be sworne vpon't, that he loues her,
For heres a paper written in his hand,
A halting sonnet of his owne pure braine,
Fashioned to *Beatrice.*
Hero. And heeres another,
Writ in my cosins hand, stolne from her pocket,
Containing her affection vnto *Benedicke.*
Bene. A miracle, here's our owne hands against our
hearts: come I will haue thee, but by this light I take
thee for pittie.
Beat. I would not denie you, but by this good day, I
yeeld vpon great perswasion, & partly to saue your life,
for I was told, you were in a consumption.
Leon. Peace I will stop your mouth.
Prin. How doft thou *Benedicke* the married man?
Bene. Ile tell thee what Prince: a Colledge of witte-
crackers cannot flout mee out of my humour, dost thou
think I care for a Satyre or an Epigram? no, if a man will
be beaten with braines, a shall weare nothing handsome
about him: in briefe, since I do purpose to marry, I will
thinke nothing to any purpose that the world can say a-
gainst it, and therefore neuer flout at me, for I haue said
against it: for man is a giddy thing, and this is my conclusion: for thy part *Claudio,* I did thinke to haue beaten
thee, but in that thou art like to be my kinsman, liue vn-
bruis'd, and loue my cousin.
Cla. I had well hop'd ỹ wouldst haue denied *Beatrice,* ỹ
I might haue cudgel'd thee out of thy single life, to make
thee a double dealer, which out of questiõ thou wilt be,
if my Cousin do not looke exceeding narrowly to thee.
Bene. Come, come, we are friends, let's haue a dance
ere we are married, that we may lighten our own hearts,
and our wiues heeles.
Leon. Wee'll haue dancing afterward.
Bene. First, of my vvord, therfore play musick. *Prince,*
thou art sad, get thee a vvife, get thee a vvife, there is no
staff more reuerend then one tipt with horn. *Enter. Mes.*
Messen. My Lord, your brother *Iohn* is tane in flight,
And brought with armed men backe to *Messina.*
Bene. Thinke not on him till to morrow, ile deuise
thee braue punishments for him: strike vp Pipers. *Dance.*

L	*FINIS.*

in line 2670 that facilitate holding Claudio's speech to four lines, and the cramming of the Messenger's entrance to the right of 2680. Only close study of the page, however, will reveal the full extent of Compositor C's adjustments. Comparison with his quarto copy indicates that at 2587 he deleted a line ("Heere comes the Prince and Claudio"); at 2633-34 he turned verse that would have usually been given three lines (one for an overrun) into two lines of prose; at 2639-41 he deleted a word in each of three consecutive lines (*that*, *that*, and *such*) to hold each long verse line to one type-line. Perhaps one should not consider this crowded page to be a sign of miscalculation in casting off. After all, when quire K was finished, there was not sufficient copy to warrant more than one additional page for the play. L1 does indicate, however, a serious error in judgment. Had the danger presented by the long final page been recognized earlier, as it should have been, compositors could easily have compressed the text (by deleting some blank lines, if nothing else) as they completed the second half of quire K. Of course, a far better solution would have been to expand in the last seven pages, thus reserving an adequate number of lines to create an attractive final page on L1^v: with rules and the ornament that had just been used for *The Comedy of Errors* and *Measure for Measure*. Exactly this kind of foresight was exercised in planning the composition of *2 Henry IV* and *Othello*.

The different kinds of adjustments that Compositor C made on L1 should warn us of a danger. We may underestimate the difficulty of casting off because, owing to the skill of the compositors, much of the evidence of miscalculation is not immediately apparent. Close attention to several pages reveals the kinds of adjustment to which we should be alert.

On N2 (Plate V) the abnormal use of two blank lines after the stage direction might catch the eye, but four adjustments in the right column probably would not. At 286 and 288, Compositor C twice spelled out speech prefixes and inserted thick spaces so that he could run the final word of each speech over onto a new line— or, to use Moxon's terms, he "set wide" so that he could "drive"

O then, what graces in my Loue do dwell,
That he hath turn'd a heauen into hell.

Lyſ. *Helen,*to you our mindes we will vnfold,
To morrow night,when *Phœbe* doth behold
Her ſiluer viſage,in the watry glaſſe,
Decking with liquid pearle,the bladed graſſe
(A time that Louers flights doth ſtill conceale)
Through *Athens* gates,haue we deuis'd to ſteale.

Her. And in the wood,where often you and I,
Vpon faint Primroſe beds,were wont to lye,
Emptying our boſomes,of their counſell ſweld :
There my *Lyſander*, and my ſelfe ſhall meete,
And thence from *Athens* turne away our eyes
To ſeeke new friends and ſtrange companions,
Farwell ſweet play-fellow, pray thou for vs,
And good lucke grant thee thy *Demetrius.*
Keepe word *Lyſander* we muſt ſtarue our ſight,
From louers ſoode, till morrow deepe midnight

Exit Hermia.

Lyſ. I will my *Hermia. Helena* adieu,
As you on him,*Demetrius* dotes on you. *Exit Lyſander.*

Hele. How happy ſome,ore otherſome can be ?
Through *Athens* I am thought as faire as ſhe.
But what of that ? *Demetrius* thinkes not ſo :
He will not know,what all,but he doth know,
And as hee errcs,doting on *Hermias* eyes ;
So I, admiring of his qualities :
Things baſe and vilde, holding no quantity,
Loue can tranſpoſe to forme and dignity,
Loue lookes not with the eyes,but with the minde,
And therefore is wing'd *Cupid* painted blinde.
Nor hath loues minde of any iudgement taſte :
Wings and no eyes, figure, vnheedy haſte.
And therefore is Loue ſaid to be a childe,
Becauſe in choiſe he is often beguil'd,
As waggiſh boyes in game themſelues forſweare;
So the boy Loue is periur'd euery where.
For ere *Demetrius* lookt on *Hermias* eyne,
He hail'd downe oathes that he was onely mine.
And when this Haile ſome heat from *Hermia* felt,
So he diſſolu'd, and ſhowres of oathes did melt,
I will goe tell him of faire *Hermias* flight :
Then to the wood will he, to morrow night
Purſue her ; and for his intelligence,
If I haue thankes, it is a deere expence :
But heerein meane I to enrich my paine,
To haue his ſight thither, and backe againe. *Exit.*

Enter *Quince the Carpenter, Snug the Ioyner, Bottome the Weauer, Flute the bellowes-mender, Snout the Tinker, and Starueling the Taylor.*

Quin. Is all our company heere ?

Bot. You were beſt to call them generally, man by man, according to the ſcrip.

Qui. Here is the ſcrowle of euery mans name, which is thought fit through all *Athens*, to play in our Enterlude before the Duke and the Dutches, on his wedding day at night.

Bot. Firſt, good *Peter Quince*, ſay what the play treats on : then read the names of the Actors : and ſo grow on to a point.

Quin. Marry our play is the moſt lamentable Comedy, and moſt cruell death of *Pyramus* and *Thisbie.*

Bot. A very good peece of worke I aſſure you, and a merry, Now good *Peter Quince*, call forth your Actors by the ſcrowle. Maſters ſpread your ſelues.

Quince. Anſwere as I call you. *Nick Bottome* the Weauer.

Bottome. Ready ; name what part I am for, and proceed.

Quince. You *Nicke Bottome* are ſet downe for *Pyramus.*

Bot. What is *Pyramus*, a louer, or a tyrant ?

Quin. A Louer that kills himſelfe moſt gallantly for loue.

Bot. That will aſke ſome teares in the true performing of it: if I do it, let the audience looke to their eies: I will mooue ſtormes ; I will condole in ſome meaſure. To the reſt yet, my chiefe humour is for a tyrant. I could play *Ercles* rarely, or a part to teare a Cat in, to make all ſplit the raging Rocks; and ſhiuering ſhocks ſhall break the locks of priſon gates, and *Phibbus* carre ſhall ſhine from farre, and make and marre the fooliſh Fates. This was lofty. Now name the reſt of the Players. This is *Ercles* vaine, a tyrants vaine : a louer is more condoling.

Quin. Francis Flute the Bellowes-mender.

Flu. Heere *Peter Quince.*

Quin. You muſt take *Thisbie* on you.

Flut. What is *Thisbie*, a wandring Knight ?

Quin. It is the Lady that *Pyramus* muſt loue.

Flut. Nay faith, let not mee play a woman, I haue a beard comming.

Qui. That's all one, you ſhall play it in a Maske, and you may ſpeake as ſmall as you will.

Bot. And I may hide my face, let me play *Thisbie* too : Ile ſpeake in a monſtrous little voyce ; *Thiſne, Thiſne*, ah *Pyramus* my louer deare, thy *Thisbie* deare, and Lady deare.

Quin. No no, you muſt play *Pyramus*, and *Flute*, you *Thuby.*

Bot. Well, proceed.

Qu. Robin Starueling the Taylor.

Star. Heere *Peter Quince.*

Quince. Robin Starueling, you muſt play *Thisbies* mother ?

Tom Snowt, the Tinker.

Snowt. Heere *Peter Quince.*

Quin. You, *Pyramus* father ; my ſelf, *Thisbies* father ; *Snugge* the Ioyner, you the Lyons part : and I hope there is a play fitted.

Snug. Haue you the Lions part written ? pray you if be, giue it me, for I am ſlow of ſtudie.

Quin. You may doe it *extemporie*, for it is nothing but roaring.

Bot. Let mee play the Lyon too, I will roare that I will doe any mans heart good to heare me. I will roare, that I will make the Duke ſay, Let him roare againe, let him roare againe.

Quin. If you ſhould doe it too terribly, you would fright the Dutcheſſe and the Ladies, that they would ſhrike, and that were enough to hang vs all.

All. That would hang vs euery mothers ſonne.

Bottome. I graunt you friends, if that you ſhould fright the Ladies out of their Wittes, they would haue no more diſcretion but to hang vs : but I will aggrauate my voyce ſo, that I will roare you as gently as any ſucking Doue ; I will roare and 'twere any Nightingale.

Quin. You can play no part but *Piramus*, for *Piramus*

TEXTUAL CHANGES BY THE COMPOSITORS   67

one word into the next line.[17] At 301 and 302, he again set wide to permit using an additional line: first by driving the word *is* into 302 and then by driving one syllable (*-ling*) into 303, Again at 341 we find the speech prefix *Bottome* rather than *Bot.*, and the result at the end of the speech is the use of another unnecessary line. Although the page appears normal, Compositor C spread out his text to use five lines more than his copy would ordinarily require.

Another method for expanding prose, one that does not mar the appearance of the page if used with care, is found on V2 (Plate VI). At 191 and 208, lines of prose have been arbitrarily divided into pseudo-verse. Because of the series of short lines in the right column, the chopped lines do not draw our attention. On the same page, we might also think that the setting of Parolles' entrance at 103 reflects standard practice, but entrances that interrupt a continuing speech are usually set with no blank lines. These adjustments stretch the text on V2 to four type-lines that would not normally have been used. A more striking example of skillful adjustment is found on X1^v (Plate VII). As Compositor B approached the end of the page, he was faced with far too little copy for the remaining space. At 1602 he gave *A Tucket afarre off* its own line, although he would normally have set it at the beginning of the ensuing stage direction. Then he set the entrance on three lines, though it required only two. (Compare his setting of the stage direction at 1539–40 in the left column.) Next he proceeded to divide five prose speeches into twenty lines of pseudo-verse, speeches that, as prose, would take about fifteen lines. Despite these adjustments, the page looks fairly normal, largely because we have come to expect partial verse lines at the beginnings and ends of verse speeches.

Expansion by means of dividing verse lines is often more obvious. On c3, for example, we find a page of solid verse with only one line divided (at 833–34). Viewed in the context of a series of long lines, the anomaly of

    Rich. Why Vncle,
What's the matter?

All's Well, that Ends Well.

Must I be comforted, not in his sphere;
Th'ambition in my loue thus plagues it selfe:
The hind that would be mated by the Lion
Must die for loue. 'Twas prettie, though a plague
To see him euerie houre to sit and draw
His arched browes, his hawking eie, his curles
In our hearts table: heart too capeable
Of euerie line and tricke of his sweet fauour.
But now he's gone, and my idolatrous fancie
Must sanctifie his Reliques. Who comes heere?

Enter Parrolles.

One that goes with him: I loue him for his sake,
And yet I know him a notorious Liar,
Thinke him a great way foole, solie a coward,
Yet these fixt euils sit so fit in him,
That they take place, when Vertues steely bones
Lookes bleake i'th cold wind: withall, full ofte we see
Cold wisedome waighting on superfluous follie.

Par. Saue you faire Queene.
Hel. And you Monarch.
Par. No.
Hel. And no.
Par. Are you meditating on virginitie?
Hel. It you haue some staine of souldier in you: Let mee aske you a question. Man is enemie to virginitie, how may we barracado it against him?
Par. Keepe him out.
Hel. But he assailes, and our virginitie though valiant, in the defence yet is weak: vnfold to vs some warlike resistance.
Par. There is none: Man setting downe before you, will vndermine you, and blow you vp.
Hel. Blesse our poore Virginity from vnderminers and blowers vp. Is there no Military policy how Virgins might blow vp men?
Par. Virginity beeing blowne downe, Man will quicklier be blowne vp: marry in blowing him downe againe, with the breach may himselfe is a Virgin: Virginitie murthers it selfe, and should be buried in highwayes out of all sanctified limit, as a desperate Offendresse against Nature. Virginitie breedes mites, much like a Cheese, consumes it selfe to the very payring, and so dies with feeding his owne stomacke. Besides, Virginitie is peeuish, proud, ydle, made of selfe-loue, which is the most inhibited sinne in the Cannon. Keepe it not, you cannot choose but loose by't. Out with't: within ten yeare it will make it selfe two, which is a goodly increase, and the principall it selfe not much the worse. Away with't.
Hel. How might one do sir, to loose it to her owne liking?

Par. Let mee see. Marry ill, to like him that ne're it likes. 'Tis a commoditie wil lose the glosse with lying: The longer kept, the lesse worth: Off with't while 'tis vendible. Answer the time of request, Virginitie like an olde Courtier, weares her cap out of fashion, richly suted, but vnsuteable, iust like the brooch & the toothpick, which were not now: your Date is better in your Pye and your Porredge, then in your cheeke: and your virginity, your old virginity, is like one of our French wither'd peares, it lookes ill, it eates drily, marry 'tis a wither'd peare: it was formerly better, marry yet 'tis a wither'd peare: Will you any thing with it?
Hel. Not my virginity yet:
There shall your Master haue a thousand loues,
A Mother, and a Mistresse, and a friend,
A Phenix, Captaine, and an enemy,
A guide, a Goddesse, and a Soueraigne,
A Counsellor, a Traitoresse, and a Deare:
His humble ambition, proud humility:
His iarring, concord: and his discord, dulcet:
His faith, his sweet disaster: with a world
Of pretty fond adoptious christendomes
That blinking Cupid gossips. Now shall he:
I know not what he shall, God send him well,
The Courts a learning place, and he is one.
Par. What one ifaith?
Hel. That I wish well, 'tis pitty.
Par. What's pitty?
Hel. That wishing well had not a body in't,
Which might be felt, that we the poorer borne,
Whose baser starres do shut vs vp in wishes,
Might vvith effects of them follow our friends,
And shew what vve alone must thinke, which neuer Returnes vs thankes.

Enter Page.

Pag. Monsieur *Parrolles*,
My Lord cals for you.
Par. Little *Hellen* farewell, if I can remember thee, I will thinke of thee at Court.
Hel. Monsieur *Parolles*, you were borne vnder a charitable starre.
Par. Vnder *Mars* I.
Hel. I especially thinke, vnder *Mars*.
Par Why vnder *Mars*?
Hel. The warres hath so kept you vnder, that you must needes be borne vnder *Mars*.
Par. When he was predominant.
Hel. When he was retrograde I thinke rather.
Par. Why thinke you so?
Hel. You go so much backward when you fight.
Par. That's for aduantage.
Hel. So is running away,
When feare proposes the safetie:
But the composition that your valour and feare makes in you, is a vertue of a good wing, and I like the weare well.
Paroll. I am so full of businesses, I cannot answere thee acutely: I will returne perfect Courtier, in the which my instruction shall serue to naturalize thee, so thou wilt be capeable of a Courtiers councell, and vnderstand what aduice shall thrust vppon thee, else thou diest in thine vnthankfulnes, and thine ignorance makes thee away, farewell: When thou hast leysure, say thy praiers: when thou hast none, remember thy Friends:

V 2 Get

242   *All's Well that ends Well.*

you written to beare along.
Fren.G. We serue you Madam in that and all your worthiest affaires.
La. Not so, but as we change our courtesies,
Will you draw neere?   *Exit.*
Hel. Till I haue no wife I haue nothing in France.
Nothing in France vntill he has no wife :
Thou shalt haue none *Rossillion*, none in France,
Then hast thou all againe : poore Lord, is't I
That chase thee from thy Countrie, and expose
Those tender limbes of thine, to the euent
Of the none-sparing warre ? And is it I,
That driue thee from the sportiue Court, where thou
Was't shot at with faire eyes, to be the marke
Of smoakie Muskets ? O you leaden messengers,
That ride vpon the violent speede of fire,
Fly with false ayme, moue the still-peering aire
That sings with piercing, do not touch my Lord :
Who euer shoots at him, I set him there.
Who euer charges on his forward brest
I am the Caitiffe that do hold him too't,
And though I kill him not, I am the cause
His death was so effected : Better 'twere
I met the rauine Lyon when he roar'd
With sharpe constraint of hunger : better 'twere,
That all the miseries which nature owes
Were mine at once. No come thou home *Rossillion*,
Whence honor but of danger winnes a scarre,
As oft it looses all. I will be gone :
My being heere it is, that holds thee hence,
Shall I stay heere to do't ? No, no, although
The ayre of Paradise did fan the house,
And Angles offic'd all : I will be gone,
That pittifull rumour may report my flight
To consolate thine eare. Come night, end day,
For with the darke (poore theefe) Ile steale away.   *Exit.*

Flourish. Enter the Duke of Florence, Rossillion,
drum and trumpets, soldiers, Parrolles.

Duke. The Generall of our horse thou art, and we
Great in our hope, lay our best loue and credence
Vpon thy promising fortune.
Ber. Sir it is
A charge too heauy for my strength, but yet
Wee'l striue to beare it for your worthy sake,
To th'extreme edge of hazard.
Duke. Then go thou forth,
And fortune play vpon thy prosperous helme
As thy auspicious mistris.
Ber. This very day
Great Mars I put my selfe into thy file,
Make me but like my thoughts, and I shall proue
A louer of thy drumme, hater of loue.   *Exeunt omnes*

Enter Countesse & Steward.

La. Alas ! and would you take the letter of her :
Might you not know she would do, as she has done,
By sending me a Letter. Reade it agen.

Letter.
I am S. *Iaques* Pilgrim, thither gone.
Ambitious loue hath so in me offended,
That bare-foot plod I the cold ground vpon
With sainted vow my faults to haue amended.

Write, write, that from the bloodie course of warre,
My deerest *Master* your deare sonne, may hie,
Blesse him at home in peace. Whilst I from farre,
His name with zealous feruour sanctifie :
His taken labours bid him me forgiue :
I his despightfull *Iuno* sent him forth,
From Courtly friends, with Camping foes to liue,
Where death and danger dogges the heeles of worth.
He is too good and faire for death, and mee,
Whom I my selfe embrace, to set him free.

Ah what sharpe stings are in her mildest words ?
Rynaldo, you did neuer lacke aduice so much,
As letting her passe so : had I spoke with her,
I could haue well diuerted her intents,
Which thus she hath preuented.
Ste. Pardon me Madam,
If I had giuen you this at ouer-night,
She might haue beene ore-tane : and yet she writes
Pursuite would be but vaine.
La. What Angell shall
Blesse this vnworthy husband, he cannot thriue,
Vnlesse her prayers, whom heauen delights to beare
And loues to grant, repreeue him from the wrath
Of greatest Iustice. Write, write *Rynaldo*,
To this vnworthy husband of his wife,
Let euerie word waigh heauie of her worth,
That he does waigh too light : my greatest greefe,
Though little he do feele it, set downe sharpely.
Dispatch the most conuenient messenger,
When haply he shall heare that she is gone,
He will returne, and hope I may that shee
Hearing so much, will speede her foote againe,
Led hither by pure loue : which of them both
Is deerest to me, I haue no skill in sence
To make distinction : prouide this Messenger :
My heart is heauie, and mine age is weake,
Greefe would haue teares, and sorrow bids me speake.
                                                  Exeunt

A Tucket afarre off.

Enter old Widdow of Florence, her daughter, Violenta
and Mariana, with other
Citizens.

Widdow. Nay come,
For if they do approach the Citty,
We shall loose all the sight.
Diana. They say, the French Count has done
Most honourable seruice.
Wid. It is reported,
That he has taken their great'st Commander,
And that with his owne hand he slew
The Dukes brother : we haue lost our labour,
They are gone a contrarie wayi harke,
you may know by their Trumpets.
Maria. Come lets returne againe,
And suffice our selues with the report of it.
Well *Diana*, take heed of this French Earle,
The honor of a Maide is her name,
And no Legacie is so rich
As honestie.
Widdow. I haue told my neighbour
How you haue beene solicited by a Gentleman
His Companion.

                                                    Maria

strikes the eye. It does not immediately strike the eye, however, on f2 (Plate VIII), a page on which prose lines are twice divided into pseudo-verse (2177–82, 2186–88) and single verse lines are twice divided into half-lines (2237–40). The irregular length of lines on the page as a whole makes division unobtrusive.

Only comparison with the authoritative text of *1 Henry IV* or close attention to metrics would reveal the extent of Compositor A's tinkering on f3^v (Plate IX). In the right column, he used a device that could prove distinctly unsettling for editors if we did not have quarto copy. At 4.4.3–5, Q5 of *1 Henry IV* reads

> This to my coosen *Scroope*, and all the rest
> To whom they are directed. If you knew
> How much they doe import, you would make haste.

But Compositor A needed to use an additional line, and at 2590–93 he realigned to create the following:

> This to my Cousin *Scroope*, and all the rest
> To whom they are directed.
> If you knew how much they doe import,
> You would make haste.

We would immediately notice the division if he had simply divided the first line and set

> This to my Cousin *Scroope*,
> And all the rest
> To whom they are directed. If you knew
> How much they doe import, you would make haste.

The same is true of 2613–15, the last lines on the page, when he again divided and realigned. The scene box and the internal entry on f3^v are set normally. We might be alerted by a divided verse line at 2508–9, but other than that we have no visual clue to the fact that a page of verse, the easiest type of copy to cast off, has been cast off inaccurately.

The settings we have just considered are not atypical. Signs of adjustment by compositors—and thus of miscalculation in coun-

The First Part of King Henry the Fourth. 65

Falst. There's no more faith in thee then a ftu'de Prunes, nor no more truth in thee, then in a drawne Fox: and for Wooman-hood, Maid-marian may be the Deputies wife of the Ward to thee. Go you nothing: go.

Host. Say, what thing? what thing?

Falst. What thing? why a thing to thanke heauen on.

Host. I am no thing to thanke heauen on, I wold thou shouldst know it : I am an honest mans wife : and setting thy Knighthood aside, thou art a knaue to call me so.

Falst. Setting thy woman-hood aside, thou art a beast to say otherwise.

Host. Say, what beast, thou knaue thou?

Fal. What beast? Why an Otter.

Prin. An Otter, sir *Iohn*? Why an Otter?

Fal. Why? She's neither fish nor flesh; a man knowes not where to haue her.

Host. Thou art vniust man in saying so ; thou, or anie man knowes where to haue me, thou knaue thou.

Prince. Thou say'st true Hostesse, and he slanders thee most grossely.

Host. So he doth you, my Lord, and sayde this other day, You ought him a thousand pound.

Prince. Sirrah, do I owe you a thousand pound?

Falst. A thousand pound *Hal*? A Million. Thy loue is worth a Million : thou ow'st me thy loue.

Host. Nay my Lord, he call'd you Iacke, and said hee would cudgell you.

Fal. Did I, *Bardolph*?

Bar. Indeed Sir *Iohn*, you said so.

Fal. Yea, if he said my Ring was Copper.

Prince. I say 'tis Copper. Dar'st thou bee as good as thy word now?

Fal. Why *Hal*? thou know'st, as thou art but a man, I dare : but, as thou art a Prince, I feare thee, as I feare the roaring of the Lyons Whelpe.

Prince. And why not as the Lyon?

Fal. The King himselfe is to bee feared as the Lyon : Do'st thou thinke Ile feare thee, as I feare thy Father? nay if I do, let my Girdle breake.

Prin. O, if it should. how would thy guttes fall about thy knees. But sirra : There's no roome for Faith, Truth, nor Honesty, in this bosome of thine : it is all fill'd vppe with Guttes and Midriffe. Charge an honest Woman with picking thy pocket? Why thou horson impudent imbost Rascall, if there were any thing in thy Pocket but Tauerne Recknings, *Memorandums* of Bawdie-houses, and one poore peny-worth of Sugar-candie to make thee long-winded : if thy pocket were enrich'd with anie other iniuries but these, I am a Villaine : And yet you will stand to it, you will not Pocket vp wrong. Art thou not asham'd?

Fal. Do'st thou heare *Hal*? Thou know'st in the state of Innocency, *Adam* fell: and what should 'poore *Iacke Falstaffe* do, in the dayes of Villany? Thou seest, I haue more flesh then another man, and therefore more frailty. You confesse then you pickt my Pocket?

Prin. It appeares so by the Story.

Fal. Hostesse, I forgiue thee :
Go make ready Breakfast, loue thy Husband,
Looke to thy Seruants, and cherish thy Guests:
Thou shalt find me tractable to any honest reason:
Thou seest, I am pacified still.
Nay, I prethee be gone.

Exit Hostesse.

Now *Hal*, to the newes at Court for the Robbery, Lad? How is that answered?

Prin. O my sweet Beefe :
I must still be good Angell to thee,
The Monie is paid backe againe.

Fal. O, I do not like that paying backe, 'tis a double Labour.

Prin. I am good Friends with my Father, and may do any thing.

Fal. Rob me the Exchequer the first thing thou do'st, and do it with vnwash'd hands too.

Bard. Do my Lord.

Prin. I haue procured thee *Iacke*, a Charge of Foot.

Fal. I would it had beene of Horse. Where shal I finde one that can steale well? O, for a fine theefe, of two and twentie, or thereabout : I am heynously vnprouided. Wel God be thanked for these Rebels, they offend none but the Vertuous. I laud them, I praise them.

Prin. Bardolph.

Bar. My Lord.

Prin. Go beare this Letter to Lord *Iohn* of Lancaster To my Brother *Iohn*. This to my Lord of Westmerland, Go *Peto*, to horse : for thou, and I,
Haue thirtie miles to ride yet ere dinner time.
Iacke, meet me to morrow in the Temple Hall
At two a clocke in the afternoone,
There shalt thou know thy Charge, and there receiue
Money and Order for their Furniture.
The Land is burning, *Percie* stands on hye,
And either they, or we must lower lye.

Fal. Rare words! braue world.
Hostesse, my breakfast, come :
Oh, I could wish this Tauerne were my drumme.

Exeunt omnes.

Actus Quartus. Scœna Prima.

Enter Harrie Hotspurre, Worcester, and Dowglas.

Hot. Well said, my Noble Scot, if speaking truth
In this fine Age, were not thought flatterie,
Such attribution should the *Dowglas* haue,
As not a Souldiour of this seasons stampe,
Should go so generall currant through the world.
By heauen I cannot flatter : I defie
The Tongues of Soothers. But a Brauer place
In my hearts loue, hath no man then your Selfe.
Nay, taske me to my word : approue me Lord.

Dow. Thou art the King of Honor :
No man so potent breathes vpon the ground,
But I will Beard him.

Enter a Messenger.

Hot. Do so, and 'tis well. What Letters hast there ?
I can but thanke you.

Mess. These Letters come from your Father.

Hot. Letters from him ?
Why comes he not himselfe?

Mess. He cannot come, my Lord,
He is greeuous sicke.

Hot. How? haz he the leysure to be sicke now,
In such a iustling time? Who leades his power?
Vnder whose Gouernment come they along?

f2 *Mes*

Worc. The number of the King exceedeth ours:
For Gods sake, Cousin, stay till all come in.

*The Trumpet sounds a Parley. Enter Sir
Walter Blunt.*

Blunt. I come with gracious offers from the King,
If you vouchsafe me hearing, and respect.
 Hotsp. Welcome, Sir *Walter Blunt*:
And would to God you were of our determination.
Some of vs loue you well: and euen those some
Enuie your great deseruings, and good name,
Becaufe you are not of our qualitie,
But stand against vs like an Enemie.
 Blunt. And Heauen defend, but still I should stand so,
So long as out of Limit, and true Rule,
You stand against anoynted anoynted Maiestie.
But to my Charge.
The King hath sent to know
The nature of your Griefes, and whereupon
You coniure from the Brest of Ciuill Peace,
Such bold Hostilitie, teaching his dutious Land
Audacious Crueltie. If that the King
Haue any way your good Deserts forgot,
Which he confesseth to be manifold,
He bids you name your Griefes, and with all speed
You shall haue your desires, with interest;
And Pardon absolute for your selfe, and these,
Herein mis-led, by your suggestion.
 Hotsp. The King is kinde:
And well wee know, the King
Knowes at what time to promise, when to pay.
My Father, my Vnckle, and my selfe,
Did giue him that same Royaltie he weares:
And when he was not sixe and twentie strong,
Sicke in the Worlds regard, wretched, and low,
A poore vnminded Out-law, sneaking home,
My Father gaue him welcome to the shore:
And when he heard him sweare, and vow to God,
He came but to be Duke of Lancaster,
To sue his Liuerie, and begge his Peace,
With teares of Innocencie, and tearmes of Zeale;
My Father, in kinde heart and pitty mou'd,
Swore him assistance, and perform'd it too.
Now, when the Lords and Barons of the Realme
Perceiu'd *Northumberland* did leane to him,
The more and lesse came in with Cap and Knee,
Met him in Boroughs, Cities, Villages,
Attended him on Bridges, stood in Lanes,
Layd Gifts before him, proffer'd him their Oathes,
Gaue him their Heires, as Pages followed him,
Euen at the heeles, in golden multitudes.
He presently, as Greatnesse knowes it selfe,
Steps me a little higher then his Vow
Made to my Father, while his blood was poore,
Vpon the naked shore at Rauenspurgh:
And now (forsooth) takes on him to reforme
Some certaine Edicts, and some strait Decrees,
That lay too heauie on the Common-wealth;
Cryes out vpon abuses, seemes to weepe
Ouer his Countries Wrongs: and by this Face,
This seeming Brow of Iustice, did he winne
The hearts of all that hee did angle for.
Proceeded further, cut me off the Heads
Of all the Fauorites, that the absent King
In deputation left behinde him heere.

When hee was personall in the Irish Warre.
 Blunt. Tut, I came not to heare this.
 Hotsp. Then to the point.
In short time after, hee depos'd the King.
Soone after that, depriu'd him of his Life:
And in the neck of that, task't the whole State.
To make that worse, suffer'd his Kinsman *March*,
Who is, if euery Owner were plac'd,
Indeede his King, to be engag'd in Wales,
There, without Ransome, to lye forfeited:
Disgrac'd me in my happie Victories,
Sought to intrap me by intelligence,
Rated my Vnckle from the Councell-Boord,
In rage dismiss'd my Father from the Court,
Broke Oath on Oath, committed Wrong on Wrong,
And in conclusion, droue vs to seeke out
This Head of safetie; and withall, to prie
Into his Title: the which wee finde
Too indirect, for long continuance.
 Blunt. Shall I returne this answer to the King?
 Hotsp. Not so, Sir *Walter.*
Wee'le with-draw a while:
Goe to the King, and let there be impawn'd
Some suretie for a safe returne againe,
And in the Morning early shall my Vnckle
Bring him our purpose: and so farewell.
 Blunt. I would you would accept of Grace and Loue.
 Hotsp. And't may be, so wee shall.
 Blunt. Pray Heauen you doe. *Exeunt.*

Scena Quarta.

Enter the Arch-Bishop of Yorke, and Sir Michell.

Arch. Hie, good Sir *Michell*, beare this sealed Briefe
With winged haste to the Lord Marshall,
This to my Cousin *Scroope*, and all the rest
To whom they are directed.
If you knew how much they doe Import,
You would make haste.
 Sir Mich. My good Lord, I guesse their tenor.
 Arch. Like enough you doe.
To morrow, good Sir *Michell*, is a day,
Wherein the fortune of ten thousand men
Must bide the touch. For Sir, at Shrewsbury,
As I am truly giuen to vnderstand,
The King, with mightie and quick-rays'd Power,
Meetes with Lord *Harry*: and I feare, Sir *Michell*,
What with the sicknesse of *Northumberland*,
Whose Power was in the first proportion;
And what with *Owen Glendowers* absence thence,
Who with them was rated firmely too,
And comes not in, ouer-rul'd by Prophecies,
I feare the Power of *Percy* is too weake,
To wage an instant tryall with the King.
 Sir Mich. Why, my good Lord, you need not feare,
There is *Douglas*, and Lord *Mortimer.*
 Arch. No, *Mortimer* is not there.
 Sir Mic. But there is *Mordake, Vernon*, Lord *Harry Percy*,
And there is my Lord of Worcester,
And a Head of gallant Warriors,
Noble Gentlemen.
                                                              Arch. And

ting off lines—are, as Hinman says, abundant. Most indicative of the problems presented by casting off are pages of solid verse, pages for which the line count should have been relatively simple. On e1, for example, we find an internal entrance placed to the right of line 451. A correct line count should have allotted one line for the entrance and one or two blank lines to set it off from the dialogue. Although compression on the last page in a quire to be set sometimes reflects pressures caused by too much copy being cast off for pages set previously, such is not the case here. The settings of e1^v through e3^v are normal. For d1^v, f2, m3, and r1— again pages of verse—too little copy was cast off. In the lower right column of each page, verse speeches are divided to waste space. These examples are representative only.[18]

Miscalculation is thus far more prevalent than meets the eye, and the demands on a compositor's skill and initiative were considerable in setting all of the Folio plays. In setting *2 Henry IV*, however, the problems created by casting off were compounded by another problem, one that is unique to this play.

Before the comedies were completed, the setting of the histories had begun, starting a new sequence of the alphabet with quires a through c for *King John* and the first two-thirds of *Richard II*. Upon completion of the comedies, the normal progression of work should have led to finishing *Richard II* with quire d and then moving in order through the Henriad to the end of the history plays. Instead, however, work jumped directly from *The Winter's Tale* to *Henry V*.[19]

At that point, someone made a serious error. The letter *h* was assigned to the first quire of *Henry V*. Thus only four quires, or forty-eight pages, were reserved to complete *Richard II* and to set the two parts of *Henry IV*: quires d through g. Since nine pages of *Richard II* remained to be set, both parts of *Henry IV* would thus have had to be accommodated in thirty-nine pages—a patent impossibility. Of the fifteen plays already set, only the four shortest had required fewer than twenty pages each. The average length had been twenty-two pages, and two plays, *All's Well* and

The Winter's Tale, had both required more than two quires (twenty-five and twenty-seven pages, respectively). Given the length of the *Henry IV* plays and their high proportion of prose, the compositors should have assigned the letter *i* to the beginning of *Henry V*, thus holding five quires in reserve: the greater part of one quire to complete *Richard II* and a little over two quires each for the two *Henry IV* plays. It is difficult to see how such a major miscalculation could have been possible. Peter Davison suggests that the compositors intended to reserve five quires but that they simply "miscounted their letters."[20] I find it more likely that only the needs of *1, 2 Henry IV* were taken into account when the compositors jumped from *The Winter's Tale* to *Henry V*. Someone may have momentarily forgotten that nine pages of *Richard II* remained to be completed.

By the time casting off began for *1 Henry IV*, the error had been discovered. If the compositors had expected to be forced to complete both parts of *Henry IV* in only thirty-nine pages, they would have conserved space at every opportunity in Part 1. Instead, they used space liberally. At times, they even seem to have wasted it.[21] As a result, *1 Henry IV* was unnecessarily extended to twenty-six pages. The only plays in the first half of the Folio that are comparable in length and in demands made on blank space (for scene divisions and internal entries) are *Richard II* and *Measure for Measure*, which take twenty-three and twenty-four pages, respectively. It is thus evident that even before work began on Part 1, an important decision had been made: a supplementary quire, marked gg, would be added at the end of Part 2 to provide twelve additional pages.[22] The decision was apparently based on the assumption that the given amount of copy for the two plays would fit into the number of pages now made available by the additional quire: a total of fifty-one, which left twenty-five pages for Part 2.

When work actually began on Part 2, that assumption proved to be wrong. *2 Henry IV* is a very long play. In fact, had space been

TEXTUAL CHANGES BY THE COMPOSITORS 75

used as liberally in Part 2 as it was in Part 1, the text would have required three or four pages more than the twenty-six used for *1 Henry IV*, not one page less. Sudden awareness of the problem is reflected in Compositor B's atypical settings in the first half of quire g. On four pages—g1^v, g2, g2^v and g3—casting off demanded that he accommodate far more copy than normal. As a result, B was driven to extreme measures, measures of major significance for an editor.[23]

May the severely cramped settings in the first half of quire g merely reflect the type of local miscalculation in casting off that we encounter throughout the Folio? I do not think so. The only other play to have a sequence of pages with such tight settings is *The Tempest*, and a comparison with plays set thereafter indicates that compositors had not yet settled on certain conventions that were later to require allotting additional lines for certain kinds of stage directions and speeches.* In plays set after *The Tempest*, tight settings reflect strictly local problems: miscalculation of the number of lines required by a given page; anticipation in the penultimate pages of a play of a final page that threatened to be too short or too long; a scene-break at the head of a column, and the like. For example, E1 of *The Merry Wives of Windsor* is very crowded. In addition to using shortened spellings, abbreviations, and turn-overs, Compositor B compressed one of the two scene divisions to four-type-lines.[24] In contrast, the scene boxes on E2 through E2^v, which B had just finished setting, are normal. Thus the problem on E1 is local, the result of miscalculation. Page-by-page miscalculation cannot, however, account for the extreme pressure under which B was working in the first half of quire g in *2 Henry IV*. Casting off was clearly based on the assumption that

---

* The text of *The Tempest* is mercilessly cramped. Only four of the thirty internal entrances are spaced; in plays set thereafter, they are usually allotted one or two blank lines. Two speakers are placed on one line eight times and ten entrances are crammed to the right of the dialogue; thereafter, these appear to be largely emergency measures. None of the songs is set off with blank space; thereafter, they usually are.

it would be possible to cram the remaining pages into two quires of twelve pages each: quires g and gg.*

Before turning to quire g, let us briefly consider the setting of the display title page, set on f6^v (Plate X), the reverse of the last page of *1 Henry IV*. As the final page in its quire, it was not cast off, but B's setting suggests that he may already have begun the task of compressing. The setting of f6^v looks fairly normal, but a comparison with two other title pages may be instructive. The only other plays in the Folio that open with prologues on the first page of text are *Henry V* (already set by Compositor A) and *Henry VIII* (shortly to be set by B). Both of their opening pages follow the same format: the prologue heading is boxed, followed by the prologue itself in double columns of italic type. Thereafter, the opening of the play is set normally: the double-column 1.1. box reading "*Actus Primus. Scoena Prima.*" is followed by the opening of the first scene. In contrast, the opening page of *2 Henry IV* treats what is surely a prologue (though it is not so marked in the Quarto) as if it were Scene 1. After the play's title, we find the 1.1 box, immediately followed by a boxed designation "INDVCTION" at the head of the left column (with the prologue occupying the remainder of the column) and "*Scena Secunda*" at the head of the right column (with the text of what is actually 1.1 ensuing). Although the setting may reflect an odd scene division in Compositor B's copy or a local problem he faced in setting the Scene 2 box, it may reflect the pressure to accommodate as much text as possible on f6^v before the work of casting off quire g began.†

---

* Such a serious error in estimating the length of *2 Henry IV* is difficult to explain. Perhaps Jaggard's staff had not yet seen the manuscript that was to serve as copy until they had completed *1 Henry IV*. Perhaps they were working with a transcript prepared by a scribe whose work was unknown to them and difficult to estimate with accuracy. For further discussion, see below, p. 175.

† Compositor B may have found the heading "induction" in his copy, but I think it quite likely that he was trying to solve first one problem, and then another. If he was, in fact, trying to compress, he could gain considerable ground if he did not center the prologue with its own boxed heading: if, that is, he did not use both columns for the prologue as Compositor A had done on the first page of *Henry V*. Instead, he could set the prologue in one column as the first scene

The Second Part of Henry the Fourth,
Containing his Death: and the Coronation
of King Henry the Fift.

Actus Primus. Scœna Prima.

INDVCTION.

Enter Rumour.

Pen your Eares: For which of you will ſtop
The vent of Hearing, when loud *Rumor* ſpeakes?
I, from the Orient, to the drooping Weſt
(Making the winde my Poſt-horſe) ſtill vnfold
The Acts commenced on this Ball of Earth.
Vpon my Tongue, continuall Slanders ride,
The which, in euery Language, I pronounce,
Stuffing the Eares of them with falſe Reports:
I ſpeake of Peace, while couert Enmitie
(Vnder the ſmile of Safety) wounds the World:
And who but *Rumour*, who but onely I
Make fearfull Muſters, and prepar'd Defence,
Whil'ſt the bigge yeare, ſwolne with ſome other griefes,
Is thought with childe, by the ſterne Tyrant, Warre,
And no ſuch matter? *Rumour*, is a Pipe
Blowne by Surmiſes, Ielouſies, Coniectures;
And of ſo eaſie, and ſo plaine a ſtop,
That the blunt Monſter, with vncounted heads,
The ſtill diſcordant, wauering Multitude,
Can play vpon it. But what neede I thus
My well-knowne Body to Anathomize
Among my houſhold? Why is *Rumour* heere?
I run before King *Harries* victory,
Who in a bloodie field by Shrewsburie
Hath beaten downe yong *Hotſpurre*, and his Troopes,
Quenching the flame of bold Rebellion,
Euen with the Rebels blood. But what meane I
To ſpeake ſo true at firſt? My Office is
To noyſe abroad, that *Harry Monmouth* fell
Vnder the Wrath of Noble *Hotſpurres* Sword:
And that the King, before the *Dowglas* Rage
Stoop'd his Annointed head, as low as death.
This haue I rumour'd through the peaſant-Townes,
Betweene the Royall Field of Shrewsburie,
And this Worme-eaten-Hole of ragged Stone,
Where *Hotſpurres* Father, old Northumberland,
Lyes crafty ſicke. The Poſtes come tyring on,
And not a man of them brings other newes
Then they haue learn'd of Me. From *Rumours* Tongues,
They bring ſmooth-Comforts-falſe, worſe then True-
  wrongs. *Exit.*

Scena Secunda.

Enter Lord Bardolfe, and the Porter.

L.Bar. Who keepes the Gate heere hoa?
Where is the Earle?
Por. What ſhall I ſay you are?
Bar. Tell thou the Earle
That the Lord *Bardolfe* doth attend him heere.
Por. His Lordſhip is walk'd forth into the Orchard,
Pleaſe it your Honor, knocke but at the Gate,
And hee himſelfe will anſwer.

Enter Northumberland.

L.Bar. Heere comes the Earle.
Nor. What newes Lord *Bardolfe*? Eu'ry minute now
Should be the Father of ſome Stratagem;
The Times are wilde: Contention (like a Horſe
Full of high Feeding) madly hath broke looſe,
And beares downe all before him.
L.Bar. Noble Earle,
I bring you certaine newes from Shrewsbury.
Nor. Good, and heauen will.
L.Bar. As good as heart can wiſh:
The King is almoſt wounded to the death:
And in the Fortune of my Lord your Sonne,
Prince *Harrie* ſlaine out-right: and both the *Blunts*
Kill'd by the hand of *Dowglas*. Yong Prince *Iohn*,
And Weſtmerland, and Stafford, fled the Field.
And *Harrie Monmouth's* Brawne (the Hulke Sir *Iohn*)
Is priſoner to your Sonne. O, ſuch a Day,
(So fought, ſo follow'd, and ſo fairely wonne)
Came not, till now, to dignifie the Times
Since *Cæſars* Fortunes.
Nor. How is this deriu'd?
Saw you the Field? Came you from Shrewsbury?
L.Bar. I ſpake with one (my L.) that came frō thence,
A Gentleman well bred, and of good name,
That freely render'd me theſe newes for true.
Nor. Heere comes my Seruant *Trauers*, whom I ſent
On Tueſday laſt, to liſten after Newes.

Enter Trauers.

L.Bar. My Lord, I ouer-rod him on the way,
And he is furniſh'd with no certainties,
More then he (haply) may retaile from me.
Nor. Now *Trauers*, what good tidings comes frō you?
              Tra.

PLATE X. Sig. f6ᵛ

Had B followed the *Henry V* format, he could not have accommodated the last seven lines now on the page.

Now the first half of quire g was cast off, and Compositor B began his first stint, working in normal order by first setting g3^v and then moving in reverse to g1. Let us, however, consider the pages in reading order, the order in which they were cast off.

The first page of the quire, g1, is set normally. A page of solid verse, it is broken by only one internal entrance and thus offered little opportunity for compression. In light of the obvious effort to compress on the next four pages, the use of blank lines framing the stage direction is slightly puzzling here. Perhaps g1 was cast off normally on the assumption that the necessary work could be done in the remaining pages of the quire, all of which are wholly or partly in prose.

On g1^v we note the first signs of pressure. The division for Scene 3 is telescoped to three type-lines: a box three lines deep, set without framing blank lines, in contrast to a normal setting of a four-line box with blank lines both preceding and following it. The opening stage direction and the one internal entry are also set without blank lines. Beyond this, there is really no place where B could have held his type-lines to fewer than normal. The page is almost half verse, and more than half of the prose is in two long speeches, the kind of copy it was difficult to compress. In general, brief prose speeches that would normally be set in two lines with only one word on the second line provided the best opportunity, but there are no such speeches on this page.

On g2 (Plate XI), local miscalculation cannot possibly explain B's concentrated effort to compress or the extraordinary measures to which he resorts. When adjusting to compensate for local miscalculation, compositors usually concentrated their efforts at

---

itself. Now, however, the middle of the Scene 2 box would have come right at the bottom of the left column. He was trapped. "*Scena Secunda*" would have to head the right-hand column. It was thus, I suggest, that B may have hit on the expedient of adding the boxed term "INDVCTION" and spacing so that the prologue would finish exactly on the last line of the left column.

The second Part of King Henry the Fourth.   77

on any side but one, it is worse shame to begge, then to be on the worst side, were it worse then the name of Rebellion can tell how to make it.

Ser. You mistake me Sir.

Fal. Why sir? Did I say you were an honest man? Setting my Knight-hood, and my Souldiership aside, I had lyed in my throat, if I had said so.

Ser. I pray you (Sir) then set your Knighthood and your Souldier-ship aside, and giue mee leaue to tell you, you lye in your throat, if you say I am any other then an honest man.

Fal. I giue thee leaue to tell me so? I lay a-side that which growes to me? If thou get'st any leaue of me, hang me: if thou tak'st leaue, thou wer't better be hang'd: you Hunt-counter, hence: Auant.

Ser. Sir, my Lord would speake with you.

Iust. Sir *Iohn Falstaffe*, a word with you.

Fal. My good Lord: giue your Lordship good time of the day. I am glad to see your Lordship abroad: I heard say your Lordship was sicke. I hope your Lordship goes abroad by aduise. Your Lordship (though not clean past your youth) hath yet some smack of age in you: some rellish of the saltnesse of Time, and I most humbly beseech your Lordship, to haue a reuerend care of your health.

Iust. Sir *Iohn*, I sent you before your Expedition, to Shrewsburie.

Fal. If it please your Lordship, I heare his Maiestie is return'd with some discomfort from Wales.

Iust. I talke not of his Maiesty: you would not come when I sent for you?

Fal. And I heare moreouer, his Highnesse is falne into this same whorson Apoplexie. (you.

Iust. Well, heauen mend him. I pray let me speake with

Fal. This Apoplexie is (as I take it) a kind of Lethargie, a sleeping of the blood, a horson Tingling.

Iust. What tell you me of it? be it as it is.

Fal. It hath it originall from much greefe; from study and perturbation of the braine. I haue read the cause of his effects in *Galen.* It is a kinde of deafenesse.

Iust. I thinke you are falne into the disease: For you heare not what I say to you.

Fal. Very well (my Lord) very well: rather an't please you) it is the disease of not Listning, the malady of not Marking, that I am troubled withall.

Iust. To punish you by the heeles, would amend the attention of your eares, & I care not if I be your Physitian

Fal. I am as poore as *Iob*, my Lord; but not so Patient: your Lordship may minister the Potion of imprisonment to me, in respect of Pouertie: but how I should bee your Patient, to follow your prescriptions, the wise may make some dram of a scruple, or indeede, a scruple it selfe.

Iust. I sent for you (when there were matters against you for your life) to come speake with me.

Fal. As I was then aduised by my learned Councel, in the lawes of this Land-seruice, I did not come.

Iust. Wel, the truth is (sir *Iohn*) you liue in great infamy

Fal. He that buckles him in my belt, cānot liue in lesse.

Iust. Your Meanes is very slender, and your wast great.

Fal. I would it were otherwise: I would my Meanes were greater, and my waste slenderer.

Iust. You haue misled the youthfull Prince.

Fal. The yong Prince hath misled mee. I am the Fellow with the great belly, and he my Dogge.

Iust. Well, I am loth to gall a new-heal'd wound: your daies seruice at Shrewsbury, hath a little gilded ouer your Nights exploit on Gads-hill. You may thanke the vnquiet time, for your quiet o're-posting that Action.

Fal. My Lord? (Wolfe.

Iust. But since all is wel, keep it so: wake not a sleeping

Fal. To wake a Wolfe, is as bad as to smell a Fox.

Iu. What? you are as a candle, the better part burnt out

Fal. A Wassell-Candle, my Lord; all Tallow: if I did say of wax, my growth would approue the truth.

Iust. There is not a white haire on your face, but shold haue his effect of grauity.

Fal. His effect of grauy, grauy, grauy.

Iust. You follow the yong Prince vp and downe, like his euill Angell.

Fal. Not so (my Lord) your ill Angell is light: but I hope, he that lookes vpon mee, will take mee without, weighing: and yet, in some respects I grant, I cannot go: I cannot tell. Vertue is of so little regard in these Costermongers, that true valor is turn'd Beare-heard. Pregnancie is made a Tapster, and hath his quicke wit wasted in giuing Recknings: all the other gifts appertinent to man (as the malice of this Age shapes them) are not woorth a Gooseberry. You that are old, consider not the capacities of vs that are yong: you measure the heat of our Liuers, with the bitternes of your gals: & we that are in the vaward of our youth, I must confesse, are wagges too.

Iust. Do you set downe your name in the scrowle of youth, that are written downe old, with all the Characters of age? Haue you not a moist eye? a dry hand? a yellow cheeke? a white beard? a decreasing leg? an increasing belly? Is not your voice broken? your winde short? your wit single? and euery part about you blasted with Antiquity? and wil you cal your selfe yong? Fy, fy, fy, sir *Iohn.*

Fal. My Lord, I was borne with a white head, & something a round belly. For my voice, I haue lost it with hallowing and singing of Anthemes. To approue my youth farther, I will not: the truth is, I am onely olde in iudgement and vnderstanding: and he that will caper with mee for a thousand Markes, let him lend me the mony, & haue at him. For the boxe of th'eare that the Prince gaue you, he gaue it like a rude Prince, and you tooke it like a sensible Lord. I haue checkt him for it, and the yong Lion repents: Marry not in ashes and sacke-cloath, but in new Silke, and old Sacke.

Iust. Wel, heauen send the Prince a better companion.

Fal. Heauen send the Companion a better Prince: I cannot rid my hands of him.

Iust. Well, the King hath seuer'd you and Prince Harry, I heare you are going with Lord *Iohn* of Lancaster, against the Archbishop, and the Earle of Northumberland

Fal. Yes, I thanke your pretty sweet wit for it: but looke you pray, (all you that kisse my Ladie Peace, at home) that our Armies ioyn not in a hot day: for if I take but two shirts out with me, and I meane not to sweat extraordinarily: if it bee a hot day, if I brandish any thing but my Bottle, would I might neuer spit white againe: There is not a daungerous Action can peepe out his head, but I am thrust vpon it. Well, I cannot last euer.

Iust. Well, be honest, be honest, and heauen blesse your Expedition.

Fal. Will your Lordship lend mee a thousand pound, to furnish me forth?

Iust. Not a peny, not a peny: you are too impatient to beare crosses. Fare you well. Commend mee to my Cosin Westmerland.

Fal. If I do, fillop me with a three-man-Beetle. A man can no more separate Age and Couetousnesse, then he can part yong limbes and letchery: but the Gowt galles the

or near the end of the right column, when the excessive amount of copy became apparent. On g2, B's consistent compression throughout both columns indicates his awareness from the beginning that he must be alert to every opportunity. He faced a formidable challenge, and he met it with the ingenuity that marks all of his work.

Only two speeches on the page could be compressed by legitimate means.

> *Fal.* My Lord? (Wolfe.
> *Iuſt.*But ſince all is wel,keep it ſo: wake not a ſleeping   416
> *Fal.* To wake a Wolfe,is as bad as to ſmell a Fox.
> *Iu.* What?you are as a candle,the better part burnt out
> *Fal.* A Waſſell-Candle, my Lord; all Tallow : if I did

At 416 Compositor B held to one line by tightening spacing and using a turn-up. At 418 he held to one line by using a shortened prefix and omitting the spaces that would normally follow the prefix and the question mark. (Here, as elsewhere, even the period had to be sacrificed.) In a normal setting he would have run the word *out* onto a second line.

The normal methods, however, did not suffice, and there can be no doubt that Compositor B was driven to take radical steps. Only twenty lines into the left column, we find evidence that, under exceptional pressure, B would even revise his copy or make deletions. None of the changes we shall note is characteristic of the scribe; none is an improvement, reflecting authorial revision. In the following quotations from the Quarto, the revised or omitted passages are italicized. First, at 1.2.98–99, we find the following:

Q: some smack of *an ague* in you, some relish of the saltnes of time *in you*

F: abroad by aduiſe. Your Lordſhip(though not clean paſt your youth)hath yet ſome ſmack of age in you: ſome relliſh of the ſaltneſſe of Time, and I moſt humbly beſeech   370 your Lordſhip,to haue a reuerend care of your health.

Almost all editors adopt both Folio variants, reading *of age* (369) and omitting the second *in you* (370). Surely neither variant gives any sign of Shakespearean revision. The context gives full warrant to the Quarto's more vivid image of *an ague*. Falstaff is playing a game with the Chief Justice: "I heard your Lordship was sick. Oh dear, you really don't look too well. You are—as I can see—getting a little creaky in the joints; time is creeping up on you." Would Shakespeare have so revised the speech that it reads, as in the Folio, "You are getting old; you are getting old"? Both *an ague* and the teasing repetition of *in you* are exactly what we would expect of Falstaff. Moreover, as the ensuing discussion will show, the revisions are exactly what we should expect of Compositor B when he was forced to compress his text. By revising *an ague* to *age*, he was able to squeeze the first syllable of *relish* into line 369. Then by cutting *in you* in the next line, he could set all of *beseech* on 370. Without both the revision and the deletion, *health* would have required a final line to itself.

The same purpose probably underlies Compositor B's deletion of one word in 1.2.109:

Q: I pray *you* let me speake with you.

F: *Fal.* And I heare moreouer, his Highneſſe is falne into this ſame whorſon Apoplexie.   (you.
    Iuſt. Well, heauen mend him. I pray let me ſpeak with   380

Given the compositors' reluctance to use a two-word turn-up (they are very rare in the Folio) and the evidence of pressure throughout the page, it is highly probable that the deletion of *you* was a conscious device to hold the speech to one line.

Two Folio deletions in 1.2.111 may have different sources:

Q: a kind of lethergie, *and't please your lordship*, a *kind of* sleeping

F: *Fal.* This Apoplexie is (as I take it) a kind of Lethargie, a ſleeping of the blood, a horſon Tingling.   382

Elsewhere, the scribe deleted what he took to be unnecessary repetitions, and he may be responsible for cutting the second *kind of.* He cannot, however, be responsible for cutting *and't please your lordship.* Occasionally he revised *and't* to *if it,* but otherwise he left the familiar expression intact throughout the play: "and't please your Lordship/worship/grace," and the like. The only time the expression appears in the Quarto but not in the Folio is in this speech. The deletion is almost certainly an expedient by Compositor B to avoid using a third line.

A deletion at 1.2.124 can also be attributed to him:

Q: I care not if I *doe become* your physitian

F: attention of your eares,& I care not if I be your Physitian   393
    Fal. I am as poore as *Iob*, my Lord; but not so Patient:

If B had set *do become* and spelled out *and,* rather than using the ampersand—which he uses almost solely when he is compressing or justifying a long line—line 393 would have ended comfortably with *your,* and *Physitian* would have required an additional line.[25]

Two clumsy variants at 1.2.138 and 140 and a deletion at 141 again bear signs of B's handiwork:

Q: buckles *himselfe* in my belt

    meanes *are* very slender ... waste *is* great

F: *Iust.* Wel, the truth is (sir *Iohn*) you liue in great infamy
    Fal. He that buckles him in my belt, cânot liue in lesse.   404
    Iust. Your Meanes is very slender, and your wast great.
    Fal. I would it were otherwise: I would my Meanes

At 404, inclusion of the Quarto's *-selfe* would have required a new line for *lesse.* In the Justice's ensuing speech, one cannot attribute *Meanes is* to B's copy. The scribe routinely corrected all grammar, and there is no reason to believe that he would have introduced such an error. Compositor B, however, had good reason to make the revision. By substituting *is* for *are* and deleting the subsequent *is,* he held the speech to one line.

We find further significant omissions in the right-hand column, some of which might be attributed to B's carelessness were it not for the many signs that he is intentionally compressing his text.

In Falstaff's long speech beginning at line 426, we find two such omissions in 1.2.169 and 174:

Q: these costar-mongers *times*, that true valour

F: I cannot tell. Vertue is of so little regard in thefe Coftor-mongers, that true valor is turn'd Beare-heard. Pregnan- 430
cie is made a Tapfter, and hath his quicke wit wafted in

Q: you *doe* measure the heate

F: Goofeberry. You that are old, confider not the capacities of vs that are yong: you meafure the heat of our Li- 435
uers, with the bitternes of your gals: & we that are in the
vaward of our youth, I muft confeffe, are wagges too.

At 430, including the word *times* would, it is true, have created a difficult problem of justification, but under normal circumstances B would have solved it by normal means: by inserting spaces and, perhaps, capitalizing *Times* and *Valour* (his preferred spelling of the latter word).[26] He probably deleted *times* to permit setting two syllables of *Pregnancie* on line 430. Similarly, he probably omitted *do* at line 435 to permit setting the first syllable of *Liuers* on the same line. In the penultimate line of Falstaff's speech, against his normal practice he used *&* and two short spellings (*bitternes* and *gals*) and thus avoided driving *in the* into the next line. Without all of the changes we have just noted, the twelve-line speech would have required thirteen lines.

In the Folio setting, the last three lines of the Justice's response to Falstaff (1.2.183–85) are crammed.

Q: your winde short, *your chinne double*, your wit single ... will you *yet* call yourselfe

F: belly? Is not your voice broken? your winde fhort? your 442
wit fingle? and euery part about you blafted with Antiquity? and wil you cal your felfe yong? Fy, fy, fy, fir *Iohn*.

Even with the major cut at 442 of *your chinne double*, Compositor B would have required an additional line for *Iohn* at the end of the speech if he had not used short spellings (*wil*, *cal*), omitted spaces

after question marks, and cut the little word *yet* at line 444.
Falstaff's ensuing speech begins as follows (1.2.187-88):

Q: My Lorde, I was borne *about three of the clock in the afternoone* with

F: *Fal.* My Lord, I was borne with a white head, & fom-   445

In this first line of Falstaff's eleven-line speech beginning at 445, Compositor B slashed the equivalent of approximately three-quarters of a Folio type-line and thus eliminated the need for a twelfth line at the end of the speech.

At this point, B was into the final half of the right-hand column and apparently getting desperate. It may be for this reason that lines 1.2.214-20 are omitted in the Folio at 469, a cut that has been difficult to explain:

Q: but it was alway yet the tricke of our English nation, if they haue a good thing, to make it too common. If yee will needs say I am an olde man, you should giue me rest: I would to God my name were not so terrible to the enemy as it is, I were better to be eaten to death with a rust, than to be scoured to nothing with perpetuall motion.

It has been suggested that this cut was made because the lines were incomprehensible or because they were considered unpatriotic. Neither explanation satisfies. However, Hinman's discoveries about the problems created by casting off copy and the specific problem faced in setting *2 Henry IV* may offer an explanation. The cut occurs only ten lines from the bottom of g2, and in the last ten lines there is no good opportunity to compress. B may simply have thrown up his hands.

The amount of compression on g2 and B's consistent adjustments throughout the page indicate a problem far more extensive than can be accounted for by mere local error in casting off. An excessive amount of copy was allotted—and consciously allotted—to g2: a minimum of eleven excess lines and perhaps, if pressures of space were responsible for the long cut, as many as seventeen or eighteen. Compositor B's work on g2 amply bears out Charlton Hinman's warning that compositors may have been driven at times to drastic measures.²⁷

On g2ᵛ, a page almost entirely in verse, the only opportunity for compression was a scene division, and B held that to three lines. On g3 (Plate XII), however, we again find a page entirely of prose, and again we find B concentrating every effort to compress throughout the page. He had several opportunities that he did not have on g2—a scene division and three internal entries—and he took full advantage of them. He held the scene division to four lines and set all of the entrances to the right of short lines (at 648, 665, and 729). In addition, he twice set two brief speeches on one line (661 and 675). All three of these measures had been reserved almost exclusively for emergencies since the setting of *The Tempest*. But these familiar methods did not suffice, and again B resorted to tampering with the text itself (2.1.11).

Q: our liues, *for* he will stabbe.

F: *Sn.*It may chance coſt ſome of vs our liues:he wil ſtab   625

Only by abbreviating the speech prefix (at 622 we find *Snare*), omitting all spaces, and deleting one small word was he able to hold Snare's speech to one line. A simple substitution sufficed at 2.1.48–49.

Q: in the channell? Ile throw thee *in the channel*

F: *Hoſt.*Throw me in the channell? Ile throw thee there.   656
    Wilt thou?wilt thou?thou baſtardly rogue.Murder,mur-
    der,O thou Hony-ſuckle villaine,wilt thou kill Gods of-
    ficers,and the Kings? O thou hony-ſeed Rogue,thou art
    a honyſeed,a Man-queller,and a woman-queller.

By the substitution of a logical *there* for the second *in the channel* in 656, B prevented the Hostess's speech from running to six lines. Even more obvious is the reason for the deletions in the following (2.1.114–16):

Q: consideration: you haue *as it appeares to me* practisde vpon the easie yeelding spirite of this woman, *and made her serue your vses both in purse and in person*.

The second Part of King Henry the Fourth. 79

And take thou this (Ô thoughts of men accurs'd)⸰
"*Paſt, and to Come, ſeemes beſt; things Preſent, worſt.*
Mow. Shall we go draw our numbers, and ſet on?
Haſt. We are Times ſubiects, and Time bids, be gon.

Actus Secundus. Scœna Prima.

Enter Hoſteſſe, with two Officers, Fang, and Snare.
Hoſteſſe. Mr. *Fang*, haue you entred the Action?
Fang. It is enter'd.
Hoſteſſe. Wher's your Yeoman? Is it a luſty yeoman?
Will he ſtand to it?
Fang. Sirrah, where's *Snare*?
Hoſteſſe. I, I, good M. *Snare*..
Snare. Heere, heere.
Fang. Snare, we muſt Arreſt Sir *Iohn Falſtaffe*.
Hoſt. I good M. *Snare*, I haue enter'd him, and all.
Sn. It may chance coſt ſome of vs our liues: he wil ſtab
Hoſteſſe. Alas the day: take heed of him: he ſtab'd me
in mine owne houſe, and that moſt beaſtly: he cares not
what miſcheefe he doth, if his weapon be out. Hee will
foyne like any diuell, he will ſpare neither man, woman,
nor childe.
Fang. If I can cloſe with him, I care not for his thruſt.
Hoſteſſe. No, nor I neither: Ile be at your elbow.
Fang. If I but fiſt him once: if he come but within my
Vice.
Hoſt. I am vndone with his going: I warrant he is an
infinitiue thing vpon my ſcore. Good M. *Fang* hold him
ſure: good M. *Snare* let him not ſcape, he comes continuantly to Py-Corner (ſauing your manhoods) to buy a ſad-
dle, and hee is indited to dinner to the Lubbars head in
Lombardſtreet, to M. *Smoothes* the Silkman. I pra'ye, ſince
my Exion is enter'd, and my Caſe ſo openly known to the
world, let him be brought in to his anſwer: A 100. Marke
is a long one, for a poore lone woman to beare: & I haue
borne, and borne, and borne, and haue bin fub'd off, and
fub'd-off, from this day to that day, that it is a ſhame to
be thought on. There is no honeſty in ſuch dealing, vnles
a woman ſhould be made an Aſſe and a Beaſt, to beare e-
uery Knaues wrong. *Enter Falſtaffe and Bardolfe.*
Yonder he comes, and that arrant Malmeſey-Noſe *Bardolfe* with him. Do your Offices, do your offices: M. *Fang*,
& M. *Snare*, do me do me, do me your Offices.
Fal. How now? whoſe Mare's dead? what's the matter?
Fang. Sir *Iohn*, I arreſt you, at the ſuit of Miſt. *Quickly*.
Falſt. Away Varlets, draw *Bardolfe* : Cut me off the
Villaines head: throw the Queane in the Channel.
Hoſt. Throw me in the channell? Ile throw thee there.
Wilt thou? wilt thou? thou baſtardly rogue. Murder, mur-
der, O thou Hony-ſuckle villaine, wilt thou kill Gods of-
ficers, and the Kings? O thou hony-ſeed Rogue, thou art
a honyſeed, a Man-queller, and a woman-queller.
Falſt. Keep them off, *Bardolfe*. *Fang.* A reſcu, a reſcu.
Hoſt. Good people bring a reſcu. Thou wilt not? thou
wilt not? Do, do thou Rogue: Do thou Hempſeed.
Page. Away you Scullion, you Rampallian, you Fuſti-
lirian: Ile tucke your Cataſtrophe. *Enter. Ch. Iuſtice.*
Iuſt. What's the matter? Keepe the Peace here, hoa.
Hoſt. Good my Lord be good to mee. I beſeech you
ſtand to me.
Ch. Iuſt. How now ſir *Iohn*? What are you brauling here?
Doth this become your place, your time, and buſineſſe?
You ſhould haue bene well on your way to Yorke.
Stand from him Fellow; wherefore hang'ſt vpon him?

Hoſt. Oh my moſt worſhipfull Lord, and't pleaſe your
Grace, I am a poore widdow of Eaſtcheap, and he is arre-
ſted at my ſuit. *Ch. Iuſt.* For what ſumme? | 675
Hoſt. It is more then for ſome (my Lord) it is for all: all
I haue, he hath eaten me out of houſe and home; hee hath
put all my ſubſtance into that fat belly of his : but I will
haue ſome of it out againe, or I will ride thee o'Nights,
like the Mare.
Falſt. I thinke I am as like to ride the Mare, if I haue
any vantage of ground, to get vp.
Ch. Iuſt. How comes this, Sir *Iohn*? Fy, what a man of
good temper would endure this tempeſt of exclamation?
Are you not aſham'd to inforce a poore Widdowe to ſo
rough a courſe, to come by her owne?
Falſt. What is the groſſe ſumme that I owe thee?
Hoſt. Marry (if thou wer't an honeſt man) thy ſelfe, & | 688
the mony too. Thou didſt ſweare to mee vpon a parcell
gilt Goblet, ſitting in my Dolphin-chamber at the round
table, by a ſea-cole fire, on Wedneſday in Whitſon week, | 691
when the Prince broke thy head for lik'ning him to a ſin-
ging man of Windſor; Thou didſt ſweare to me then (as I
was waſhing thy wound) to marry me, and make mee my
Lady thy wife. Canſt ÿ deny it? Did not goodwife *Keech*
the Butchers wife come in then, and cal me goſſip *Quickly*? comming in to borrow a meſſe of Vinegar: telling vs,
ſhe had a good diſh of Prawnes: whereby ÿ didſt deſire to
eat ſome : whereby I told thee they were ill for a greene
wound? And didſt not thou (when ſhe was gone downe
ſtaires) deſire me to be no more familiar with ſuch poore | 701
people, ſaying, that ere long they ſhould call me Madam?
And did'ſt ÿ not kiſſe me, and bid mee fetch thee 30. s? I | 703
put thee now to thy Book-oath, deny it if thou canſt?
Fal. My Lord, this is a poore mad ſoule: and ſhe ſayes
vp & downe the town, that her eldeſt ſon is like you. She
hath bin in good caſe, & the truth is, pouerty hath diſtra-
cted her : but for theſe fooliſh Officers, I beſeech you, I
may haue redreſſe againſt them.
Iuſt. Sir *Iohn*, ſir *Iohn*. I am well acquainted with your
maner of wrenching the true cauſe, the falſe way. It is not
a confident brow, nor the throng of wordes, that come
with ſuch (more then impudent) ſawcines from you, can
thruſt me from a leuell conſideration, I know you ha' pra- | 714
cti'sd vpon the eaſie-yeelding ſpirit of this woman.
Hoſt. Yes in troth my Lord.
Iuſt. Prethee peace: pay her the debt you owe her, and
vnpay the villany you haue done her: the one you may do
with ſterling mony, & the other with currant repentance.
Fal. My Lord, I will not vndergo this ſneape without
reply. You call honorable Boldnes, impudent Sawcineſſe:
If a man wil curt'ſie, and ſay nothing, he is vertuous : No, | 722
my Lord (your humble duty remebred) I will not be your
ſutor. I ſay to you, I deſire deliu'rance from theſe Officers
being vpon haſty employment in the Kings Affaires.
Iuſt. You ſpeake, as hauing power to do wrong : But
anſwer in the effect of your Reputation, and ſatisfie the
poore woman.
Falſt. Come hither Hoſteſſe. *Enter M. Gower.* | 729
Ch. Iuſt. Now Maſter *Gower*; What newes?
Gow. The King (my Lord) and *Henrie* Prince of Wales
Are neere at hand: The reſt the Paper telles.
Falſt. As I am a Gentleman.
Hoſt. Nay, you ſaid ſo before.
Fal. As I am a Gentleman. Come, no more words of it
Hoſt. By this Heauenly ground I tread on, I muſt be
faine to pawne both my Plate, and the Tapiſtry of my dy-
ning Chambers.

g 3   *Falſt.*

TEXTUAL CHANGES BY THE COMPOSITORS 87

F: thruſt me from a leuell confideration,I know you ha' pra- 714
ctis'd vpon the eafie-yeelding ſpirit of this woman.

It has been suggested that the second passage was cut as improper, but lines that might have been far more offensive are retained elsewhere in the play. At this point, B was approaching the end of the page. Both deletions enabled him to avoid using two lines.

The purpose of other revisions and deletions on g3 is not readily apparent without considering the passages in their full context. If the Hostess's long speech beginning at line 635 (again refer to Plate XII), note the effect of the following changes in the Folio at 2.1.23, 29, and 34–35:

Q: I warrant *you* hees an infinitiue thing

F: *Hoſt*. I am vndone with his going:I warrant he is an 635

Q: master Smooths the silk man, I *pray you* since my exion

F: Lombardſtreet,to M.*Smoothes* the Silkman.I pra'ye,ſince 640
my Exion is enter'd,and my Cafe fo openly known to the
world,let him be brought in to his anſwer: A 100.Marke
is a long one,for a poore lone woman to beare: & I haue

Q: and haue bin fubd off, and fubd off, *and fubd off*

F: borne,and borne,and borne, and haue bin fub'd off, and
fub'd-off, from this day to that day, that it is a ſhame to 645
be thought on.There is no honeſty in fuch dealing, vnles
a woman ſhould be made an Affe and a Beaſt, to beare e-
uery Knaues wrong.   *Enter Falſtaffe and Bardolfe.*

By deleting *you* in 635, B could set one additional word in the line: *an*. The change is a small one, one that might be attributed to B's carelessness were it not for his consistent efforts to compress throughout the Hostess's long speech. In 640, had he not omitted the space between *Lombard* and *street* and substituted *pra'ye* for *pray you*, he would have had to set *since* in the next line. If he had then set 641–643 normally—if, that is, he had set *since* on 641, used *hundred* instead of *100* on 642, and spelled out *and* on 643—and if he had retained the third *fub'd-off* at 645, line 648 would have been almost full and he would have had to center the entrance of Falstaff and Bardolph on a new line, as he normally would have done. I do not, of course, suggest that B was anticipating the stage direction when he began setting the speech, but throughout he capitalized on every opportunity to compress.

His single-minded concentration may explain his curious setting of the last three lines of the Hostess's speech as well as his omission of a word in 2.1.39.

Q: that arrant malmsie-nose *knaue* Bardolfe

F: Yonder he comes, and that arrant Malmcsey-Nofe *Bar-*   649
    dolfe with him. Do your Offices, do your offices: M. *Fang*,
    & M. *Snare*, do me do me, do me your Offices.

In contrast to his almost invariable practice, B here used & in a short line and, for no good reason, cut *knaue*. This setting suggests a possible tendency of B to which we should be alert. When compressing copy, he may have tended to make gratuitous deletions and to vary unnecessarily from some of his normal practices (in regard to spelling, spacing, and abbreviations), just as—and this we shall note shortly—he may have tended to make gratuitous additions when he was expanding.

In the second long speech by the Hostess on g3, three minor changes at 2.1.88, 90, and 99–100 again require attention to the full context.

Q: *vpon* wednesday

F: table, by a fea-cole fire, on Wednefday in Whitfon week,   691

Q: for *liking his father* to a singing man of Winsor

F: when the Prince broke thy head for lik'ning him to a fin-   692
    ging man of Windfor; Thou didft fweare to me then (as I

Q: to be no more *so familiarity*

F: ftaires) defire me to be no more familiar with fuch poore   701

The substitution of *on* for *vpon* at 691 may be a revision by the scribe; it may be Compositor B's solution to a problem of justification. One notes, however, that if B had set *vpon*, he would normally have completed 691 with *Whitson* by adding spaces and, probably, capital letters. The substitution may be his expedient to enable squeezing an extra word, *week*, into the line. At 692, the substitution of *lik'ning* for *liking* should undoubtedly be attributed to the scribe, for he consistently eliminated archaisms. But who substituted *him* for *his father*? The scribe's sense of decorum (which we shall consider in detail in Chapter IV) may have made him eliminate this insult to the King; if so, however, would such a heightened sensitivity to *lèse majesté* lead him to transfer the insult to the heir apparent? Moreover, to England's great national hero?* The revision may well be Compositor B's, enabling him to set *to a sin-* on line 692. At 701, the reduction of Quickly's delightful *familiarity* to a pedestrian *familiar* raises similar questions. Such obtuse "correction" is typical of the scribe's work, but deletion of the unoffending *so* is not. Do we again see B's hand? On this page, any reading shorter than that in the Quarto should be automatically suspect. Unmistakable signs of compression are found in the rest of the speech. Three substitutions of y^u for *thou* at first look like normal expedients to justify lines, but two are not. At 698, the substitution enabled B to squeeze the word *to* into the line. At 703, his normal setting—using *thou*, spelling *me* both times, and spelling out *thirty*—would have driven *shillings* (normally spelled out) and *I* into 704, requiring an additional line for the speech.

In the last speech on the page that can be compressed, we find the following (2.1.124, 126):

Q: if a man wil *make* curtsie
    I *do* desire deliuerance

* Attributing this revision to the scribe is even more doubtful if the scribe understood "the singing-man of Windsor" to refer to John Magdalene, a priest who served as Richard II's double during the Abbot of Westminster's conspiracy against Henry IV. If the scribe hesitated to refer to the King as a pretender even in jest, one doubts that he would have revised to create such an innuendo about Prince Henry. See E. Brennecke, "Shakespeare's Singing-Man of Windsor," *PMLA*, 66 (1951), 1189–92.

F: If a man wil curt'fie,and fay nothing,he is vertuous: **No,** 722
my Lord(your humble duty remēbred)I will not be your
futor.I fay to you,I defire deliu'rance from thefe Officers
being vpon hafty employment in the Kings Affaires.

The deletion of *make* at 722 prevented setting *No,* on a new line, just as the deletion of *do* and the clipping of *deliu'rance* at 724 prevented dividing *Officers* after the first syllable. With the Quarto reading restored, B might have been able to squeeze *-icers* into 725, but the deletion of *make* and the tight setting throughout the speech indicate a determined effort to hold it to as few lines as possible.

B's unremitting efforts throughout g3 thus indicate that casting off allotted a minimum of thirteen lines more than customary. I say "minimum" because I have hesitated to draw specific conclusions about the absence of blank lines on the page. When he was not under the constraints of cast-off copy, B's settings of stage directions vary to such a degree (as, indeed, do those of all compositors) that it is as yet impossible to ascertain either his habitual practice or the customary allotment for blank lines made when casting off. In the history plays set prior to *2 Henry IV*, however, we do observe that opening entrances are usually preceded by, and often both preceded and followed by, blank lines. Internal entries, here placed to the right of short lines, are usually centered. In stints that were not cast off, internal entries are usually preceded and often followed by a blank line. Entrances that interrupt a speech, as does that of Falstaff and Bardolph at 648, are usually centered but not spaced. Under normal conditions, then, one would expect the copy allotted to g3 to require somewhere between three and nine lines more than the thirteen already noted.

When we consider the severe compression of copy on g2 and g3, together with the narrow scene boxes and the lack of blank lines with stage directions on g1^v and g2^v, only one conclusion seems possible. Casting off the first half of quire g was still based on the assumption that, by cramping the text at every opportunity, compositors could complete *2 Henry IV* in the twenty-five pages available: f6^v and two quires (g and gg) of twelve pages each.

TEXTUAL CHANGES BY THE COMPOSITORS 91

Thus the radical measures to which B was driven in the first half of quire g were caused by a problem unique to *2 Henry IV*.

Settings throughout the second half of quire g are in striking contrast to those in the first. Scene boxes return to a normal complement of five lines. Blank lines are used liberally: before and after all scene boxes, all opening stage directions, and all internal entries. The original hope of cramping the long play into two normal quires had obviously been abandoned. Because two compositors were working simultaneously—B frantically compressing copy in the first half of the quire as his co-worker, Compositor A, was using open settings in the second half—it is self-evident that they had realized the severity of the problem and determined the solution before beginning work on the second half. The play could not possibly be accommodated in the twenty-five pages originally allotted. It was therefore decided to expand quire gg by adding another sheet, making an abnormal quire of eight, rather than six, leaves.

There is one objection to this hypothesis: the setting of $g3^v$, a cast-off page that we have not yet considered. If pages of prose in the first half of quire g were all to be compressed, $g3^v$ should show the same signs of pressure that we find on g2 and g3. But it does not. The setting looks normal. The one scene box is a normal five lines deep. Blank lines precede the box, the opening stage direction, and the one internal entry. A further question arises when we note the abnormal order of setting at this point. According to Hinman's study of type, B began his first stint with $g3^v$ but then, before continuing with g3 and working in reverse order to g1, he paused to set g4, the first page of the second half of the quire.[28] We are thus faced with a contradiction. B's normal setting of $g3^v$ followed by his sudden cramping of the text on g3 suggests that the problem did not become evident until he reached g3. On the other hand, his open setting of g4 suggests that the decision to add four pages to quire gg had been made before he began g3. It suggests, in short, that the decision was made by the time B had completed setting $g3^v$.

Is there, then, anything abnormal about $g3^v$ to indicate sufficient awareness of the problem to warrant deciding at that point to expand quire gg? Yes: the very fact that the setting appears to be normal. In the context of four crowded pages in the first half of the quire, it is extremely odd that B should have set g3^v with the same freedom he exhibits in stints that were not cast off. The abnormal order of composition at this point suggests a logical explanation. If B knew as he set g3^v that he himself would next set g4, he could end g3^v wherever he wished. It may be that he realized the severity of the problem as he began g3^v, warned A to stop work on g4 (if, indeed, he had begun), and paused to discuss the problem with his colleagues. Once it had been decided to expand quire gg, work could be held up on g4 while B continued setting g3^v. And now he could set it as if it were not cast off.

Open settings in the second half of quire g reflect the decision to expand the next quire. Both compositors set scene boxes normally, used blank space liberally, and spaced generously within lines. When work actually began on quire gg, however, a new problem arose. Since the quire had been expanded to eight leaves, sixteen pages had to be used for the rest of the play, but the remaining copy would not stretch to sixteen pages if it were set normally.

Again, normal procedure was suspended. Given the inadequate amount of copy remaining, it was decided to complete the text of the play on gg7^v, to devote gg8 to the epilogue, and to set a cast list on gg8^v. According to established procedure, the next step would have been to cast off the first half of the quire. Because the addition of an extra sheet to gg created an abnormal quire, an unwieldy eight pages—two more than normal—would need to be cast off. Accurate casting off was probably difficult under the most ideal circumstances, and the problems with *2 Henry IV* were especially difficult. Thus composing began by an unusual procedure, undoubtedly in order to reduce the number of pages to be cast off. The epilogue and the cast list required no fixed starting point and could therefore be set immediately. As a result, the first two pages of the quire could also be set immediately, and in their reading order. B began by setting the first and sixteenth pages, gg1 and gg8ᵛ (the cast list). Then A set the second page, gg1ᵛ, while B set the fifteenth, gg8 (the epilogue), to complete the outer sheet.

Throughout quire gg, B's work shows that the problem had only partially been solved. The remaining copy was apparently still inadequate, for B now exercised the same resourcefulness in expanding the text that he had shown in compressing it in the first half of quire g. He got off to a good start on gg1. Twice he divided a single line of prose into two lines.

>   *Shal.* Shall I pricke him downe,   1677
>   Sir *Iohn* ?
>
>   *Shal.* Ha,ha,ha, you can do it fir: you can doe it : I   1682
>   commend you well.
>   *Francis Feeble.*

The setting of 1698 can also be explained only as the result of conscious effort to waste an additional type-line.

>   mans Taylour well Mafter *Shallow,* deepe Maifter *Shal-
>   low.*

By spelling out *Master* and *Maister* (rather than using his preferred abbreviation of *M.*) and by varying from his normal spelling of *Taylor*, B barely succeeded in driving *-low* into line 1699. He also expanded four additional lines by highly unorthodox methods, but to these we shall return.★

Compositor A's setting of gg1ᵛ is fairly open, but for A such is to be expected. The amount of copy cast off for gg2–gg4, also set by him, suggests that he was expected to follow his normal procedure.²⁹ While A was completing the first half of gg, Compositor B proceeded to the final six pages, expanding his copy at almost every opportunity. Clearly the yeoman's job was left to him, and he succeeded superbly in his task.

Rather than proceeding seriatim, as did B, let us first consider one page in detail: gg5ᵛ (Plate XIII). At first glance, the setting looks normal. In point of fact, it is not. By means of various

★ For discussion of lines 1669, 1677, 1706, and 1731–32, see below, pp. 98–99, 110–11, and 108–9.

The second Part of King Henry the Fourth.

Where is my Lord of Warwicke?
P-in. My Lord of Warwicke.
King. Doth any name particular, belong
Vnto the Lodging, where I firſt did ſwoon'd?
War. 'Tis call'd *Ieruſalem*, my Noble Lord.
King. Laud be to heauen:
Euen there my life muſt end.
It hath beene propheſi'de to me many yeares,
I ſhould not dye, but in *Ieruſalem*:
Which (vainly) I ſuppos'd the Holy-Land.
But beare me to that Chamber, there Ile lye:
In that *Ieruſalem*, ſhall *Harry* dye. *Exeunt.*

Actus Quintus. Scœna Prima.

Enter Shallow, Silence, Falſtaffe, Bardolfe, Page, and Dauie.

Shal. By Cocke and Pye, you ſhall not away to night.
What *Dauy*, I ſay.
Fal. You muſt excuſe me, M. *Robert Shallow.*
Shal. I will not excuſe you: you ſhall not be excuſed.
Excuſes ſhall not be admitted: there is no excuſe ſhall
ſerue: you ſhall not be excus'd.
Why *Dauie.*
Dauie. Heere ſir.
Shal. Dauy, Dauy, Dauy, let me ſee (*Dauy*) let me ſee:
William Cooke, bid him come hither. Sir *Iohn*, you ſhal
not be excus'd.
Dauy. Marry ſir, thus: thoſe Precepts cannot bee
ſeru'd: and againe ſir, ſhall we ſowe the head-land with
Wheate?
Shal. With red Wheate *Dauy.* But for *William* Cook:
are there no yong Pigeons?
Dauy. Yes Sir.
Heere is now the Smithes note, for Shooing,
And Plough-Irons.
Shal. Let it be caſt, and payde: Sir *Iohn*, you ſhall
not be excus'd.
Dauy. Sir, a new linke to the Bucket muſt needes bee
had: And Sir, doe you meane to ſtoppe any of *Williams*
Wages, about the Sacke he loſt the other day, at *Hinckley*
Fayre?
Shal. He ſhall anſwer it:
Some Pigeons *Dauy*, a couple of ſhort-legg'd Hennes: a
ioynt of Mutton, and any pretty little tine Kickſhawes,
tell *William* Cooke.
Dauy. Doth the man of Warre, ſtay all night ſir?
Shal. Yes *Dauy*:
I will vſe him well. A Friend i'th Court, is better then a
penny in purſe. Vſe his men well *Dauy*, for they are ar-
rant Knaues, and will backe-bite.
Dauy. No worſe then they are bitten. ſir: For, they
haue maruellous fowle linnen.
Shallow. Well conceited *Dauy*: about thy Buſineſſe,
Dauy.
Dauy. I beſeech you ſir,
To countenance *William Viſor* of Woncot, againſt *Cle-
ment Perkes* of the hill.
Shal. There are many Complaints *Dauy*, againſt that
Viſor, that *Viſor* is an arrant Knaue, on my know-
ledge.

Dauy. I graunt your Worſhip, that he is a knaue Sir:)
But yet heauen forbid Sir, but a Knaue ſhould haue ſome
Countenance, at his Friends requeſt. An honeſt man ſir,
is able to ſpeake for himſelfe, when a Knaue is not. I haue
ſeru'd your Worſhippe truely ſir, theſe eight yeares: and
if I cannot once or twice in a Quarter beare out a knaue,
againſt an honeſt man, I haue but a very litle credite with
your Worſhippe. The Knaue is mine honeſt Friend Sir,
therefore I beſeech your Worſhip, let him bee Counte-
nanc'd.
Shal. Go too,
I ſay he ſhall haue no wrong: Looke about *Dauy*.
Where are you Sir *Iohn*? Come, off with your Boots.
Giue me your hand M. *Bardolfe.*
Bard. I am glad to ſee your Worſhip.
Shal. I thanke thee, with all my heart, kinde Maſter
Bardolfe: and welcome my tall Fellow:
Come Sir *Iohn.*
Falſtaffe. Ile follow you, good Maſter *Robert Shallow.*
Bardolfe, looke to our Horſſes. If I were ſaw'de into
Quantities, I ſhould make foure dozen of ſuch bearded
Hermites ſtaues, as Maſter *Shallow.* It is a wonderfull
thing to ſee the ſemblable Cohetence of his mens ſpirits,
and his: They, by obſeruing of him, do beare themſelues
like fooliſh Iuſtices: Hee, by conuerſing with them, is
turn'd into a Iuſtice-like Seruingman. Their ſpirits are
ſo married in Coniunction, with the participation of So-
ciety, that they flocke together in conſent, like ſo many Wilde-Geeſe. If I had a ſuite to Mayſter *Shallow,* I
would humour his men, with the imputation of beeing
neere their Mayſter. If to his Men, I would currie with
Maiſter *Shallow,* that no man could better command his
Seruants. It is certaine, that either wiſe bearing, or ig-
norant Carriage is caught, as men take diſeaſes, one of
another: therefore, let men take heede of their Companie. I will deuiſe matter enough out of this *Shallow,* to
keepe Prince *Harry* in continuall Laughter, the wearing
out of ſixe Faſhions (which is foure Tearmes) or two Ac-
tions, and he ſhall laugh with *Interuallums.* O it is much
that a Lye (with a ſlight Oath) and a ieſt (with a ſadde
brow) will doe, with a Fellow, that neuer had the Ache
in his ſhoulders. O you ſhall ſee him laugh, till his Face
be like a wet Cloake, ill laid vp.
Shal. Sir *Iohn.*
Falſt. I come Maſter *Shallow,* I come Maſter *Shallow.*
Exeunt

Scena Secunda.

*Enter the Earle of Warwicke, and the Lord
Chieſe Iuſtice.*

Warwicke. How now, my Lord Chiefe Iuſtice, whe-
ther away?
Ch. Iuſt. How doth the King?
Warw. Exceeding well: his Cares
Are now, all ended.
Ch. Iuſt. I hope, not dead.
Warw. Hee's walk'd the way of Nature,
And to our purpoſes, he liues no more.
Ch. Iuſt. I would his Maieſty had call'd me with him,
The ſeruice, that I truly did his life,
Hath left me open to all iniuries.
War.

TEXTUAL CHANGES BY THE COMPOSITORS 95

adjustments, B succeeded in making his copy stretch to a minimum of seventeen lines more than it would normally require. Moreover, he did so in addition to any adjustments he may have made in blank space. His two scene boxes are ample and the opening stage directions are framed by blank lines, but it is impossible to know whether or not he was consciously deviating from his normal practice.[30]

On gg5ᵛ Compositor B overran several lines by using standard compositorial techniques, though he exercised considerable ingenuity in applying them. By spacing alone, he was able to make one syllable, the *-ledge* of *knowledge*, run over to a new line at 2831.

   Vifor, that *Vifor* is an arrant Knaue, on my knowledge.

By spelling out speech prefixes and using thick spaces, he was able to use an additional line at 2825

   Shallow. Well conceited *Dauy*: about thy Bufineffe,
Dauy.

and at 2881

   Warwicke. How now, my Lord Chiefe Iuftice, whether away?

Instead of using his customary abbreviation of *M*., he spelled out *Master* twice to expand line 2876 and thus to require setting the *Exeunt* at the end of 5.1 on a separate line.

   Falft. I come Mafter *Shallow*, I come Mafter *Shallow*.
                                                                  Exeunt

From the beginning of Falstaff's long monologue in the right column (2850–74), we see B's determination to stretch his copy. He spelled out the speech prefix, using *Falstaffe* instead of his usual *Fal.*, and thereafter rejected his customary abbreviation of *M*. five times—setting *Maister* and *Mayster* as well as *Master*. Without this close attention throughout, the long speech would have run one line shorter.

One of B's most frequently used devices is amply demonstrated on gg5ᵛ. He expanded verse copy by the simple expedient of dividing one line into two. Ideally, division is used in the opening line of a speech at a strong caesura, as in 2778-79.

> *King.* Laud be to heauen :
> Euen there my life muſt end.
> It hath beene propheſi'de to me many yeares,

Pushed to extremes, however (as he often seemed to be toward the end of a page), B might arbitrarily divide anywhere in the line, as in 2884-85.

> *Warw.* Exceeding well : his Cares
> Are now, all ended.

In its present setting, the line is too long for the Folio column, but B could have set it on one line had he used his usual prefix of *War.*, omitted the extraneous comma, and closed spacing.

Compositor B was especially skillful at a far more difficult task: dividing lines of prose in such a way that the expedient has a certain dramatic logic. In speeches that are solid prose in the Quarto and were undoubtedly prose in the scribe's transcript, he divided at a transition. This device is least obtrusive at the end of a speech, as at 2848-49

> *Shal.* I thanke thee, with all my heart, kinde Maſter
> *Bardolfe* : and welcome my tall Fellow :
> Come Sir *Iohn.*

and at 2793-94.

> *Shal.* I will not excuſe you : you ſhall not be excuſed.
> Excuſes ſhall not be admitted : there is no excuſe ſhall
> ſerue : you ſhall not be excus'd.
> Why *Davie.*

At times there is a certain logic in such division at the opening of a speech, as at 2813.

> *Shal.* He ſhall anſwer it :
> Some Pigeons *Davy*, a couple of ſhort-legg'd Hennes : a
> ioynt of Mutton, and any pretty little tine Kickſhawes,
> tell *William* Cooke.

Here a strong transition justifies dividing the line, but at 2818–19 B divided where there is no shift in thought. Where the Quarto reads "Yea Dauy I will vse him well," Compositor B set

> *Shal.* Yes *Dauy* :
> I will vse him well. A Friend i'th Court, is better then a

Here the Folio's colon seems an arbitrary heavy stop, designed to justify the line division. In some cases, the divided lines are excused by the pretense that they are verse, as at 2804–06

> *Dauy.* Yes Sir.
> Heere is now the Smithes note, for Shooing,
> And Plough-Irons.

and at 2842–45.

> *Shal.* Go too,
> I fay he fhall haue no wrong: Looke about *Dauy.*
> Where are you Sir *Iohn?* Come, off with your Boots.
> Giue me your hand M. *Bardolfe.*

In one case on this page (2826–28), B began by setting prose as verse but carelessly forgot how he started.

> *Dauy.* I befeech you fir,
> To countenance *William Vifor* of Woncot, againft *Cle-*
> *ment Perkes* of the hill.

On gg5^v, Compositor B used nine additional type-lines solely by means of dividing. His skill is shown in exercising a certain restraint. He seems to have realized that successive prose speeches could not be divided without making the typographical expedient obvious. Since speeches of chopped prose alternate with speeches of solid prose, the page looks normal to a casual reader. It is nonetheless clear that, given this restriction, B divided at every possible opportunity.

Another creative solution to the problem of expanding copy is found in the opening stage direction to 5.2. As noted in Chapter II, the scribe omitted all titles in his stage directions, and his transcript probably read "*Enter Warwicke and Chiefe Iustice.*" In the

Folio, this is expanded to create two lines: "*Enter the Earle of Warwicke and the Lord | Chiefe Iustice.*"

By these methods B stretched his copy so that it takes fifteen type-lines more than it would normally require. In light of his concentrated effort, there can be little doubt that he resorted to one last desperate measure: adding words. Three such additions on gg5^v have been adopted by almost all editors. One is found at 5.1.24.

Q: about the sacke he lost at Hunkly Faire?

F: Wages, about the Sacke he loft the other day, at *Hinckley* 2811
Fayre ?

The inserted *the other day* is surely B's invention, added to force *Fayre?* into an additional line. At 5.1.49 and 51, two additions facilitated eking out one syllable for an extra line.

Q: against an honest man, I haue litle credit with your worship: the knaue is mine honest friend sir, therefore I beseech you let him be countenaunst.

F: againſt an honeſt man, I haue but a very litle credite with your Worſhippe. The Knaue is mine honeſt Friend Sir, therefore I befeech your Worſhip, let him bee Counte- 2840
nanc'd.

The substitution of *your Worship* (2840) for *you* was an ideal device, given the opening words of Davy in this speech to Shallow: "I graunt your Worship." That and the addition of *but a very* (2838) show the ingenuity B was to use throughout his final stint.

On five pages of quire gg, it is surely B who added words and phrases that have been adopted by almost all editors as authoritative corrections, corrections proving that a revised manuscript was consulted in preparing copy for the Folio.* On gg1—where,

---

* I omit detailed discussion of gg6 and gg6^v because on neither page did B tamper with his copy. On gg6, a page of solid verse, his only adjustment was to expand a stage direction so that it took two lines. On gg6^v, he set an atypical blank line before a break-in entrance (3104), divided two prose lines (3128–29, 3135–36), and expanded 3116 by using thick spaces, capital letters, and atypical

TEXTUAL CHANGES BY THE COMPOSITORS 99

as we have already noted, B stretched his copy so as to waste three additional type-lines—we find the following reading for 3.2.134-35:

Q: we haue a number of shadowes fill vp the muster booke.

F: wee haue a number of shadowes to fill vppe the Mufter- 1669
Booke.

He drove *Booke* into a new line by using expanded spellings (he prefers *we* and *vp*) and by adding one little word: *to*.

On gg7 (Plate XIV), the penultimate page of the play, B was expanding his text as much as possible so as to finish it in the middle of gg7^v. In a ten-line speech (3155-64), he again used the simple device of spelling out *Master* three times in order to drive one word into an additional line. Four times he expanded by dividing prose into pseudo-verse: 3146-47, 3148-51, 3197-98, and 3202-3. At the opening of 5.4 and at 3247-49, he undoubtedly expanded the entrances to excuse setting each with an additional line. Although it is usually difficult to draw conclusions about the use of blank space, sufficient evidence exists to suggest that B also stretched his copy at the 5.5 scene division that heads the right column. The scene box itself is an ample five lines deep, and it is preceded by a blank line. Throughout the Folio, B set a total of eighteen boxes at the top of a column; of these, thirteen are set without a preceding blank line. In the four cases other than on gg7 when he did use an additional blank line, two occur in cast-off stints.[31] His open spacing of the scene box was probably intentional. Thus far, then, B set nine type-lines on gg7 that were not required by his copy.

In light of these adjustments, let us consider a series of Folio additions on gg7. The first is at 5.4.5-6.

---

spellings of *luckie* and *happie* to drive one word into 3117. His adjustments on these pages are minor compared with those on pages both preceding and following. For the moment, he may have felt that his Herculean efforts on gg5^v—stretching the text to an additional seventeen type-lines—had been sufficient. On gg7, he again began making major adjustments.

The second Part of King Henry the Fourth.

Fal. What, is the old King dead?
Pift. As naile in doore.
The things I speake, are iuſt.
Fal. Away *Bardolfe*, Sadle my Horſe,
Maſter *Robert Shallow*, chooſe what Office thou wilt
In the Land, 'tis thine. *Piſtol*, I will double charge thee
With Dignities.
Bard. O ioyfull day:
I would not take a Knighthood for my Fortune.
Piſt. What? I do bring good newes.
Fal. Carrie Maſter *Silence* to bed : Maſter *Shallow*, my
Lord *Shallow*, be what thou wilt, I am Fortunes Steward.
Get on thy Boots, wee l ride all night. Oh ſweet Piſtoll :
Away *Bardolfe* : Come Piſtol, vtter more to mee : and
withall deuiſe ſomething to do thy ſelfe good. Boote,
boote Maſter *Shallow*, I know the young King is ſick for
mee. Let vs take any mans Horſſes : The Lawes of Eng-
land are at my command'ment. Happie are they, which
haue beene my Friendes : and woe vnto my Lord Chiefe
Iuſtice.
Piſt. Let Vultures vil'de ſeize on his Lungs alſo :
Where is the life that late I led, ſay they?
Why heere it is, welcome thoſe pleaſant dayes. *Exeunt*

Scena Quarta.

Enter Hoſteſſe Quickly, Dol Teare-ſheete, and Beadles.

Hoſteſſe. No, thou arrant knaue : I would I might dy,
that I might haue thee hang'd : Thou haſt drawne my
ſhoulder out of ioynt.
Off. The Conſtables haue deliuer'd her ouer to mee :
and ſhee ſhall haue Whipping cheere enough, I warrant
her. There hath beene a man or two (lately) kill'd about
her.
Dol. Nut-hooke, nut-hooke, you Lye : Come on, Ile
tell thee what, thou damn'd Tripe-viſag'd Raſcall, if the
Childe I now go with, do miſcarrie, thou had'ſt better
thou had'ſt ſtrooke thy Mother, thou Paper-fac'd Villaine.
Hoſt. O that Sir *Iohn* were come, hee would make
this a bloody day to ſome body. But I would the Fruite
of her Wombe might miſcarry.
Officer. If it do, you ſhall haue a dozen of Cuſhions
againe, you'haue but eleuen now. Come, I charge you
both go with me : for the man is dead, that you and Piſtoll beate among you.
Dol. Ile tell thee what, thou thin man in a Cenſor ; I
will haue you as ſoundly ſwindg'd for this, you blew-
Bottel'd Rogue : you filthy famiſh'd Correctioner, if you
be not ſwing'd, Ile forſweare halfe Kirtles.
Off. Come, come, you ſhee-Knight-arrant, come.
Hoſt. O, that right ſhould thus o'recome might. Wel
of ſufferance, comes eaſe.
Dol. Come you Rogue, come :
Bring me to a Iuſtice.
Hoſt. Yes, come you ſtaru'd Blood-hound.
Dol. Goodman death, goodman Bones.
Hoſt. Thou Anatomy, thou.
Dol. Come you thinne Thing :
Come you Raſcall.
Off. Very well. *Exeunt.*

Scena Quinta.

Enter two Groomes.

1. *Groo.* More Ruſhes, more Ruſhes.
2. *Groo.* The Trumpets haue ſounded twice.
1. *Groo.* It will be two of the Clocke, ere they come
from the Coronation. *Exit Groo.*

Enter Falſtaffe, Shallow, Piſtoll, Bardolfe, and Page.

Falſtaffe. Stand heere by me, M. *Robert Shallow*, I will
make the King do you Grace. I will leere vpon him, as
he comes by : and do but marke the countenance that hee
will giue me.
Piſtol. Bleſſe thy Lungs, good Knight.
Falſt. Come heere *Piſtol*, ſtand behind me. O if I had
had time to haue made new Liueries, I would haue be-
ſtowed the thouſand pound I borrowed of you. But it is
no matter, this poore ſhew doth better : this doth inferre
the zeale I had to ſee him.
Shal. It doth ſo.
Falſt. It ſhewes my earneſtneſſe in affection.
Piſt. It doth ſo.
Fal. My deuotion.
Piſt. It doth, it doth, it doth.
Fal. As it were, to ride day and night,
And not to deliberate, not to remember,
Not to haue patience to ſhift me.
Shal. It is moſt certaine.
Fal. But to ſtand ſtained with Trauaile, and ſweating
with deſire to ſee him, thinking of nothing elſe, putting
all affayres in obliuion, as if there were nothing els to bee
done, but to ſee him.
Piſt. 'Tis *ſemper idem* : for *obſque hoc nihil eſt*. 'Tis all
in euery part.
Shal. 'Tis ſo indeed.
Piſt. My Knight, I will enflame thy Noble Liuer, and
make thee rage. Thy *Dol*, and *Helen* of thy noble thoghts
is in baſe Durance, and contagious priſon : Hall'd thither by moſt Mechanicall and durty hand. Rowze vppe
Reuenge from Ebon den, with fell Alecto's Snake, for
Dol is in. Piſtol, ſpeakes nought but troth.
Fal. I will deliuer her.
Piſtol. There roar'd the Sea : and Trumpet Clangour
ſounds.

The Trumpets ſound. Enter King Henrie the Fift, Brothers, Lord Chiefe Iuſtice.

Falſt. Saue thy Grace, King *Hall*, my Royall *Hall.*
Piſt. The heauens thee guard, and keepe, moſt royall
Impe of Fame.
Fal. 'Saue thee my ſweet Boy.
King. My Lord Chiefe Iuſtice, ſpeake to that vaine
man.
Ch. Iuſt. Haue you your wits?
Know you what 'tis you ſpeake?
Falſt. My King, my Ioue ; I ſpeake to thee, my heart.
King. I know thee not, old man : Fall to thy Prayers :
How ill white haires become a Foole, and Ieſter?

I haue

Q: and shee shal haue whipping cheere I warrant her, there hath beene a man or two kild about her.

F: and shee shall haue Whipping cheere enough, I warrant 3175
her. There hath beene a man or two (lately) kill'd about her.

The Folio's additions of *enough* and *lately* have been widely adopted as authoritative, but the evidence suggests that they were both invented by Compositor B to drive *her* into an unnecessary line. Another widely adopted addition is found at 5.4.9.

Q: the child I go with do miscarry, thou wert better thou hadst strook

F: Childe I now go with, do miscarrie, thou had'ft better 3180
thou had'ft ftrooke thy Mother, thou Paper-fac'd Villaine.

In 3180, B used three legitimate methods of expanding copy: setting thick spaces, substituting a longer spelling (his preferred spelling is *carry*),[32] and, probably, adding punctuation (the comma after *with*). In addition, he even substituted a reasonably comparable but longer synonym (*had'st* for *wert*).[33] Nonetheless, without that little added word—*now*—he could not have reserved a syllable for line 3182.

A final addition on gg7 might not seem due to the compositor (5.5.5).

Q: maister Shallow, I will

F: *Falftaffe*. Stand heere by me, M. *Robert Shallow*, I will 3212
make the King do you Grace. I will leere vpon him, as he comes by: and do but marke the countenance that hee will giue me.

That B was consciously stretching his copy is indicated by his use of *Falstaffe*, rather than an abbreviated prefix. In such cases one would expect him to have spelled out *Master* too, but perhaps he rejected that expedient on the grounds that he could then justify the line only by using abnormally thick spaces. With *Robert* added, the line justified easily. Of course the added name was not needed to ensure a fourth line for the speech; spelling out the speech prefix alone would have sufficed. This, then, may be one of several added words we find in B's settings that do not facilitate using extra lines. Three Folio additions of *good* are highly suspicious: "O that this good Blossome" (875; 2.2.94), "Well, my good Lord" (880; 2.2.99) and "What's the newes (my good Lord?)" (761; 2.1.167).[34] The first probably echoes "good Interpretation" found in the preceding line. With the second two, B probably held too much copy in his head and carelessly echoed a familiar phrase. The same type of carelessness may explain B's addition of *Robert*. (Perhaps he automatically echoed the full name, which he had already set at 1620, 2790, and 2850.)

Most editors have rejected the three additions of *good*. The majority, however, have adopted not only the *Robert* but two more gratuitous Folio additions that I find equally suspect. For the Quarto's "come pricke Bul-calfe til hee roare againe" (3.2.175–76), the Folio reads "Come, pricke me *Bulcalfe* ..." (1711). The context argues against the Folio reading. Shakespeare's idiom throughout the scene is "prick him," and the Folio's added *me* blunts the edge of Falstaff's pun.[35] Another addition open to question is *new* in "the Ale-wiues new Petticoat" (865; 2.2.82). The significance of the ale-wife's petticoat is that it is red. A "new" petticoat for such a disreputable creature would be as improbable in life as it is meaningless in context. B's lack of disciplined attention to the exact wording of his copy at this point is seen in his omission of *so* only three words later in the line.

Several Folio variants in *1 Henry IV* further confirm B's tendency to add gratuitous words. In addition to conjunctions, articles, and other minor words (e.g., at 46, 270, 645, and 1015), he interpolated *light* in "a plague light vpon you all" (764) and *wond'rous* in 606:

> *Hot.* I smell it:
> Vpon my life, it will do wond'rous well.

This speech occurs in the lower right column of e1^v, and B divided the quartos' single line to waste space. Did he add *wond'rous* to create a full pentameter line or merely because he was holding too much copy in his mind? Elsewhere he did not try to regularize part-lines resulting from division, and I tend toward the latter explanation.*

On gg7^v (Plate XV), which completes the text of the play, B continued to stretch the text. In his copy, he probably found *Exit* set to the right of 3283 to mark the exit of the King and his train. Instead of using the available space to the right of the King's last line, B expanded the direction to *Exit King* to excuse setting it on a new line. We also find one line of verse divided into two lines (3315-16) and two more additions that appear to be compositorial in origin (5.5.81).

Q: I cannot perceiue how, vnlesse you giue me

F: **Shal. I cannot well perceiue how, vnleſſe you ſhould**   3292
        giue me your Doublet, and ſtuffe me out with Straw. I
        beſeech you, good Sir *Iohn*, let mee haue fiue hundred of
        my thouſand.

The added *well* and *should* both weaken the sharp bite of Shallow's retort, and there is no conceivable reason why the scribe, much less Shakespeare, would have made such a revision. B probably added the words to drive *giue me your* into 3293, thus requiring a fourth line for the speech.

In the cases above, Compositor B inserted words or brief phrases merely to expand the given sentences of the Folio copy. When B operated under extreme pressure, however, it seems highly probable that he occasionally resorted to adding longer phrases and even lines entirely of his own invention. We are, in fact, ready to consider three of the puzzling additions that gave rise to the present study.

* An interpolation at 723 near the end of e2—*rather* in "Nay, I think rather, you are more beholding to the Night"—might seem gratuitous, but B added it so that he could expand a two-line speech to three lines. His need to expand on this page is confirmed by the ensuing three lines, where he divided two lines of prose into three lines of verse.

100 *The second Part of King Henry the Fourth.*

I haue long dream'd of such a kinde of man,
So surfeit-swell'd, so old, and so prophane:
But being awake, I do despise my dreame.
Make lesse,thy body (hence) and more thy Grace,
Leaue gourmandizing; Know the Graue doth gape
For thee, thrice wider then for other men.
Reply not to me, with a Foole-borne Ieft,
Presume not, that I am the thing I was,
For heauen doth know (so shall the world perceiue)
That I haue turn'd away my former Selfe,
So will I those that kept me Companie.
When thou dost heare I am, as I haue bin,
Approach me, and thou shalt be as thou was't
The Tutor and the Feeder of my Riots:
Till then, I banish thee, on paine of death,
As I haue done the rest of my Misleaders,
Not to come neere our Person, by ten mile.
For competence of life, I will allow you,
That lacke of meanes enforce you not to euill:
And as we heare you do reforme your selues,
We will according to your strength, and qualities,
Giue you aduancement. Be it your charge (my Lord)
To see perform'd the tenure of our word. Set on.
Exit King.

Fal. Master *Shallow,* I owe you a thousand pound.
Shal. I marry Sir *Iohn,* which I beseech you to let me haue home with me.
Fal. That can hardly be, M. *Shallow,* do not you grieue at this: I shall be sent for in priuate to him: Looke you, he must seeme thus to the world: feare not your aduancement: I will be the man yet, that shall make you great.

Shal. I cannot well perceiue how, vnlesse you should giue me your Doublet, and stuffe me out with Straw. I beseech you, good Sir *Iohn,* let mee haue fiue hundred of my thousand.
Fal. Sir, I will be as good as my word. This that you heard, was but a colour.
Shall. A colour I feare, that you will dye, in Sir *Iohn.*
Fal. Feare no colours, go with me to dinner:
Come Lieutenant *Pistol,* come *Bardolfe,*
I shall be sent for soone at night.
Ch. Iust. Go carry Sir *Iohn Falstaffe* to the Fleete,
Take all his Company along with him.
Fal. My Lord, my Lord.
Ch. Iust. I cannot now speake, I will heare you soone:
Take them away.
Pist. Si fortuna me tormento, spera me contento.
Exit. Manet Lancaster and Chiefe Iustice.
Iohn. I like this faire proceeding of the Kings:
He hath intent his wonted Followers
Shall all be very well prouided for:
But all are banisht, till their conuersations
Appeare more wise, and modest to the world.
Ch. Iust. And so they are.
Iohn. The King hath call'd his Parliament,
My Lord.
Ch. Iust. He hath.
Iohn. I will lay oddes, that ere this yeere expire,
We beare our Ciuill Swords, and Natiue fire
As farre as France. I heare a Bird so sing,
Whose Musicke (to my thinking) pleas'd the King.
Come, will you hence? *Exeunt*

FINIS.

PLATE XV. Sig. gg7ᵛ

As yet I have not discussed gg5 (Plate XVI), primarily because it is solid verse and thus did not lend itself to the many techniques used to expand prose. The copy for gg5 presented B with a major challenge. Covering part of the reconciliation scene (4.5.110-230), the page is devoted almost entirely to two long speeches by the King and one by the Prince. A one-line speech in verse can now and then be divided into two lines without seriously marring the appearance of the page, but for aesthetic reasons long speeches resist such tinkering. This page was the first of B's final stint, and he had to begin using additional lines immediately. But how? Beginning with the left column, he faced the long conclusion of the King's rebuke. After twenty-eight lines, he had been unable to add one line. Now he began the Prince's speech of repentance. Here, at last, was an opportunity. Although the opening line could easily have been accommodated in the Folio column, B divided it at the caesura: "O pardon me (my Liege) / But for my Teares . . ." (2671-72). Now, however, he faced unbroken verse for thirty-eight lines. As he approached the end of the left column, he saw a strong transition where a division into two lines could be tolerated.

> But thou, most Fine, most Honour'd, most Renown'd,
> Hast eate the Bearer vp.
> Thus (my Royall Liege)
> Accusing it, I put it on my Head. . . .

At 2698-99 he created what is, in effect, a two-line "waist" in the middle of a long speech. The device is useful but it has limitations. To be rhetorically justifiable, it can be employed only at a point of major transition; to be aesthetically acceptable, it can be employed only rarely.

As B began the right column, he had been able to expand the text by only two type-lines, and ahead of him lay similar problems. The only legitimate place to do further spreading would be at the bottom of the right column, where he found an entrance and three brief verse speeches totaling only six lines. Fortunately three

The second Part of King Henry the Fourth.

Then get thee gone, and digge my graue thy selfe,
And bid the merry Bels ring to thy eare
That thou art Crowned, not that I am dead.
Let all the Teares, that should bedew my Hearse
Be drops of Balme, to sanctifie thy head:
Onely compound me with forgotten dust.
Giue that, which gaue thee life, vnto the Wormes:
Plucke downe my Officers, breake my Decrees;
For now a time is come, to mocke at Forme.
Henry the fift is Crown'd: Vp Vanity,
Downe Royall State: All you sage Counsailors, hence:
And to the English Court, assemble now
From eu'ry Region, Apes of Idlenesse.
Now neighbor-Confines, purge you of your Scum:
Haue you a Ruffian that swill sweare? drinke? dance?
Reuell the night? Rob? Murder? and commit
The oldest sinnes, the newest kinde of wayes?
Be happy, he will trouble you no more:
England, shall double gill'd, his trebble guilt.
England, shall giue him Office, Honor, Might:
For the Fift Harry, from curb'd Licenfe pluckes
The muzzle of Restraint; and the wilde Dogge
Shall flesh his tooth in euery Innocent.
O my poore Kingdome (sicke, with ciuill blowes)
When that my Care could not with-hold thy Ryots,
What wilt thou do, when Ryot is thy Care?
O, thou wilt be a Wildernesse againe,
Peopled with Wolues (thy old Inhabitants.

2671 *Prince.* O pardon me (my Liege)
But for my Teares,
The most Impediments vnto my Speech,
I had fore-stall'd this deere, and deepe Rebuke,
Ere you (with greefe) had spoke, and I had heard
The course of it so farre. There is your Crowne,
And he that weares the Crowne immortally,
Long guard it yours. If I affect it more,
Then as your Honour, and as your Renowne,
Let me no more from this Obedience rise,
Which my most true, and inward duteous Spirit
Teacheth this prostrate, and exteriour bending.
Heauen witnesse with me, when I here came in,
And found no course of breath within your Maiestie,
How cold it strooke my heart. If I do faine,
O let me, in my present wildenesse, dye,
And neuer liue, to shew th'incredulous World,
The Noble change that I haue purposed.
Comming to looke on you, thinking you dead,
(And dead almost (my Liege) to thinke you were)
I spake vnto the Crowne (as hauing sense)
And thus vpbraided it. The Care on thee depending,
Hath fed vpon the body of my Father,
Therefore, thou best of Gold, art worst of Gold.
Other, lesse fine in Charract, is more precious,
Preseruing life, in Med'cine potable:
But thou, most Fine, most Honour'd, most Renown'd,
2698 Hast eate the Bearer vp.
Thus (my Royall Liege)
Accusing it, I put it on my Head,
To try with it (as with an Enemie,
That had before my face murdred my Father)
The Quarrell of a true Inheritor.
But if it did infect my blood with Ioy,
Or swell my Thoughts, to any straine of Pride;
If any Rebell, or vaine spirit of mine,
Did, with the least Affection of a Welcome,
Giue entertainment to the might of it,

Let heauen, for euer, keepe it from my head,
And make me, as the poorest Vassaile is,
That doth with awe, and terror kneele to it.
King. O my Sonne! 2712
Heauen put it in thy minde to take it hence,
That thou might'st ioyne the more, thy Fathers loue,
Pleading so wisely, in excuse of it.
Come hither *Harrie,* sit thou by my bedde,
And heare (I thinke, the very latest Counsell
That euer I shall breath: Heauen knowes, my Sonne)
By what by-pathes, and indirect crook'd-wayes
I met this Crowne: and I my selfe know well
How troublesome it sate vpon my head.
To thee, it shall descend with better Quiet,
Better Opinion, better Confirmation:
For all the soyle of the Atchieuement goes
With me, into the Earth. It seem'd in mee,
But as an Honour snatch'd with boyst'rous hand,
And I had many liuing, to vpbraide
My gaine of it, by their Assistances,
Which dayly grew to Quarrell, and to Blood-shed,
Wounding supposed Peace. 2730
All these bold Feares,
Thou seest (with perill) I haue answered:
For all my Reigne, hath beene but as a Scene
Acting that argument. And now my death
Changes the Moode: For what in me, was purchas'd,
Falles vpon thee, in a more Fayrer sort.
So thou, the Garland wear'st successiuely.
Yet, though thou stand'st more sure, then I could do,
Thou art not firme enough, since greefes are greene:
And all thy Friends, which thou must make thy Friends
Haue but their stings, and teeth, newly tak'n out,
By whose fell working, I was first aduanc'd,
And by whose power, I well might lodge a Feare
To be againe displac'd. Which to auoyd,
I cut them off: and had a purpose now
To leade out many to the Holy Land;
Least rest, and lying still, might make them looke
Too neere vnto my State. 2748
Therefore (my *Harrie*)
Be it thy course to busie giddy Mindes
With Forraigne Quarrels: that Action hence borne out,
May waste the memory of the former dayes.
More would I, but my Lungs are wasted so,
That strength of Speech is vtterly deni'de mee.
How I came by the Crowne, O heauen forgiue:
And grant it may, with thee, in true peace liue.
Prince. My gracious Liege: 2757
You wonne it, wore it: kept it, gaue it me,
Then plaine and right must my possession be;
Which I, with more, then with a Common paine,
'Gainst all the World, will rightfully maintaine.

*Enter Lord Iohn of Lancaster,
and Warwicke.*

King. Looke, looke,
Heere comes my *Iohn* of Lancaster:
Iohn. Health, Peace, and Happinesse,
To my Royall Father.
King. Thou bring'st me happinesse and Peace
(Sonne *Iohn:*)
But health (alacke) with youthfull wings is flowne
From this bare, wither'd Trunke. Vpon thy sight
My worldly businesse makes a period.
Where

of the six lines were too long for the Folio column, so that he would be able to divide two of them and overrun one. The only place he could expand his copy was at the stage direction. There, instead of the brief one-line entry that we would expect—*Enter Prince Iohn and Warwicke*—he would set *Enter Lord Iohn of Lancaster, | and Warwicke*. If he did no more, on the entire page he would be able to use only three type-lines more than his copy would require. Apparently he felt that a total of three lines was inadequate.

Let us return to the beginning of the right column. There B faced the three-line completion of Hal's speech of penitence, lines in which nothing could be divided. Next was the King's long reply of forty-two lines. As the King's speech stands in the Quarto —and also, I believe, as it stood in Compositor B's copy—the first line is "God [F: Heauen] put it in thy mind to take it hence" (2713), a line with no strong caesura to justify division. Where could he spread his copy? In the eighteenth line, he saw a major transition that could be divided to form a "waist" (2730–31). After a decent interval of sixteen lines, he saw another transitional line suitable for another "waist" (2748–49). Further division of lines within the speech would have looked awkward. The Prince's four-line response concluding the reconciliation sequence provided no further opportunity for division. As the speech stands in the Quarto—and, again as I believe, it stood in B's copy—the first line offers no sharp division into two logical halves: "You won it, wore it, kept it, gaue it me" (2758). Apparently two more lines were needed; apparently B wrote them. Although, as we shall note, the scribe deleted short verse lines wherever possible, here we find two speeches in the right column that both begin with short lines. The King begins his speech of reconciliation with "O my Sonne!" (2712), surely an appropriate opening, and the Prince's response begins with an equally logical "My gracious Liege" (2757). Neither of the two short lines is in the Quarto; neither is dramatically essential. I grant that both lines have a certain appeal. Actors, given the choice, might want to adopt them. Unless, however, we can be sure that some corrected manuscript of independent authority underlies the Folio copy, the evidence suggests that Compositor B, not Shakespeare, wrote these two lines.

In light of the many words and phrases added by Compositor B, let us return to an addition on gg1, the page on which B began his concentrated push to expand copy, The copy for gg1 would be very difficult to spread. It is all prose, and so many of the speeches consist of one short line that the expedient of dividing the few longer speeches into chopped prose was probably ruled out by aesthetic considerations. In the second half of the right column, there is no opportunity to expand into additional type-lines by any of the standard methods. As B faced this predicament, only twelve lines before the end of the page, he set the third of the major puzzling additions with which this study began (3.2.196–97).

Q: *Fal.* No more of that master Shallow.

F: *Falstaffe.* No more of that good Mafter *Shallow :* **No**   1731
more of that.

Yes, the line does sound like Falstaff, and the repetition of *No more of that*, though not the *good*, has been almost universally adopted. The line is appealing, but the accumulation of evidence makes it suspect. As we have seen, B interpolated *good* three times elsewhere in the play, and this addition may mean little other than that B was thinking in terms of adding words. Another fact, however, is significant. B spelled out the speech prefix for Falstaff only three times in the play—here and at 2850 and 3212—and he did so only when he could overrun to an extra line by so doing. If the scribe's transcript had given the repetition as it appears in the Folio, the line would normally have been set as follows: "*Fal.* [or *Falst.*] No more of that M. *Shallow*: no more of that." That line would have required merely judicious spacing and the spelling out of *Master* to ensure two lines. There would have been no need to spell out the speech prefix. The full form of *Falstaffe*, found only three times in the play, is the telling sign that B had

TEXTUAL CHANGES BY THE COMPOSITORS 109

decided to expand the one-line speech to two lines, by whatever means might be necessary, at the moment he began to set it.

Throughout the preceding discussion of compositorial deletions and additions in *2 Henry IV*, we have focused primarily on one problem: the need either to compress too much copy into the allotted pages or to stretch copy to fill more pages than the copy would normally require. The Folio compositors faced another problem, one that is aesthetic. I have touched on this fact briefly in discussing the apparent attempts by compositors to avoid setting short "break-lines" at the head of a column, to avoid placing scene boxes at the bottom of a column, and to avoid dividing both prose and verse lines too frequently. In following such policies, compositors would rarely have needed to add words.

In certain instances, however, aesthetic considerations apparently did lead Compositor B to add words unauthorized by his copy. One has been briefly noted but deserves further attention. Five times in quire gg, we find stage directions that are atypically amplified. At the opening of 5.4 on gg7, the scribe probably wrote his usual terse stage direction: "*Enter Hostesse, Dol, and Beadles.*" On this, the penultimate page of the play, B was intent upon spreading copy and wanted to divide the stage direction into two lines. Why did he not merely set the following?

Enter Hostesse, Dol,
and Beadles.

The bunched type is aesthetically unpleasing and the compositorial expedient would have been far too obvious. Instead, B added words that were surely not in his copy.

Enter Hostesse Quickly, Dol Teare-sheete,
and Beadles.

To justify dividing stage directions, the first line must be of sufficient length to suggest that the second—and, for aesthetic reasons, the shorter—line is required. Another example was noted in the discussion of B's work on gg5^v: the expansion of the copy's expected "*Enter Warwicke and Chiefe Iustice*" to "*Enter the Earle of Warwicke, and the Lord | Chiefe Iustice.*" Similarly, although the scribe probably used the consistent designation *Prince Iohn*, B expanded to *Lord Iohn of Lancaster* at 2762–63 on gg5 and to *Iohn of Lancaster* at 2897 on gg6 to create two lines.* It is difficult to know what the scribe provided for the coronation entry in the final scene, but one cannot doubt that B's need to add lines combined with his aesthetic concerns:

> *The Trumpets sound. Enter King Henrie the*
> *Fift, Brothers, Lord Chiefe*
> *Iustice.*

At the very least, B probably added *Lord*, and possibly *The* and *the Fift*.³⁶

Two curious additions in the Folio suggest a second type of situation in which B may have added words for reasons of either aesthetics or self-justification—it is difficult to determine which. Compare the following versions of 3.2.142 on gg1:

Q: *Shal.*   Shall I pricke him sir Iohn?

F: *Shal.*   Shall I pricke him downe,   1677
      Sir *Iohn* ?

Why is *downe* added? Elsewhere in the scene, the idiom is simply "prick him." Perhaps there was a certain compositorial sense of decorum. B was determined to divide the line, but "Shall I pricke him" would take less than half the width of the Folio column. Was *downe* added to balance the two lines better, to make the arbitrary division less obvious? A similar sense of decorum may underlie the following addition to 3.2.171:

Q: *Fal.*   I am bound to thee reuerend Feeble, who is next?

F: *Falst.*   I am bound to thee, reuerend *Feeble.* Who is   1706
      the next ?

---

* We find *Prince Iohn* at 2100 and 2259. In stage directions, Harry is regularly *the Prince* or *Prince Henry/Henrie*. The two brothers are simply *Clarence* and *Gloucester*.

By expanding the speech prefix, inserting spaces, and adding punctuation, B had already gained his extra line. Was the extraneous *the* added to keep *next* from looking awkward?

> *Falst.* I am bound to thee, reuerend *Feeble.* Who is next?

The addition of both *downe* and *the* may result from B's known carelessness, but we cannot rule out the possibility that aesthetic considerations operated.[37]

A third instance in which a word may have been added for aesthetic reasons occurs in the epilogue on gg8 (Plate XVII). The three paragraphs of prose, easily separable from the text of the play proper since the epilogue is not spoken by one of the play's characters, provided copy for a page that would otherwise have been blank. To justify giving the epilogue an entire page to itself, B set out to make it a work of art. He began with an ornament and set the three paragraphs in large italic type. He did not set blank lines between the paragraphs, but a glance at the page shows that they are not needed. Each paragraph ends with less than half a line, making the paragraph divisions clear. Thus all three paragraphs make neatly balanced units. I doubt that this was sheer luck. In the penultimate line of the second paragraph, the Folio reads "which was neuer seene before" in contrast to the Quarto's "which was neuer seene." The word *before* may have been a scribal addition in the Folio's copy but the context does not require such a logical subtlety. "Of course," the epilogue implies, "the gentlemen will agree with the gentlewomen. It has never been otherwise. Nor will it be now." The *before* allows possibility of disagreement on this particular occasion. Compositor B, however, had the best of reasons for adding *before*, followed by an extraneous comma: he could drive the last two syllables of *Assembly* into a new line.

Finally, a major aesthetic consideration leading Compositor B to add words has been implicit in the discussion of his work throughout quire gg: the need to spread the text of *2 Henry IV* so

EPILOGVE.

FIRST, *my Feare*: then, *my Curtsie*: last, *my Speech*. *My Feare, is your Displeasure: My Curtsie, my Dutie: And my Speech, to Begge your Pardons. If you looke for a good speech now, you undoe me: For what I haue to say, is of mine owne making: and what (indeed) I should say, will (I doubt) prooue mine owne marring. But to the Purpose, and so to the Venture.* Be it knowne to you (as it is very well) I was lately heere in the end of a displeasing Play, to pray your Patience for it, and to promise you a Better: I did meane (indeede) to pay you with this, which if (like an ill Venture) it come vnluckily home, I breake; and you, my gentle Creditors lose. Heere I promist you I would be, and heere I commit my Bodie to your Mercies: Bate me some, and I will pay you some, and (as most Debtors do) promise you infinitely.

If my Tongue cannot entreate you to acquit me: will you command me to vse my Legges? And yet that were but light payment, to Dance out of your debt: But a good Conscience, will make any possible satisfaction, and so will I. All the Gentlewomen heere, haue forgiuen me, if the Gentlemen will not, then the Gentlemen do not agree with the Gentlewowen, which was neuer seene before, in such an Assembly.

One word more, I beseech you: if you be not too much cloid with Fat Meate, our humble Author will continue the Story (with Sir Iohn in it) and make you merry, with faire Katherine of France: where (for any thing I know) Falstaffe shall dye of a sweat, vnlesse already he be kill'd with your hard Opinions: For Old-Castle dyed a Martyr, and this is not the man. My Tongue is wearie, when my Legs are too, I will bid you good night; and so kneele downe before you: But (indeed) to pray for the Queene.

TEXTUAL CHANGES BY THE COMPOSITORS 113

that it extended to approximately the middle of gg7^v (Plate XV). B's goal was apparently to ensure the desired format for a final page: approximately one-half page of text followed by "FINIS," then a line, and then the ornament. With the exception of *Hamlet*, all plays with two columns of twenty-five lines or less on the final page are given abnormal treatment: four have cast lists appended and four have two or three additional lines following "FINIS." Similarly, with the exception of *Twelfth Night*, all plays with parallel columns of forty-one lines or more lose the ornament (nine plays) or the "FINIS" (*King John*). The ideal length for a final page seems to have been a half column of thirty-three lines, with a deviation of perhaps no more than eight lines longer or eight lines shorter. B came out almost exactly on target with parallel columns of thirty-one lines each. Had it not been for his concentrated effort to expand throughout quire gg, forty-seven of the sixty-two type-lines now used on gg7^v would have been set on gg7. Of these forty-seven, the need for fourteen was created by B's addition of words.[38]

For those concerned with the integrity of Shakespeare's text— as, of course, are all readers of this study—it will seem ludicrously ironic that I pause briefly to rise in defense of the notorious Compositor B. Few anonymous workmen of history have had such opprobrium cast upon them. And, from one point of view, rightly so. His careless typographical errors, and there are many, present little problem because they are easily detected. Unfortunately, however, his settings are littered with unconscious substitutions, probably the result of glancing at his copy, trying to hold too much in his mind, and then setting what his memory dictated.[39] He undoubtedly worked too fast, but he was usually thinking and he was an intelligent man. If his substitutions did not so often make excellent sense, textual critics would not be so frustrated by his work. Perhaps he was too quick, too bright— perhaps he had too creative a mind—to do the doggedly faithful copywork required of a compositor. One notes an implied warning by Joseph Moxon that a trained scholar need not apply for the job.*

Compositor B's conscious revisions—his deletions, his rewordings, his additions—are even more frustrating for a textual scholar. As we have noted, several of the widely accepted readings in *2 Henry IV* are, in all probability, his work. Nonetheless, it is at this point that I rise to his defense. Given the task that he was assigned to do, he did it brilliantly. As Hinman has shown, Jaggard was not concerned with the purity of the texts. He was concerned primarily with pressroom efficiency and, to a degree, with typographical aesthetics.[40] And there can be little doubt that he was delighted with B's work. Studying the work of different compositors in the Folio, one soon becomes aware that several of the most difficult or important tasks were assigned to him. It was B who set the first page of *The Tempest;* B who got apprentice Compositor E off to the right start by setting his first pages for *Titus Andronicus, Romeo and Juliet,* and *King Lear*; B who divided twelve lines of verse on the last three pages of *Othello* to ensure an adequate number of lines for the final page;[41] B who was given the difficult stints in *2 Henry IV*.

In fairness, we must remember that B and his colleagues were required to solve many problems that their modern counterparts do not face. In Linotype, for example, the dominant method of typesetting in the United States until very recently, the operator of the typesetting machine is typically responsible only for setting the type. As lines of type are cast in metal by the machine, they are placed in long trays, or "galleys," which are then placed on the "bank," a special table with various equipment used in making up pages and pulling proof. Commonly, then, it is the bank man,

---

* "*In a strict sence, a good* Compositor *need be no more than an English Scholler, or indeed scarce so much; for if he knows but his Letters and Characters he shall meet with in his* Printed *or* Written *Copy, and have otherwise a good natural capacity, he may be a better* Compositor *than another Man whose Education has adorn'd him with* Latin, Greek, Hebrew, *and other Languages, and shall want a good natural Genius: For by the Laws of* Printing, *a* Compositor *is strictly to follow his* Copy . . ." (*Mechanick Exercises*, pp. 191-92).

TEXTUAL CHANGES BY THE COMPOSITORS 115

working from galleys, who divides the type into pages, and thus it is he who first faces problems created by too much or too little copy for a given page. Perhaps he finds that a page break falls in the middle of a tabulation or immediately after a heading. Perhaps the text for the final page of a chapter is running too short. A bank man can make certain legitimate adjustments in such cases, but when a problem in page length can be solved only by revision of the text wording, he refers the problem to the publisher's editor rather than trying to solve it himself. The staff of a responsible printing house today never tampers with an author's wording. It has no need to. If four words must be cut near the end of a paragraph to avoid a "widow," or if a line must be added to the text preceding a sonnet in order to carry two lines of the sonnet over to the next page, rather than just one line, the publisher's editor either makes the necessary change or refers the problem back to the author.*

Compositor B had to serve as bank man, editor, and author. In certain emergency situations, such as those pertaining in the setting of *2 Henry IV*, standard methods of adjusting copy were wholly inadequate, and he had no choice but to tamper with his copy. Given the requirements of his job and the restrictions under which he worked, it is a sign of Compositor B's high degree of professional skill, not of his incompetence or sheer willfulness, that he could revise his copy so artfully that editors have sometimes been unable to distinguish his work from that of Shakespeare.[42]

My study of adjustments by the Folio compositors in plays other than *2 Henry IV* has been only cursory, but my chance discoveries offer additional warning that editors must be alert to the specific problems compositors faced at any given moment and to their characteristic solutions.

* Contemporary methods of phototypesetting present other configurations, in some of which, as in Jaggard's shop, the compositor and the bank man are in effect one and the same person. I have used Linotype rather than phototypesetting as an example because of the complexity and great variety of phototypesetting methods.

The work of Compositor A has concerned us little because as yet I have found no evidence that he solved typesetting problems by changing the words of his copy. He did, however, have one disconcerting habit of which editors should be aware. In one-line verse speeches and in the first line of longer speeches, he often faced a line too long for the Folio measure. He freely overran speeches of only one line, but he was clearly uncomfortable with overrunning or dividing long lines in multilined verse speeches. We have already noted two instances on f3^v in which he divided lines to compensate for miscalculation in casting off and then realigned for aesthetic reasons. Elsewhere, his sole concern was aesthetic. At 2310-12 on f2^v, the first line of a two-line speech was too long. Rather than simply dividing it—

> *Dowg.* As heart can thinke:
> There is not such a word
> Spoke of in Scotland, at this Dreame of Feare.

—he set the following:

> *Dowg.* As heart can thinke:
> There is not such a word spoke of in Scotland,
> At this Dreame of Feare.

Faced with the same problem at 2177-80 on gg3, he set

> *West.* I pledge your Grace:
> And if you knew what paines I haue bestow'd
> To breede this present Peace,
> You would drinke freely: but my loue to ye. . . .

rather than

> *West.* I pledge your Grace
> And if you knew what paines
> I have bestow'd to breede this present Peace,
> You would drinke freely: but my loue to ye. . . .

In both cases, the realignments require the same number of lines as if he had merely divided the long line in question. The anomaly of one short line in the middle of a verse speech did not bother him, for he freely created short lines, as in his setting of 2564-71 on gg4ᵛ.

> My due from thee, is this Imperiall Crowne,
> Which (as immediate from thy Place and Blood)
> Deriues it selfe to me. Loe, heere it sits,
> Which Heauen shall guard:
> And put the worlds whole strength into one gyant Arme,
> It shall not force this Lineall Honor from me.
> This, from thee, will I to mine leaue,
> As 'tis left to me.

One line—"Which Heauen shall guard: and put the worlds whole strength"—is too long for the Folio column. Since Compositor A avoided turn-overs whenever possible, he divided the line and then realigned to the end of the speech. Apparently he tried to avoid setting two short lines in succession when they were preceded and/or followed by lines of full length. There is abundant evidence of this particular trick by Compositor A in plays for which we have good quarto copy as well as in plays for which we do not.[43] Most of the lineation problems that he created have been solved by analyzing the meter, but remaining puzzles—for example, in *Macbeth*—may be illuminated by our awareness of this habit.

Rarely can verbal corruption by a compositor be so easily detected, and thus our primary concern has been with Compositor B. In the present chapter I have argued the strong probability that he added, deleted, and revised words found in his copy solely to meet a pressing need of the moment. Additional evidence supports this probability. One setting from *2 Henry IV* has not yet been discussed because B's corruption there was not occasioned by the need to compensate for casting off. On g2ᵛ, a tight page we have already considered, B set 501 as follows:

> *Ar.*Thus haue you heard our caufes,& kno our Means :
> And my moft noble Friends, I pray you all

Here B abbreviated the speech prefix, used an ampersand, and substituted *kno* for *knowne* (which was surely in his copy) only to avoid a turn-down. If we did not have the Quarto for comparison, we would certainly adopt *know* as authoritative on the grounds that the structure is elliptical—"and [now you] know our means."

When the Folio provides our only substantive text, we should be alert to similar cases in which we see Compositor B working under pressure. A case in point is his setting of 1.2.59 in *2 Henry VI*. In the lower right column of m3^v, we find the following setting:

> *Meſſ.* My Lord Proteƈtor,'tis his Highnes pleaſure,
> You do prepare to ride vnto S. *Albons,*
> Where as the King and Queene do meane to Hawke.
> *Hu.* I go. Come *Nel* thou wilt ride with vs?*Ex. Hum*   334
> *Eli.* Yes my good Lord,Ile follow preſently.

The page is solid verse, and casting off had not allowed for two long verse lines earlier on the page: at 272 an exit had to be placed on a line of its own, and at 298 a line had to be overrun. B compensated for the two additional lines by setting an entry to the right of 344 and, I believe, by truncating a line. At 334, we find

> Hu. I go. Come *Nel* thou wilt ride with vs?

A foot is missing. To be sure, Shakespeare often writes short lines, but usually for specific dramatic effect. Here there is no such purpose. However, B faced a problem: he could not set Humphrey's exit to the right of Eleanor's line; he could not use a turn-over; and he could not divide or overrun Humphrey's line because he had no extra line available. His solution was to cut something, and the crippled line is adopted almost universally. Arguing that the Folio copy for *2 Henry VI* was a manuscript supplemented by one or two reprintings of the bad quarto (*The First Part of the Contention*), Andrew S. Cairncross emends the line by adding the Quartos' "I'm sure."[44] Whether or not one accepts his theory about the copy underlying the Folio text, the addition of "I'm sure" is an excellent emendation. It exactly suits the good Duke's half-command, half-entreaty to his willful wife. It would

TEXTUAL CHANGES BY THE COMPOSITORS 119

be dangerous to emend such a line solely on metrical grounds, but when metrical and bibliographical evidence support each other, emendation would seem valid.

Another chance discovery supports the probability that Compositor B would add not only words but part verse lines when he needed to expand. In the lower right column of d1^v, he stretched five lines of verse to eight type-lines, and not merely by dividing lines. For 4.1.60–64 of *Richard II*, the copy used for the Folio text (Q3) reads as follows:

> *Sur.* My Lord Fitzwater, I do remember well
> The verie time Aumerle and you did talke.
> *Fitz.* Tis very true, you were in presence then,
> And you can witnesse with me this is true.
> *Sur.* As false by heauen, as heauen it selfe is true.

In order to spread his text to three additional lines, Compositor B needed only to divide the first line of each speech. Had he done so, however, the only two full lines remaining would have made his expedient setting flagrantly obvious. And so B set the passage as follows:

> *Surrey.* My Lord *Fitz-water*:
> I do remember well, the very time
> *Aumerle*, and you did talke.
> *Fitz.* My Lord,
> 'Tis very true: You were in presence then,
> And you can witnesse with me, this is true.
> *Surrey.* As false, by heauen,
> As Heauen it selfe is true.

Not only did he divide and realign, he even added a part-line of his own invention: "My Lord." Moreover, he did all this in such a way that the sequence of speeches almost scans. His realignment created a new pentameter line ("I do remember well, the very time"), and Surrey's half-line (as Heauen it selfe is true") is a perfect complement to Fitzwater's ensuing challenge ("Surrey, thou Lyest"). At 536 on e1ᵛ, where B was again wasting space, we find another part-line that he undoubtedly invented:

Wor. He apprehends a World of Figures here,
But not the forme of what he should attend:
Good Cousin giue me audience for a-while,
And list to me.

Worcester's redundant final line was not in B's copy, Q5. Accustomed as we are to part-lines at the beginning and ending of Shakespeare's verse speeches, we might think both of B's interpolations authoritative—if, that is, we did not have good quartos for both plays.

In the Folio version of *2 Henry IV*, we are fortunate in having just such a check on Compositor B's work. If the conclusions of the present study are valid, nineteen Folio variants that have been widely or universally adopted can be attributed to him.

1.2.98	of an ague	(F: *of age*)
1.2.99	saltnes of time in you	(F: om. *in you*)
2.2.82	ale wiues peticote	(F: *new Petticoat*)
2.2.94	that this blossome	(F: *this good Blossome*)
3.2.134	of shadowes fill vp	(F: *to fill vppe*)
3.2.175	come pricke Bul-calfe	(F: *pricke me Bulcalfe*)
3.2.196–97	master Shallow.	(F: Shallow: *No more of that.*)
4.5.177	om.	(F: *O my Sonne!*)
4.5.220	om.	(F: *My gracious Liege:*)
5.1.24	he lost at Hunkly	(F: *lost the other day at*)
5.1.49	I haue litle	(F: *haue but a very litle*)
5.1.51	I beseech you	(F: *beseech your worship*)
5.4.5	whipping cheere I warrant	(F: *cheere enough, I*)
5.4.6	a man or two kild	(F: *or two lately kill'd*)
5.4.9	child I go with	(F: *I now go with*)
5.5.5	maister Shallow	(F: *M. Robert Shallow*)
5.5.81	I cannot perceiue how	(F: *cannot well perceiue*)
5.5.81	vnlesse you giue me	(F: *you should giue me*)
Ep. 25	which was neuer seene in	(F: *seene before, in*)

With the possible exception of *No more of that*, none of these Folio variants suggests consultation of a version of the play revised by Shakespeare himself. Only this one line can be considered an improvement. Indeed, the majority weaken the line in question. All of the above should be rejected and the Quarto reading adopted—unless, that is, other variants prove conclusively that Jaggard was handed a manuscript incorporating authentic Shakespearean revisions. Let us, then, turn to the many Folio variants that cannot be compositorial in origin.

CHAPTER IV

Textual Changes by the Scribe

The major types of changes by the transcriber-editor who prepared the Folio copy for *2 Henry IV* have been listed and classified by Greg, Shaaber, and others, and a brief summary with only a few examples will suffice here.[1] Spelling errors are corrected, even when Shakespearean spelling reflects character pronunciation: *Berod* becomes *Beare-heard* (1.2.169), *Wheeson* becomes *Whitson* (2.1.89). Grammatical errors are removed, with no attention paid to the speaker or to the dramatic situation. Verbs are made to agree with subjects: *beards wags* is revised to *Beards wagge* (5.3.34), *white heires becomes* to *white haires become* (5.5.48). Pronoun case is regularized: *of he* becomes *of him* (5.2.16), *who I sent* becomes *whom I sent* (1.1.28). Personal pronouns are made to accord with sophisticated usage: *which* is substituted for *who* when it refers to "things" (3.1.84) and for *whom* when it refers to "daggers" (4.5.107). Double negatives are resolved: *you shall not hardely offend her* becomes *you shall hardly offend her* (2.4.116–17). Noun agreement in number is "corrected": *their sleepe* becomes *their sleepes* (4.5.68), and even common Elizabethan idiom is rejected when it results in apparent solecisms such as *thirtie mile* (2.4.165) and *fiftie fiue yeare ago* (3.2.210).

This attention to the most refined standards of correctness reflects a distinctive kind of literary sophistication found in several types of changes. Contractions have been expanded: *tis* to *it is*, *toot* to *to it*, *nere* to *neuer*. The changed tone of a character such as Falstaff is apparent in the Folio's expansion of *hee'd a prickt you* to *he would haue prick'd you* (3.2.153). Archaic colloquial forms—or, rather, what the sensitive ear of the scribe took to be archaic or

TEXTUAL CHANGES BY THE SCRIBE 123

unsuitably rustic forms—are eliminated. Not only does *a* become *he*, *and* become *if*, *moe* become *more*, and *enow* become *euen now*; those "horson smoothy-pates" must be given "smooth pates" (1.2.37–38). Archaic words such as *letherne* (2.2.171), *shrieue* (4.4.99), and *thorough* for *through* (1.3.59) are modernized. Even *bed hangers* must conform to sophisticated usage and become *Bed-hangings* (2.1.146). The scribe probably viewed certain archaic words as imprecise diction: thus *I will inset you* becomes *I will set you* (1.2.17); *any thing that intends to laughter* becomes *any thing that tends to laughter* (1.2.8). He may not even have understood *downe faters*, for he changes to a completely nonsensical *downe Fates* (2.4.159). Prepositions are made to accord with accepted idiom: Bardolph must be gone "into Smithfield," not "in" (1.2.50); a hair must be "on" a face, not "in" it (1.2.160); Pistol would be revenged "on" Mistress Quickly, not "of" her (2.4.154). Some of these changes in prepositions may reflect an evolving idiom, as does the substitution of *I am well spoken of* for *I am well spoke on* (2.2.65); but some show a dogged pursuit of logic that marks all of the scribe's revisions. Apoplexy cannot be "a kind of sleeping in the blood"; it is a sleeping "of" the blood (1.2.113). A man cannot, it would seem, flatter himself "in proiect of a power"; he must flatter himself "with" it (1.3.29). And can a wild dog "flesh his tooth on euery innocent"? No, if the tooth is, indeed, "fleshed," it must be "in" (4.5.132).

In addition to these easily identifiable changes, certain revisions have been introduced that were probably regarded as literary niceties. *Hath* is substituted for *has* and *doth* for *does*. *At your returne* becomes *As you returne* (3.2.293–94). Falstaff's cutting "I would you had the wit" loses its edge in the Folio's more delicate "I would you had but the wit" (4.3.86). One consistent revision throughout may reflect a similar concern: the change from the Quarto's *vile* to *vilde*, a form that we may sense to be archaic but that was not in common use until the late sixteenth century.*

* Compositors A and B each set *vilde* two times; B used *vild* once to justify a line and, for no reason, used *vil'de* once. (We find the same addition of a gratuitous

One of the most striking changes is the radical expurgation of anything that might even smack of profanity. All references to the deity are omitted: *Before God* becomes *Trust me* (2.2.1), *the God of heauen brighten it* becomes *may heauenly glory brighten it* (2.3.17), *O Lord* becomes merely *Oh* (3.2.177). All oaths—even the mildest—are deleted or revised: one can understand the deletion of *by heauen* (3.2.76–77), but surely only excessive zeal would require cutting *By this hand* (2.2.45) or revising the seemingly innocuous *By this light* to *Nay* (2.2.65). Someone other than the scribe could have been responsible for such censorship, but in the revisions of the Quarto we find the same distinctive attention to literary values that marks all of the scribe's work. For example, *by my troth* appears twelve times in the Quarto. Twice it slips into the Folio, undoubtedly through oversight, and four times it is deleted. In the other six instances, it is revised in such a way as to reflect considerable care. It would have been simple to substitute *in troth* in each case, but that variant is used only once (2.2.10). Elsewhere we find *why* (2.4.55), *Nay truely* (2.4.269), *Truly* (3.2.39), *Trust me* (3.2.83), and *in good troth* (3.2.192). The scribe—for it would seem to be his work—varied his substitutions rather than methodically deleting or merely using an obvious and safe variant.

All of the kinds of revisions that we have noted thus far have long been recognized and classified. Little or no attempt has been made, however, to analyze the exact type of mind behind such revisions. Moreover, there are other types of changes that have received little if any attention, and editors have widely adopted some of the variants on the assumption that the Folio version of the play reflects revisions by Shakespeare himself. In order to ascertain the validity of many Folio variants, let us then turn to these other types of revisions. We shall have to analyze the

---

apostrophe in his setting of *vil'd* in *Othello* (F1380). There can be little doubt that the scribe's form was *vilde* but that Shakespeare's was *vile*. In the good quartos that are probably based on foul papers, we find *vile* thirty-one times, *vild* once (*Titus*) and *vilde* twice (*Dream*).

TEXTUAL CHANGES BY THE SCRIBE   125

revisions in considerable detail in order to determine why such changes were felt to be necessary: that is, to determine the precise kind of mind and sensibility underlying the revised version of the play presented to Jaggard.

Throughout the Folio, close attention is paid to certain niceties of sentence structure, no matter who is speaking. Given Shakespeare's interest in character and situation over matters of grammatical or syntactical correctness, revisions of this kind cannot be authoritative. Such scrupulous attention to literary propriety reflects exactly the same concerns we have already noted in revisions universally attributed to the scribe. He is, for example, concerned about propriety in syntax.

Q: He sure meanes breuity in breath
F: *Sure he*   (2.2.124)

Q: Coleuile shalbe still your name
F: *shall still be*   (4.3.6–7)

He is especially alert to structures that are not parallel.

Q: I would my meanes were greater and my waste slender
F: *slenderer*   (1.2.143)

Q: To wake a wolfe, is as bad as smell a fox
F: *as to smell a fox*   (1.2.155)

Q: either to vtter them, or conceale them
F: *or to conceale them*   (5.3.111)

At times one can in all fairness only call him persnickety.

Q: as one for superfluitie, and another for vse
F: *and one other for vse*   (2.2.18)

Q: they, by obseruing him . . . hee, by conuersing with them
F: *by obseruing of him*   (5.1.66)

Totally deaf to the raciness of elliptical colloquial prose, he applies pedestrian logic to fill out structures that he considers incomplete. When Hal shifts his attention to a letter in hand with a simple "but the letter," the scribe must clarify with "but to the Letter" (2.2.118). When Falstaff's mind characteristically leaps in

"Pregnancie is made a Tapster, & his quick wit wasted...," the scribe insists on adding the unnecessary ligature: "and hath his quicke wit wasted" (1.2.170–71). When Falstaff revives Doll's flagging spirits with a clucking "shalt haue a cap to morrow," the scribe plunks in the appropriate subject *thou* (2.4.275). After shrieking the word *captain* six times in less than a minute, the Hostess makes herself abundantly clear when she says "these villaines will make the word as odious as the word occupy...." Yet the scribe must make the reference transparent to the meanest intelligence. What "word"? Why, "the word Captaine" (2.4.148). One such insertion is often taken to be a legitimate correction. When Falstaff charges "You make fat rascals mistris Dol," Doll counterattacks with "I make them? gluttonie, and diseases make, I make them not" (2.4.42–43). Doll jumps on Falstaff's word *make* and spits it back at him three times. She, she snorts, does not do the "making." In the omitted *them*—which, of course, the scribe inserts—I sense the actor-playwright's clue to the way Doll should speak the line.

Almost all of the revisions and additions noted above could be the work of any qualified scribe trained to edit for literary tastes as he copies a manuscript. Many of the revisions, however, reveal a man of rather distinctive mind and sensibilities. His determined imposition of logic approaches the fanatic. To change *The time... that* to *The time... when* is an inevitable change given his cast of mind (2.3.10), as is his change of "Where lay the King to night?" to "Where lay the King last night?" (2.1.168). Consider, however, the thought process underlying a change from *being awakt* to *being awake* (5.5.51). In the past, one was "awakt" by someone or something, but the new King refers to his present state of "being." Now, at this time—"being awake"—he despises the dream of his youth. When the Chief Justice tells Falstaff that "the King hath seuerd you," are we to believe that the King has chopped Falstaff in half? The absolute logic of diction requires what the Folio, in fact, supplies: "The King hath seuer'd you and Prince *Harry*" (1.2.203). When Hastings warns Prince John that failure to redress the rebels' grievances will lead to enduring mischief—for "heire from heire shall hold his quarrell vp"—the scribe reasons that such a dispute would be the continuing quarrel of successive generations, not the specific quarrel of each heir. Thus *his quarrell* must become *this Quarrell* (4.2.48). When Hastings announces (4.2.102–3)

> My lord our army is disperst already,
> Like youthfull steeres vnyoakt they take their courses,

the scribe stops. The army has already dispersed. The action of dispersing is, therefore, in the past, and he revises to "they took their course[s]." (The Folio's *their course* should not be blamed on the scribe. Compositor A ran out of space at the end of the line and omitted the final -*s*.) Whatever else we may think of his work as an "improver," this man was moving slowly, thinking carefully, and doing his very best to tidy up what must have seemed to him a very rude piece of work indeed.

The scribe's strained sense of logic may also account for another revision.

Q: But being moody, giue him time and scope,
   Till that his passions, like a whale on ground
   Confound themselues with working....
F: *giue him Line, and scope* (4.4.39)

Dover Wilson adopts the Folio reading, as do other editors, on the ground that "'line and scope' suggests fishing and fishing suggests whales."[2] Such may have been exactly the reasoning of the scribe. If so, he knew little of fishing or of whales, nor did he grasp the meaning of the King's charge. One does not fish for a whale from the land, giving him "line" as a trick to make him tire and then hauling him ashore. Shakespeare was quite capable of strained images but this seems too inept to be accepted as a sign of authorial revision. Here the King is pleading for patience with the Prince, asking his sons to give their brother "time," not suggesting that they cannily play him on a "line" as a hooked fish.

In addition to a rigid and methodical sense of logic, the scribe had a highly developed sense of decorum. The Chief Justice is permitted to refer informally to "Prince *Harry*" when speaking to Falstaff, but when Gower announces to the Chief Justice that the King and "Harry prince of Wales" are approaching, this simply will not do. A mere messenger refer to his royal prince by a nickname? Decorum requires that Gower use "*Henrie* Prince of Wales" in announcing the approach of a royal entourage (2.1.134). And would a lowly officer arrest a knight, even such an arrant knight as Falstaff, without the courtesy of addressing him formally? Decorum requires that Fang's abrupt "I arrest you, at the suit of Mist. *Quickly*" be prefaced by a civil "Sir *Iohn*" (2.1.45). Perhaps the most amusing application of the scribe's overly refined sense of decorum is an addition to Falstaff's challenge to Colevile at the opening of 4.3. Surely Colevile is a comic character. Why else is Falstaff able to take him using bombast as his only weapon? If, in the heat of battle, Colevile were to enter in a fighting stance, the Falstaff we know so well would suddenly find occasion to be elsewhere. Instead, Falstaff is given reason— probably by the cowering behavior of the luckless Colevile—to issue a confident, peremptory challenge: "Whats your name sir, of what condition are you, and of what place?" This man is no threat. Once again, the scribe is uneasy. A knight deserves more chivalrous treatment, and thus he appends a ludicrously inappropriate "I pray" at the end of the challenge.

This sense of decorum is reflected not only in changes to accord due respect to men of title and royalty, but also in the treatment of names. The name of Mistress Quickly's minister, one "maister Dumbe," is an unacceptable offense to the church. "Master *Dombe*" is the Folio's innocuous—and pointless—substitute (2.4.88). A similar type of concern may account for the scribe's renaming of Falstaff's idiot tailor as "*Dombledon*" (1.2.29). The Quarto's *Dommelton* vividly identifies a dolt, a blockhead. Was the word deemed too vulgar?

The scribe's acute awareness of the fitness of language probably accounts for other changes. Can the gallows "haue wrong"?

TEXTUAL CHANGES BY THE SCRIBE 129

No, "the gallowes shall be wrong'd" (2.2.97). The scribe's concern here may relate to idiom, but it may equally reflect an uneasiness over attributing personal moral injury to the inanimate. (Being strictly logical, one fails to see that the revision really solves the "problem.") And can Falstaff follow the young prince like an "ill angell"? No, such an angel must be precisely defined by the moral epithet of "euill" (1.2.164). One of the more puzzling changes in the Folio may result from a similar sense of decorum. For the Quarto's "Come you vertuous asse," the Folio substitutes *pernitious* (2.2.75). *Pernitious* cannot be explained as a graphic misreading by Compositor B, and I doubt that it is one of his careless substitutions. Sometimes B's substitutions make sense: for example, *knolling* for *tolling* (1.1.103), and *bitter* for *better* (2.1.166). Sometimes they do not: for example, *declension* for *descension* (2.2.173), *Imperiall* for *impartiall* (5.2.36), and *most* for *moist* (4.5.139). But his errors almost always bear some recognizable relationship to the form of the given word in his copy. It may well be that the idea of an "ass" being "virtuous" struck the scribe as incongruous. If one is determined to be logical, *pernitious* is far more appropriate.

The scribe's total lack of dramatic sense, apparent in many of the examples above, deserves close attention because some editors have adopted his revisions as legitimate corrections. Falstaff defends his overheard aspersions on Hal by answering Poins: "I dispraisde him before the wicked, that the wicked might not fall in loue with thee" (2.4.319-21). The Folio change from *with thee* to *with him* is eminently logical if one does not realize that Falstaff begins by addressing Ned, who has taunted him, but immediately turns to Hal, to whom his defense is primarily addressed. The scribe saw a similar type of "error" in the Hostess's wail of anguish at Doll's arrest: "O the Lord that sir Iohn were come! I would make this a bloody day to some body" (5.4.11-12). Logically, *I* must be revised to *he*—logically, but not dramatically. With the support of her old friend, the Hostess herself would see to it that the officers were made to suffer for their outrage. The scribe must also have been bothered by the logical contradiction in Falstaff's mockery of Shadow's announcement that he is his mother's son. Indeed, says Falstaff; and thus he is the shadow of his father, "but much of the fathers substance" (3.2.130–31). The scribe replaces *much* with *not*, completely missing Falstaff's irony. A less obvious example is found in a Folio revision of the following passage (1.2.45–49):

> well he may sleepe in security, for he hath the horne of aboundance, and the lightnesse of his wife shines through it: wheres Bardolf, & yet can not he see though he haue his owne lanthorne to light him.

With impeccable logic, the scribe moves "Where's *Bardolfe*?" to the end of Falstaff's speech, making it a new sentence, and editors have unanimously adopted the change. But is the Quarto version necessarily wrong? Falstaff has been roaring on for ten lines about that blockhead of a tailor, Dommelton, and winds up with an aspersion on his wife. At this point, according to the Quarto, he asks for Bardolph—but then cannot resist one last stab as he thinks of a further witty cuckold joke. Such breaks in thought are typical of Falstaff. He is quite capable of having his fun while simultaneously thinking of the most mundane matters: witness his command to "empty the jordan," which scarcely interrupts his singing of an old song about King Arthur (2.4.34).

Blind as he is to dramatic situation, the scribe is even more deaf to speech rhythms, dialectal pronunciations, malapropisms, and intentional errors that are major devices of Shakespearean characterization. I beg the reader's patience for a further series of examples because once again the scribe's determined pursuit of accuracy, literary refinement, and decorum has resulted in several readings that editors have accepted as evidence that the copy underlying the Folio has independent authority.

In addition to the assaults on Quickly's distinctive speech already noted, consider the following changes:

Q: he stabd me in mine owne house, most beastly in good faith
F: *and that most beastly* (2.1.14)

Q: Lumbert Streete
F: *Lombard street* (2.1.28)
Q: bring a reskew or two, thou wot, wot thou, thou wot, wot ta
F: *bring a rescu. Thou wilt not? Thou wilt not?* (2.1.56–58)
Q: for liking his father to a singing man of Winsor
F: *lik'ning him, Windsor*³ (2.1.90)
Q: to be no more so familiarity, with such poore people
F: *no more familiar** (2.1.99–100)
Q: debuty
F: *Deputie* (2.4.85)
Q: Heres goodly stuffe
F: *good* (2.4.200)
Q: vitlars
F: *Victuallers* (2.4.346)

We see here the scribe's typical concerns: correcting apparent misspellings, removing archaic diction, adding ligatures, expanding colloquial forms, and revising what he deems to be illogical ("a reskew *or two*"?).⁴ For the actor, these Quarto readings are important clues to Quickly's pronunciation and speech patterns throughout the play. Few editors have accepted any of the above Folio readings, but they have unanimously accepted the Folio's *Hinckley* for Davy's *Hunkly Faire* in the Quarto (5.1.24). It is easy to see how *Hunkly* could be a graphic error for *Hinckly* (with *inc* being misread as *un*), but why should we assume that the Quarto is wrong? Davy is a superb comic character, a solid country type who thumps energetically about on his duties. Shakespeare knew of the famous fair (only thirty miles northeast of Stratford), but he also knew how some country folk pronounced its name. In the Quarto spelling, the actor has a clue to the entire characterization of Davy.

* This might conceivably be a compositorial change. Line 701 is packed in the Folio, but B could have accommodated the *-ity* by dropping the *e*'s from *staires* and *poore*. Given the scribe's habits elsewhere, this offense against Quickly would seem to be his.

The same is undoubtedly true of Silence's reference to his daughter as, "Alas, a blacke woosel" (3.2.8). The scribe remedied Shakespeare's deficiencies by correcting to *Ouzell*, and most editors follow suit (with *ousel*). When Bottom sings of "The Woosell cock, so blacke of hewe" (*A Midsummer Night's Dream*, 3.1.125), Compositor D was faithful to his copy, but most editors again have felt the need to correct the spelling. Unfortunately, none of Shakespeare's sophisticated Londoners uses the word, but in the absence of counter-evidence we would be wise to assume that with Silence and Bottom he is indicating a provincial pronunciation.

Consider also the many crimes against Shallow. Naturally, the scribe corrects his grammar:

Q: I see him [in the past]
F: *saw* (3.2.29)

Q: There is many complaints
F: *are* (5.1.40)

Q: It is best certain
F: *most certaine* (5.5.23)

And Shallow's repetitions are really, the scribe must feel, excessive —an offense against decorum. At 3.2.97–98, Shallow's seven *so*'s in a row are reduced to four. At 5.1.53–54, two of his *come*'s are deleted in "come, come, come, off with your boots." At 5.1.9–11, all of the italicized words in the following have been deleted: "Dauy, Dauy, Dauy, *Dauy*, let me see Dauy let me see *Dauy, let me see, yea mary* William Cooke...."[5] Certainly Shallow's many inaccuracies must also be corrected. The scribe knows, as Shallow does not, that the word in sophisticated circles is *cauileroes*, not *cabileros* (5.3.59). It has been suggested that Shallow is using the Spanish form of the word or that the Quarto compositor made the common v/b misreading; but Shallow is scarcely a world traveler, nor need we suspect Quarto error. As with *Hunkly*, Shakespeare is probably suggesting a speech pattern. The same is true, I would suggest, of Shallow's reference to "Samforth faire," though the Folio's accurate *Stamford* is universally adopted (3.2.38). Another universal adoption that should be questioned is the Folio's *Double* for Shallow's neighbor "Dooble" (3.2.40, 52). True, *Dooble* makes no sense as the comic name for a type, but neither does *Double*. *Double* seems merely the result of trying to create an intelligible word out of gibberish. *Dooble*, on the other hand, is a comic name solely by reason of its sound, and I can well imagine (having heard the line brilliantly delivered) "And is old Dooble dead?" becoming a popular backstage joke.[6]

Ironically, the scribe's misplaced sense of accuracy led him to an actual error at 3.2.30. Did Shallow see Falstaff break "Skoggins" head (Q) or "*Scoggan's*" (F)? Our scribe knew his history. Since Henry Scogan was court poet to Henry IV, the scribe revised to get the right man in the right period. But Shallow's hapless acquaintance was probably given the generic name of *Scoggin*, a term that in the sixteenth century came to mean a buffoon because of the reputation of John Scoggin, Edward IV's jester. *Skoggin* derives from a dramatic imagination rooted in folk knowledge; *Scoggan*, from the logic of a literalist.

Pistol is especially vulnerable. His blatant errors must be corrected. Of course he must refer to "Troian"—not "troiant"— Greeks (2.4.167). Of course he must mean the one conquering hero "*Caesar*," not several "Caesars" (2.4.166). Of course he must say "giue me some Sack" rather than "giues [giue's] some sacke"; he is demanding wine for himself alone (2.4.180). And what oaf would say "and are & caeteraes, no things?" (2.4.184). Pistol, to be sure, but the Folio line is tidied to "and are *et cetera's* nothing?" One cannot but feel compassion for a man of such orderly mind faced with the incomprehensible gibberish of Pistol. What is he to do with "*si fortune me tormente sperato me contento*"? (2.4.181). The motto is familiar but scarcely the language. Well, at the very least he can make the sentence structure a little clearer by inserting a comma after *tormente*, and he can create the required rhyme and make a pretense of grammatical consistency by changing *contento* to *contente*. The second time he hits the garbled motto, he is even more sure-footed. Compare the two versions of 5.5.96:

Q: *Si fortuna me tormenta spero contenta.*
F: *Si fortuna me tormento, spera me contento.*

He must have been proud of that! A missing word replaced, the grammar made logical, and the whole thing given a neat aphoristic sound. I doubt, however, that correcting Pistol's grammar or regularizing his quotations is proof of the scribe's reference to a corrected manuscript, much less an improvement of Pistol's characterization. It would surely befit Pistol to pronounce resoundingly, "Omna Gallium est divisum in trios partes."*

Two more corrections of Pistol's rhetoric in the Folio are also open to question. In the Quarto reading of 5.5.28–29—"Tis *semper idem*, for, *obsque hoc nihil est*, tis in euery part"—Pistol not only cannot tell his *obsque* from his *absque* (surprisingly the scribe did not correct that error), he cannot even get the familiar saying right. Editors adopt the Folio's revision of "'Tis all in euery part." To be sure, it makes better sense. But does Pistol make sense? He is, one suspects, partly insane. His mind is a chaos of rhetorical rags and tags, ill-understood and faultily remembered. The Elizabethan audience probably found hilarious the botching of familiar quotations that the scribe must have attributed to Shakespeare's own ignorance. One more example (though I grant this to be highly debatable) is Pistol's roar in the Quarto: "Men like dogges giue crownes like pins" (2.4.174). If one is familiar

* In *Love's Labour's Lost*, Holofernes has received the same treatment at the hands of learned editors. At one point he proudly displays his erudition with the following quotation, here quoted from Q1: "*Facile precor gellida, quando pecas omnia sub vmbra ruminat*, and so foorth. Ah good olde *Mantuan* . . ." (4.2.93–95). Crowing happily about his intimate knowledge of the poet, Holofernes has, in fact, made a miserable botch of the quotation by beginning with the wrong word. The correct *Fauste* was substituted for *Facile* in the Second Folio, and it is adopted by most editors to this day. The line opens the first eclogue of Mantuan, regularly read by schoolboys—a line that had become notorious in the recent battles between Harvey and Nashe. Correcting Holofernes' error—for the error is surely his, not Shakespeare's—ruins the joke. For further details, see Richard David's New Arden edition of the play (London, 1951), p. 81n.

with the proverb "Men die like dogs," Pistol's nonsensical rant is far more comic than the revised Folio line: "Die men, like Dogges; giue Crownes like Pinnes." Would the Quarto compositor have overlooked the first word in the line, and a key verb at that?[7]

None of the changes I have discussed thus far would have required reference to any source other than the Quarto. Considered as a group, all of the above changes reflect a man of literary training and sensibility together with a precisely logical mind and an overly developed sense of decorum. With only a few exceptions the kinds of variants just considered have been easily recognized and rejected in favor of the Quarto readings. Many Folio variants, however, are so clearly valid corrections that they not only have been adopted but are offered to support the theory that an independent manuscript was consulted. When closely considered, all but a few can be easily attributed to the scribe, once we recognize his characteristic approach and bent of mind.

A number of valid corrections can be readily accounted for by the most rudimentary logic, even if we were to assume only a fairly competent scribe who was doing little more than copying from the Quarto mechanically. For example,

Q: The liues of all your louing complices
   Leaue on you health
F: *Leane on your*   (1.1.164)

Q: For his diuisions, as the times do brawle,
   And in three heads
F: *Are in three Heads*   (1.3.71)

Q: this is a poore made soule
F: *mad soule*   (2.1.104)

Q: these flie bitten tapestrie
F: *Tapistries*   (2.1.147)

Q: When you were more endeere to it then now
F: *endeer'd*   (2.3.11)

Q: a souldiour is better accommodate than with a wife
F: *accommodated*   (3.2.66–67)

Q: God put in thy mind to take it hence
F: *put it in*   (4.5.178)
Q: Olde-castle died Martyre
F: *a Martyr*   (Ep. 32)

Many other corrections, however, show close attention to the meaning of a line in its context, analyzed with the precise logic we have seen to be characteristic of this particular scribe. Where the Quarto compositor methodically copied what was possibly a Shakespearean abbreviation in Bardolph's joyful whoop, "I would not take a Knight for my fortune," the scribe makes the sensible expansion to *Knighthood* (5.3.126–27). At 4.2.122, the Quarto reads "Some guard this traitour to the blocke of death," but the scribe recalls that Hastings, the Archbishop, and Mowbray have all been condemned and substitutes the required *these Traitors*. Some corrections reflect even more careful thought about the exact meaning of a given line.

Q: a came ouer in the rereward of the fashion
F: *hee came euer*   (3.2.315)
Q: But you misuse the reuerence of your place,
   Imply the countenance and grace of heau'n
   As a false fauorite doth his princes name
F: *Employ the Countenance*   (4.2.24)

Other corrections required reading beyond the line or lines in question.

Q: The dangers of the daie's but newly gone
F: *dayes*   (4.1.80)

The Archbishop has been justifying the rebels' decision to take arms by referring to the griefs of many past days, not one. The scribe had just returned to the Quarto copy after a long addition from his supplementary manuscript, and he may have taken a glance back to the manuscript to confirm the Quarto reading. Since it is doubtful that Shakespeare used the apostrophe, the scribe may have found *daies*—which might mean either "days" or "day is." Only by checking ahead four lines would he have seen that *days* and *examples* form the compound subject of *hath put.*

I have suggested in Chapter II that the scribe probably skimmed the speech prefixes of an entire scene to determine who were the speaking characters before he wrote the opening stage direction. If he also skimmed speeches before beginning to copy them, corrections such as the following would require no access to a corrected manuscript:

Q: Iacke Falstaffe with my family, Iohn with my brothers and sisters, and sir Iohn with all Europe
F: Iacke Falstaffe *with my Familiars* (2.2.132–33)

The scribe first sees that brothers and sisters are obviously "family," and next that Falstaff gives the preferred form of his name in an ascending order of formality. It necessarily follows that he is "Jack" to his intimate friends. *Familiars* is thus the logical solution and undoubtedly the correct one.

Certain Folio corrections might seem to be beyond the ability of a mere scribe, but this particular man was evidently highly trained and had an astute mind. Even the following, I believe, are fully within his demonstrated capabilities:

Q: Away you horson vpright rabble, away
F: *rabbit* (2.2.85)

Q: [he is] lisping to his master, old tables, his note booke
F: *to his Masters old Tables* (2.4.266)

Faced with such problems, the scribe may have checked the manuscript, but logic alone could have sufficed. How can one man be a "rabble"? Even if he could, a "rabble" is, by connotation at least, always "upright." Lying down, a group would scarcely be termed a "rabble." *Rab*—? Ah, the page is a small boy. Suddenly the solution dawns. "Rabbit," of course! The same kind of logical process might explain the correction of Poins's comment about Bardolph. The line in the Quarto makes no sense. Bardolph is not talking to "his master" Falstaff, so he must be talking to the Hostess. And she is "his [whose?] note booke." Part of the solution is simple: his "old tables" means the same thing as "his note booke." Perhaps Bardolph is talking to "his mistress, old tables, his note booke," but how could the Quarto compositor so seriously have misread his manuscript? *Master* must be right, referring to Falstaff. And suddenly the solution is simple: the Quarto compositor misread an *s* for a comma. (I do not put such conjectures beyond the ability of a trained professional scribe.)

Methodical thought can also account, I believe, for the Folio change from the Quarto's *Billingsgate* to *Basingstoke* (2.1.169). Two things may have made the scribe pause. In the first place, why would the King of England stay in the area of the fishmarket? It was surely unfitting. Moreover, it was illogical. If the King were returning from the west, what possible reason could he have to cross London Bridge for a stop-over at Billingsgate? He would be approaching Westminster from the wrong direction. At such a puzzle, the scribe may well have checked the manuscript before him, but it may have been of little help. It is difficult to see how the Quarto compositor could have misread *Basingstoke* as *Billingsgate*.[8] The scribe was thus probably left to his own devices. "What would be a logical stopover before entering London, one that begins with the letter *B* and is a word of equal length? Why not Basingstoke, which is forty-six miles southwest of London?" Why not indeed? *Basingstoke* may be merely a good guess by an alert mind. The chronicles mention no royal stopover at Basingstoke and thus we cannot be sure it is what Shakespeare wrote. That *Basingstoke* is a superior reading seems indisputable; that the reading is Shakespeare's, however, cannot be certain.

Once one suspends the assumption that superior readings are necessarily the result of an authentic corrected manuscript that supersedes Shakespeare's foul papers, one immediately begins to suspect a particular type of Folio variant: the variant that seems to improve on a Quarto reading even though that reading is acceptable. The Folio's "Then was that Noble Worcester / Too soone

TEXTUAL CHANGES BY THE SCRIBE 139

ta'ne prisoner" (1.1.125-26) may seem to make better sense than the Quarto's "So soone," but in context the Quarto's reading makes adequate sense. Similarly, the Quarto's "how vildly did you speake of me now" (2.4.301) is adequate, though the Folio's "euen now" seems more idiomatic for Hal's specific jab at Falstaff. There is no reason to believe that, given the scribe's sense of logic and his sharp ear for idiom, he could not in fact have occasionally improved on Shakespeare. Consider the Quarto version of 2.2.13-16:

> What a disgrace is it to mee ... to take note how many paire of silke stockings thou hast with these, and those that were thy peach coloured once. ...

The passage makes sense as it stands: "how many pair of silk stockings you have—with, for example, these—and (as I now remember) the peach-colored [ones] you wore at one time." Given a pause and a gesture, *with* need not be a misreading, nor need *once*. In the loose idiom of conversation, we frequently leave out *ones* in similar constructions: for example, "Give me a pound of red grapes and a pound of green." The passage is even more acceptable if we merely emend *once* to read *ones*. The Quarto compositor may have found *ons* in his copy (*on* being a recognized Shakespearean spelling for *one*) and, left to his own devices to translate, chose *once*. As the Quarto reading stands, however, it is undeniably awkward. The improvement in the Folio—"(Viz. these, and those that were thy peach-colour'd ones)"—may well have been the scribe's thoughtful revision.

Even less problematic are the following Quarto readings:

Q: It was yong Hot-spurs cause at Shrewsbury
F: *case* (1.3.26)
Q: Eating the ayre, and promise of supplie
F: *on promise* (1.3.28)

Cause is probably right, given Shakespeare's use of the word in *The Rape of Lucrece*: "The cause craves haste" (1295). Similarly, "eating the air and promise" makes perfectly good sense and is, moreover, confirmed by Hamlet's taunt to Claudius that he eats the air, "promise crammed" (3.2.94). Another Quarto reading almost universally rejected seems to me equally valid: "a rascall: yea forsooth knaue" (1.2.35–36). Editors adopt the Folio's "a Rascally-yea-forsooth-knaue" on the assumption that Falstaff is sneering at the mild oaths of Puritan tradesmen, just as Hotspur scorns "in good sooth" as the oath of a "comfit-maker's wife" (*1 Henry IV*, 3.1.248). However, several of Shakespeare's sturdiest characters resort to a *forsooth* now and then—including Hotspur (1.3.140, 4.3.78). The Quarto reading requires only modern punctuation to clarify Falstaff's explosive scorn: "a rascall—yea forsooth, knave!—. . . ."

One Folio variant that is universally thought to correct a Quarto error I find particularly suspect. Not only does it weaken the dramatic potential of the scene in question, it is thoroughly characteristic of the scribe's particular cast of mind. In the opening scene of Act II, Mistress Quickly has summoned the sergeants Fang and Snare to arrest Falstaff. Snare is decidedly uneasy—"It may chaunce cost some of vs out liues, for he will stabbe"—and the Hostess gives warrant to his fear: "Alas the day, take heed of him, he stabd me in mine owne house . . . , he will spare neither man, woman, nor child." But Fang is not to be daunted:

> If I can close with him, I care not for his thrust.

The Hostess urges him on and he reasserts his unshakable determination:

> And I but fist him once, and a come but within my view.

Fang's series of vaunts are exactly the sequence one expects from the conventional braggart warrior: "If I once get the chance to grapple with him—if I can even get a hand on him—nay, if he even so much as comes into my sight, I'll show you!" Of course the minute Fang tries to make the arrest, Falstaff has him screaming for help. The conventional one, two, three buildup in Fang's boasts is destroyed by the Folio revision of *vice* for *view* (2.1.22). The scribe exercises his impeccable logic. If Fang can but "fist"

TEXTUAL CHANGES BY THE SCRIBE 141

Falstaff, it necessarily follows that he will have his victim in his "vice." Thus Fang is made merely to repeat himself: "If I can but grasp him, if I can but grasp him." Surely the Quarto reading —*within my view*—is Shakespeare's.⁹

In light of all the evidence pointing to the scribe's heightened literary sensitivity, his sense of decorum, and his close attention to even the most minute matters of sentence structure and diction, the close attention to regularizing meter in the Folio should probably also be attributed to him. The metrics are remarkably regular in the Quarto text of *2 Henry IV*, but most of the few anomalies have been corrected in the Folio. Three lines (4.1.173, 4.5.161 and 178) are regularized by the introduction of words that were carelessly omitted either by Shakespeare or, more probably, by the Quarto compositor. Freak seven-foot lines have been eliminated and the verses regularized either by realignment (4.5.60–61) or by deletion of the extra-metrical feet (4.5.53–54).¹⁰ Verse lines that are set as prose in the Quarto are realigned and regularized (1.3.78–80, 4.3.84–85, 4.5.16–17 and 51–52). One speech—the Prince's breezy greeting when he enters the antechamber of his father's sickroom (4.5.9–10)—appears to be set in verse because of the width of the Quarto column, but the Folio, rightly I believe, sets it as prose. In addition to these corrections, most of the very few lines that a rigid prosodist might consider faulty have been regularized in the Folio: for example,

Q: So lookes the strond whereon the imperious floud
F: *when*   (1.1.62)

Q: But who is substituted against the French
F: *gainst*   (1.3.84)

Q: Stand from him fellow, wherefore hang'st thou vpon him.
F: om. *thou*   (2.1.68)

Q: That now to see you here, an yron man talking
F: om. *talking*¹¹   (4.2.8)

Q: Yet notwithstanding being incenst, he is flint
F: *hee's*   (4.4.33)

Q: We hope no otherwise from your maiesty
F: *other*   (5.2.62)

Although I doubt that compositors played a significant role in regularizing meter, such minor changes might conceivably be attributed to them. Further evidence, however, indicates such precise attention to metrics that some kind of deliberate editorial revision must have taken place in preparing the Folio.

Pointed evidence is provided by an analysis of the spelling of the past tense and past participles of weak verbs in which the *-ed* ending is non-syllabic. In the Quarto of *2 Henry IV*, twenty-one such forms that should be clipped in pronunciation are spelled out. In the Folio, eighteen of the twenty-one are properly given clipped spellings. This is a very high percentage of efficiency in correction: 86 percent. The attention paid to this one aspect of prosody in *2 Henry IV* is noteworthy in light of the other Folio texts that derive from good quartos. Only for *Richard II*, a play that was heavily edited to regularize meter, is the percentage of efficiency higher.[12] The accompanying table is offered for comparison, listing the plays in the order in which they were set.

Such marked variation in efficiency from play to play cannot be attributed solely to the Folio compositors. In the work set by a given compositor, the rate of efficiency may vary drastically from play to play. For example, the efficiency in C's stints ranges from 0 percent in *Dream* to 23 percent in *Merchant* to 57 percent in *Much Ado*. If we exclude *Richard II* and *2 Henry IV*, we find that the efficiency in B's work in plays on the preceding list averages only 68 percent; in *2 Henry IV*, it is 86 percent; in *Richard II* it is 89 percent. A high rate of efficiency would seem to indicate careful editing.

The probability that it is the scribe to whom such metrical precision in *2 Henry IV* should be attributed receives support from the Folio treatment of short lines. In the Quarto text, there are approximately thirty short lines, most consisting of two or three feet. (I say "approximately" because in two sequences it is difficult to determine what is prose and what is verse.) Approximately half of these have been regularized in the Folio, and the remaining half are allowed to stand for good reasons. Given the scribe's apparent

Efficiency of Folio Corrections

Play	Quarto Errors[a]	Folio Corrections	Efficiency[b]
Much Ado About Nothing	12	9	75%
Love's Labor's Lost	28	14	50
Midsummer Night's Dream	14	2	14
Merchant of Venice	24	3	13
Richard II	38	34	89
1 Henry IV	25	14	56
2 Henry IV	21	18	86
Titus Andronicus	40	14	35
Romeo and Juliet	36	20	56

[a] That is, errors received in whichever quarto the Folio used as copy. Intervening quartos had often made corrections and introduced errors. Omitted from consideration are words ending in -ied or -yed preceded by a consonant (buryed, dried, unhappied, etc.). The spelling of such words when the -ed is non-syllabic (as it usually is) is too inconsistent to provide useful information for comparison. Words such as rescued are included on the grounds that we often find argu'd, valew'd, and the like in the Folio. My figures for Richard II are based on the assumption that it was printed from a copy of Q3 with a few leaves substituted from Q5.

[b] The efficiency figure does not take into account the introduction of a common error: the spelling out in the Folio of words that were properly clipped in the received text. Tracing the evolution of a text through successive quartos to the Folio, one notes a tendency of compositors to spell out clipped verbs and verbals as well as syncopated forms (such as *flattry*). For example, seven -ed forms that are properly clipped in Q2 of *Romeo and Juliet* are incorrectly spelled out in Q3, and nine such errors are introduced in Qq 2–5 of *1 Henry IV*. There is, moreover, wide variation in the number of errors introduced by different Folio compositors. In the four comedies derived from good quartos, there are six such errors, five of them by C. In all of the plays listed on the preceding chart, there is only one by B. In *2 Henry IV*, A introduced four; B, none.

attempt to eliminate as many short lines as possible, it is ironic that Compositor B found it necessary to create so many short verse lines by division in order to spread copy. The scribe and the compositor were working at cross purposes.

The elimination of four short lines was incidental, occurring as the result of other corrections. Three short lines are completed by the Folio's restoration of passages omitted in the Quarto: 1.3.85, 2.3.45, and 4.1.101. One, as will be noted, is completed by a valid correction (1.3.78). Nine short lines, however, have been eliminated in the Folio by revision of the line itself. Not one of these nine revisions can be considered a necessary correction. Not one, I believe, is even an improvement. On the contrary, in several instances the revision destroys a dramatic effect. In short, none of the nine revised lines suggests that an authoritative manuscript subsequent to the foul papers was consulted in order to correct Quarto readings. The conclusion seems inescapable that the scribe believed incomplete lines to be metrical blemishes and took it upon himself to "improve" Shakespeare.

Let us first consider the types of short lines that the scribe allowed to stand and his probable reasons for so doing. Four short lines immediately following entrances that have been preceded by prose scenes are accepted: 2.4.354, 4.1.1, 4.3.71, and 5.2.2. In each case, having just completed copying a block of prose, the scribe may not have noticed the irregularity. On the other hand, he may have let the short lines stand because the pentameter rhythm had not been established. If the latter was his reason, his instinct was right. In each case, the given entrance provides a sharp break in rhythm. Not only is the short line dramatically right; it "looks right" on the page because it follows a prose sequence. As we shall note, the "look" of a line—that is, whether or not the eye immediately notices the anomaly—may have been a factor in the scribe's choice of lines needing revision.

Five metrically irregular sequences of brief speeches (including a total of approximately nine short lines) are also allowed to stand. A typical example is 4.4.11–18. After the King's opening speech of ten pentameter lines, we find the following in the Quarto:

>   *War.*   Both which we doubt not, but your maiestie
> Shal soone enioy.
>   *King*   Humphrey my sonne of Gloster, where is the prince your brother?
>   *Glo.*   I thinke hees gone to hunt, my lord, at Winsor.
>   *King*   And how accompanied?

TEXTUAL CHANGES BY THE SCRIBE 145

Glo. I do not know, my lord.
King Is not his brother Thomas of Clarence with him?
Glo. No, my good lord, he is in presence here.
Clar. What would my lord and father?

And the King responds in a long speech of regular pentameter lines. The sequence seems highly irregular, and editors have realigned in the attempt to get a series of pentameter lines. It cannot be done. As set in the Quarto, the sequence is as follows: pentameter, dimeter, alexandrine, pentameter, two trimeter lines forming an alexandrine (a convention the scribe accepts throughout the play), pentameter, pentameter, and trimeter. Technically, there are only two irregular lines: Warwick's second line and Clarence's question. (If, as seems likely, the King's "Humphrey my sonne of Gloster" completes Warwick's "Shal soone enioy," the King's "where is the prince your brother?" should be considered the second short line.) Nonetheless, for a sequence of eight speeches the basic pentameter rhythm is broken. The scribe's reason for leaving the sequence intact may be precisely this fact: no established pentameter rhythm is conspicuously violated. Moreover, in a sequence of short lines, one or two metrically incomplete lines do not look wrong.

The same reasons may underlie his acceptance of one short line in 3.1.32–37 (pentameter / trimeter, trimeter / pentameter / pentameter / *dimeter* / pentameter) and one in 4.2.110–13 (pentameter / trimeter, trimeter / *dimeter* / pentameter). In each sequence, the pentameter norm is broken for more than one line, and— given the legitimate pairs of trimeter lines forming an alexandrine —the shortness of the two irregular dimeter lines does not stand out visually.

Two related sequences, 4.5.7–17 and 5.5.88–109, present special problems. In both, lines of prose and of verse alternate and we cannot be sure that the Quarto setting accurately reflects Shakespeare's intended arrangement. Nor can we be sure that the Folio compositor followed the scribe's transcript accurately. In the

Quarto version of 4.5.7–17, the Prince, unaware of the severity of his father's illness, cheerily arrives at the palace to announce his good news.

> *War.* Less noyse, less noyse. *Enter Harry*
> *Prince* Who saw the duke of Clarence?
> *Clar.* I am here brother, ful of heauinesse.
> *Prince* How now, raine within doores, and none abroad? How doth the King?
> *Hum.* Exceeding ill.
> *Prince* Heard he the good newes yet? tell it him.
> *Hum.* He alter'd much vpon the hearing it.
> *Prince* If he be sicke with ioy, heele recouer without phi-sicke.
> *War.* No so much noyse my Lords, sweete prince, speake lowe, the King your father is disposde to sleepe.

Apparently the Prince is speaking prose. Only the setting of his second speech looks like verse but that fact can be attributed to chance: because of the Quarto column width, his second sentence, necessarily beginning with a capital letter, begins a new line. If the Prince were speaking verse, it would be very bad verse indeed. The clash of rhythms seems authorial: the Prince rushing into the chamber in high spirits, chattering in prose, to be greeted by the measured pentameter responses of his grieving brothers.

The Folio setting of this passage cannot accurately reflect the scribe's lineation. We find eight partial verse lines, but six are undoubtedly compositorial in origin. Although Warwick's request that the Prince "speake lowe" is set incorrectly as prose in the Quarto, the scribe probably aligned it as verse. Because of the width of the Folio column, however, Compositor A had to divide the first line of Warwick's two-line speech:

> *War.* Not so much noyse (my Lords) 2538
> Sweet Prince speake lowe,
> The King, your Father, is dispos'd to sleepe.

He also divided two of the Prince's prose speeches into short lines of verse:

> *P.Hen.* Heard hee the good newes yet?   2533
> Tell it him.
>
> *P.Hen.* If hee be ficke with Ioy,   2536
> Hee'le recouer without Phyficke.

I doubt that the scribe aligned these two speeches as verse; witness the Folio setting of the Prince's second speech:

> *P.Hen.* How now?' Raine within doores, and none   2530
> abroad? How doth the King?

Had Compositor A seen two lines of verse in his copy, he would have divided the first. Apparently, then, the scribe recognized that the Prince is speaking prose. He probably wrote Henry's third and fourth speeches each on one line. When Compositor A found the lines too long for the Folio measure, he simply assumed they were verse and divided them. Thus six of the eight partial verse lines in the Folio would seem to be his. In his copy, it is likely that only two lines of verse remained short: Warwick's "less noyse, lesse noyse" and Humphrey's "Exceeding ill." The scribe may have allowed both short lines to stand for the reasons that he accepted them in the three sequences discussed above: the pentameter rhythm is broken, and the anomalies are not visually striking in a sequence of lines of such irregular length.

As to the concluding sequence of the play, 5.5.88–109, I can only assume that the scribe threw up his hands. After the King's exit with his coronation train, the exchange between Falstaff and Shallow is in prose. But from Falstaff's speech beginning "Feare no colours"—which unaccountably is set in the Quarto as verse, and irregular verse at that—to the end of the play is metrical chaos. Does Falstaff rouse his comrades in verse and then beg the Chief Justice for a hearing in prose? Does the Chief Justice order Falstaff to prison in verse and then reject his plea in prose? Finally, in the concluding verse colloquy with Prince John, the

Chief Justice has two flagrantly irregular lines. Perhaps Shakespeare was running downhill at this point. Perhaps the scribe was too. He may have made one gesture to decorum by dividing the Chief Justice's seven-foot rejection of Falstaff's plea into verse. But that is all.

All of these short verse lines retained in the Folio have one thing in common: none of them breaks a firmly established pentameter rhythm. Two lines that break the rhythm for specific dramatic effect are also retained in the Folio, although it is surprising to find the scribe showing here a sense of dramatic situation that he does not reveal elsewhere. In 5.2.20–21, the grieving princes enter and greet Warwick:

> *Iohn* Good morrow coosin Warwicke, good morrow.
> *Prin. ambo* Good morrow coosin.

Whether one considers that all three princes speak simultaneously or whether one considers their combined speeches to be one alexandrine, the Quarto's short line is acceptable and is retained in the Folio. The other short line occurs later in the same scene as all await with apprehension the entrance of the new King. Suddenly Warwick breaks off the Chief Justice's courageous defense with a curt "Heere comes the Prince" (5.2.42). The three-foot silence as Henry enters is dramatically essential.

Eleven short Quarto lines remain to be discussed. Two present a special problem and are reserved for later discussion. The other nine have all been either eliminated or "corrected" in the Folio.

One short line was eliminated by what is undoubtedly an authoritative correction. In the Quarto, 1.3.76–80 reads as follows:

> *Bish.* That he should draw his seuerall strengths togither,
> And come against vs in full puissance,
> Need not to be dreaded.
> *Hast.* If he should do so, French and Welch he leaues his back vnarmde, they baying him at the heeles neuer feare that.

The unwarranted setting of verse as prose and the jumble of

TEXTUAL CHANGES BY THE SCRIBE 149

phrases suggest that the Quarto compositor could not sort out marginal insertions in his copy. The Folio corrects as follows:

> Need not be dreaded.*
> *Hast.* If he should do so,
> He leaues his back vnarm'd, the French, and Welch
> Baying him at the heeles: neuer feare that.

Here the scribe may indeed have consulted his supplementary manuscript for help. In this particular scene, he restores three passages omitted in the Quarto. One of the passages he completed only twenty-four lines earlier. The next passage to be added is only six lines ahead. If the manuscript used for the additions was Shakespeare's foul papers, he had the sheet of foolscap before him with the questionable passage in view. More sophisticated in literary matters than the Quarto compositor, he would be better equipped to decipher the confusing insertions. Probably the Folio revision of Hastings' speech is to be trusted. The correction automatically completes the Archbishop's incomplete line.

All of the remaining "corrections" of incomplete lines are open to suspicion. One irregularity has been solved by minor revision. At 4.2.101–2, the Quarto reads,

> *Prince* They know their dueties.
> *Hastings* My lord our army is disperst already

John's short line fits both his character and the situation. Westmoreland has just announced that, despite John's explicit command that the royal forces disband—a command Westmoreland fully understood was not to be issued—the army's leaders will not give orders to disperse until the Prince himself gives the word. John's brief "They know their dueties" is, of course, ironic.

* Note that the Quarto's extra-metrical *to* has been deleted. Although the Folio reading has been widely adopted, the Quarto gives a better line for the actor. When speaking the Folio line aloud—"Need not be dreaded"—one tends to stress *Need*. In the Quarto line—"Need not to be dreaded"—stress falls naturally on the more important *not*. Shakespeare often uses additional light syllables as in "Let me see, let me see: is not the leaf turn'd down / Where I left reading?" (*Julius Caesar*, 4.3.273–74).

They do indeed. They stand in readiness as he has intended from the first, despite the truce into which he has tricked the rebels. The three-foot pause fits his cold savoring of the situation, which is broken by the entrance of Hastings to announce that the trick has worked. Shakespeare often uses short lines to mark such dramatic pauses and transitions. Only a concern for metrical regularity, then, can account for the Folio's revision of Hastings' five-foot speech to a trim three-foot fragment that dovetails with the Prince's two-foot line:

> *Iohn.* They know their duties.
> *Hast.* Our Army is dispers'd

One short line has been solved by simply cutting the offending member. The Quarto gives 4.5.53–54 as one long line of verse: "The prince of Wales, where is he? let me see him: he is not here." Since it is doubtful that Shakespeare considered a seven-foot line to be a normal variant in blank verse, proper alignment gives us

> The prince of Wales, where is he? let me see him:
> He is not here.

The offending "He is not here" is omitted in the Folio, even though, as so often in Shakespeare, the short line is essential dramatically. The King awakens, calls Warwick and the two young princes. They rush in and are chided for leaving him alone. But he has not been alone, they say: they left Prince Henry watching at the bedside. Eagerly, the King asks to see him. At this point "He is not here" is not the redundant statement of an obvious fact. The short line is a clue to the action. Probably Warwick and the princes step back from the bed and turn, expecting Henry to step forward from behind. In their swift response to the King's urgent call, they had not noticed that the Prince is gone. The pause and the King's deep disappointment are emphasized by the very shortness of "He is not here."

One other short line has been avoided by means of a deletion.

Among the several brief cuts of two or more lines in the Folio is 3.1.53-56, the passage italicized in the following:

how chances mockes,
And changes fill the cup of alteration,
With diuers liquors! *O if this were seene,*
The happiest youth viewing his progresse through,
What perills past, what crosses to ensue?
Would shut the booke and sit him downe and die:
Tis not ten yeeres gone,
Since Richard and Northumberland great friends,
Did feast togither. . . .

The omission of this particular passage in the Folio has been perplexing. Shaaber's conjecture that it may have been expurgated as profane and skeptical has satisfied few. The following explanation may not fully satisfy everyone either, but I believe it is at least possible. In the uncut Quarto version, we find an effective use of the "waist line": "Tis not ten yeeres gone." Such a short line often appears in the middle of long speeches in Shakespeare's mature plays at a point of strong transition and usually of strong emotion. Several of the most compelling lines in *Hamlet*, for example, are of this type: "And prey on garbage," "Did nothing," "For Hecuba?" and "O most pernicious woman!" "Waist lines" are found in five speeches in the Quarto of *2 Henry IV*. In the Folio, they have been eliminated in all but one. Given the scribe's aversion to short lines and particularly to "waist lines" (to be documented more fully below), may he have cut the passage in question to eliminate the "irregularity"? As a result of the deletion, "Tis not tenne yeeres gone" is made a perfect complement to "With diuers Liquors."*

* Humphreys argues on the grounds of metrics that the Folio preserves Shakespeare's original draft, whereas Qb preserves a marginal addition that the scribe preparing the Folio transcript overlooked. "If Shakespeare meant it ['Tis not ten years gone'] as a separate line he would surely have written, e.g., 'It is not ten . . .' or 'tis not yet ten . . .'" (New Arden edition [London, 1966], p. lxxxii). Shakespeare, however, used truncated lines throughout his career, lines with the first unaccented syllable omitted: for example, "Tear for tear, and loving kiss for kiss"

In addition to revising and cutting to avoid short lines, the scribe also, I am convinced, invented "fillers" of from one to three feet to create full pentameter lines. At this point we return to the series of puzzling additions in the Folio that prompted the present study. Six Folio additions must each be considered in detail because all six have been accepted as authorial.

In three instances, the addition regularizes a "waist line." The first occurs at 1.1.96 in the middle of Northumberland's reaction to Hotspur's death.

> Yet for all this, say not that Percie's dead,
> I see a strange confession in thine eie,
> Thou shakst thy head, and holdst it feare, or sinne,
> To speake a truth: if he be slaine,
> The tongue offends not that reports his death....

Northumberland is saying, in effect, "Speak, man, speak!—Why are you silent?" Following "To speake a truth," he probably pauses before the painful outcry of "if he be slaine." The dramatic impact of this strangled pause, as he waits for some response, is destroyed in the Folio version:

> Thou shak'st thy head, and hold'st it Feare, or Sinne,
> To speake a truth. If he be slaine, say so:
> The Tongue offends not, that reports his death....

It would take no great effort of the imagination for a rigid metricist to add the totally unnecessary and thoroughly pedestrian "say so." The Folio addition is a metrical gain but a dramatic loss. In the Quarto, *slaine* at the end of the line has a strength that is undercut by the two added words.

In John's icy answer to the arrested traitors' charges that he has broken faith with them, we find a particularly effective use of the "waist" (4.2.117).

(*Titus Andronicus*, 5.3.156); "Quick, dispatch, and send the head to Angelo" (*Measure for Measure*, 4.3.93); "She I kill'd? I did so; but thou strik'st me" (*The Winter's Tale*, 5.1.17); "Twelve year since, Miranda, twelve year since" (*The Tempest*, 1.2.54).

TEXTUAL CHANGES BY THE SCRIBE 153

I pawnde thee none,
I promist you redresse of these same grieuances
Whereof you did complaine, which by mine honour
I will performe, with a most christian care.
But for you rebels, looke to taste the due
Meete for rebellion:
Most shallowly did you these armes commence,
Fondly brought heere, and foolishly sent hence.

The irony of John's protestations of "christian care" increases in the ensuing four lines of the speech as he gives God credit for the victory and sends the rebels to immediate execution. In context, the short "Meete for rebellion" is a knife. In the pause, as he lets the full shock of his words sink in, John reveals his utter scorn of the rebels. By his trick and his words, he dismisses them as shallow fools to be exterminated. What, then, do we find in the Folio?

But for you (Rebels) looke to taste the due
Meet for Rebellion, and such Acts as yours.

"And such Acts as yours" has all the dramatic impact and intelligibility of "and etcetera." What act "such as" rebellion could have any meaning in this context? For John, rebellion is the most heinous of crimes. The feeble addition cannot be Shakespeare's.

The dramatic usefulness of another "waist line" has been confused not only by the scribe's addition but also by the faulty scene division of modern editors. In act four, the King suddenly feels ill and asks for assistance (4.4.131–32; 4.5.1–3).

I pray you take me vp, and beare me hence,
Into some other chamber.
Let there be no noyse made, my gentle friends,
Vnlesse some dull and fauourable hand
Will whisper musique to my weary spirite.

In both the Quarto and the Folio, the scene is continuous, and the short line in the Quarto indicates action. The King asks to be moved. In the interval following the short line, he is moved to his bed, probably revealed upstage behind an arras. Once settled, he asks for quiet while he rests. The scribe misses the significance and seeks only to regularize the meter.

> I pray you take me vp, and beare me hence
> Into some other Chamber: softly 'pray.
> Let there be no noyse made (my gentle friends). . . .

The King's line is easily filled out merely by making him repeat himself. In production, what is suggested? As the King is carried to bed, his "Softly pray" becomes the equivalent of "Take it easy," which, when immediately followed by "Let there be no noyse made," makes him a whining complainer. Editors would, I believe, have been made uneasy by this particular addition long ago were it not for the imposed scene break. When one reads "Softly pray" followed by a stage direction and then "Scene V" followed by a scene location and yet another stage direction before "Let there be no noyse made," the dramatic ineptness of the addition is not readily apparent.

Although not "waist" lines, three other short lines that break the established pentameter rhythm have also been completed in the Folio. At the opening of 4.4, it will be recalled that the King asked Gloucester of Hal's whereabouts and, receiving the answer "At Windsor," immediately asked in a curt short line, "And how accompanied?" There, as we have noted, the scribe probably let the short line stand because it occurred in a sequence of irregular lines. Forty lines later, however, the situation is different.

> *King* Why art thou not at Winsore with him Thomas?
> *Tho.* He is not there to day, he dines in London.
> *King* And how accompanied?
> *Tho.* With Poines, and other his continuall followers.

The King asks Thomas exactly the same question he has asked Clarence, the question that is always foremost in his mind. Dramatically, the repetition is important, as is the choked quality of the three words "And how accompanied?"—words loaded with implication. Here, however, the scribe will not let the short line stand. The pentameter rhythm has been firmly established for over thirty lines and the short line breaks the rhythm; moreover, the shortness of the line—set as it is in a sequence of full lines—is immediately apparent visually. The problem is solved in the Folio by completing the line with pure "filler": "And how accompanyed? Canst thou tell that?" (4.4.52). Not only is the addition redundant; it destroys the echo of the clipped question that is pregnant with the King's concern.

The same type of mind saw the following exchange as faulty. At 4.5.48, the King suddenly wakes and, finding himself alone, calls out,

> *King* Warwicke, Gloucester, Clarence.
> *Clar.* Doth the King cal?
> *War.* What would your Maiestie?
> *King* Why did you leaue me here alone, my lords?

If the lines of the King and Clarence are read to form one pentameter line, Warwick's question is metrically incomplete. Thus the Folio reads "What would your Maiestie? how fares your Grace?" —another simple, and wholly unnecessary, addition. The King has called. What does he want? That is Warwick's sole question. It is perhaps gracious of him to inquire after the King's health, but the question is dramatically irrelevant at this moment.

At 4.4.117–22 we find the third of the Quarto's short lines that break the established pentameter rhythm and have been completed in the Folio. Clarence's speech follows Warwick's attempt to reassure the princes that their father will recover:

> *Clar.* No, no, he cannot long hold out these pangs,
> Th'incessant care and labour of his mind,
> Hath wrought the Mure that should confine it in
> So thin that life lookes through.
> *Hum.* The people feare me, for they do obserue
> Vnfather'd heires, and lothly births of nature. . . .

Clarence's short line is completed in the Folio to read "So thinne, that Life lookes through, and will breake out." It could be argued that the added part-line clarifies an obscure image, but such density is characteristic of Shakespeare. So too is the device of ending, as well as beginning, speeches with half-lines. All the evidence accumulated thus far suggests that "and will break out" is another piece of redundancy, inserted by the scribe for metrical reasons.

Only two incomplete lines in the Quarto remain to be discussed. Both are in the King's bitter response to his son's removing of the crown (4.5.59–81). Both break the established pentameter rhythm and yet both are retained in the Folio. In addition, three more incomplete lines are created in the Folio that no alignment can resolve into regular verse. The problem is complex and requires extensive quotation. First, from the Quarto:

> The Prince hath tane it hence, go seeke him out:
> Is he so hastie, that he doth suppose my sleepe my death?
> Finde him, my lord of Warwicke, chide him hither.
> This part of his conioynes with my disease,
> And helps to end me: see, sonnes, what things you are,
> How quickly nature falls into reuolt,
> When gold becomes her obiect?
> For this, the foolish ouer-carefull fathers
> Haue broke their sleepe with thoughts,
> Their braines with care, their bones with industry:
> For this they haue ingrossed and pilld vp,
> The cankred heapes of strange atcheeued gold:
> For this they haue beene thoughtfull to inuest
> Their sonnes with arts and martiall exercises,
> When like the bee toling from euery flower,
> Our thigh, packt with waxe our mouthes with hony,
> We bring it to the hiue: and like the bees,
> Are murdred for our paines, this bitter taste
> Yeelds his engrossements to the ending father,
> Now where is he that will not stay so long,
> Till his friend sicknesse hands determind me.   *Enter Warwicke.*

In the Folio version, the first line of the speech is divided, but solely because of column width.

> The Prince hath ta'ne it hence:
> Goe seeke him out.

Immediately thereafter, beginning with the second line, we find an attempt to regularize.

> Is hee so hastie, that hee doth suppose
> My sleepe, my death? Finde him (my Lord of Warwick)
> Chide him hither: this part of his conioynes
> With my disease, and helpes to end me.

The scribe, for the work is probably his, began well. Faced with an unacceptable seven-foot line, he divided it at *suppose* and proceeded to realign successfully for two more lines. But suddenly his prospects dimmed. He had been trapped into a four-foot line—"With my disease, and helpes to end me"—and ahead lay three three-foot lines: "See, sonnes, what things you are," "When gold becomes her obiect" and "Haue broke their sleepe with thoughts." Only by arbitrarily dividing at the completion of every five-foot unit could he make a pretense of regularity, but at the expense of rhetoric. Even so, he could not possibly come out right at the end of the speech. I suggest that he quite simply gave up at this point, and it is to his credit that he did so. He finished his attempt with "See Sonnes, what things you are," thus creating yet another short line, and then proceeded for ten lines to follow the Quarto's lineation.[13]

But his problems were not over. New difficulties arose in the following:

> When like the bee toling from euery flower,
> Our thigh, packt with waxe our mouthes with hony,
> We bring it to the hiue. . . .

To the type of logical mind we have seen operating in the scribe, these lines must have presented four errors. In the second line, "Our thigh" is an error in agreement, and the line lacks an unaccented syllable in the second foot. And what is the bee "tolling"? There should be a direct object. If, moreover, the bee is "tolling" something, is "tolling" really the apt word? As the result of such reasoning, it was, I believe, the scribe and not Shakespeare who revised the diction, wrote an additional half-line (here italicized), and then, necessarily realigned the rest of the speech.

> When like the Bee, culling from euery flower
> *The vertuous Sweetes,* our Thighes packt with Wax,
> Our Mouthes with Honey, wee bring it to the Hiue;
> And like the Bees, are murthered for our paines.
> This bitter taste yeelds his engrossements,
> To the ending Father.
> *Enter Warwicke.*
> Now, where is hee, that will not stay so long
> Till his Friend Sicknesse hath determin'd me?[14]

The scribe has, of course, created still another half-line, but one that can be partially excused by moving up the entrance of Warwick. In fact, despite the five lines that are metrically short, the speech as it is set in the Folio looks, on the whole, fairly normal. The only visual anomaly is the short line created by the compositor when he was forced to divide the first line of the speech.

Do any of these revisions bear the stamp of Shakespeare? He often failed to resolve agreement in constructions such as *our thigh*. We find related instances not only throughout the Quarto of *2 Henry IV* (all systematically corrected in the Folio) but throughout the canon as well. Moreover, the apparently irregular line of the Quarto is a stronger, more "Shakespearean," verse line than the apparently regular line of the Folio.

Q: Our thigh, packt with waxe our mouthes with hony
F: The vertuous Sweetes, our Thighes packt with Wax

The pentameter line can far better tolerate the omission of a light syllable following the second foot—an omission at a caesura, which is pointed by a comma in the Quarto—than it can tolerate a clash of accents in the last half of the line where there is no caesura. Note a similar juxtaposition of accents in *Richard II:* "In rage, deaf as the sea, hasty as fire" (1.1.19). With the Folio's alignment, the unmetrical phrase is contained in a line that counts out to the required ten syllables, but the accents are faulty.

The added half-line—"The vertuous Sweetes"—has been

adopted almost without question, but again do not all the signs point to the scribe? The half-line could not have been in Shakespeare's foul papers. Almost all editors realize that the Quarto's lineation is superior to that of the Folio and thus combine the Quarto alignment with the Folio addition to provide the following:

When, like the bee, tolling from every flower
The virtuous sweets,
Our thighs pack'd with wax, our mouths with honey,
We bring it to the hive. . . .

It has been conjectured that the Quarto compositor overlooked the half-line, but such an irregular line would be too obvious to be easily overlooked. Simmes' Compositor A had difficulties with single letters and words, but there is no evidence to suggest that he was capable of such a major oversight.[15] A more telling argument against the authority of the line is that, given the preferred Quarto lineation, it would be a "waist line" that serves no purpose. Here there is no major transition, no rush of emotion, no required pause for action.

As it stands in the Quarto, the image makes perfect sense—once we recognize the early use of *toll* as an intransitive verb. Some editors have probably been misled by the fact that the OED cites "tolling . . . the virtuous sweets"—thus conflating the Quarto's *tolling* with the Folio's interpolation—under the entry for the transitive verb. If one looks further, however, one finds *toll* as an intransitive verb meaning "to take or collect toll," and an appropriate Shakespearean line is cited: "no Italian Priest / Shall tythe or toll in our dominions" (*King John*, 3.1.153-54). No direct object is required. Indeed, the Quarto version seems much stronger, much more Shakespearean, without the gratuitous addition. The King's simile is straightforward. The bee is a literal bee exacting a certain amount of honey as "toll" from every flower. The ethical content is in the application of the simile, not in the simile itself. To me, the Quarto version sounds like Shakespeare; the Folio addition, like a rigidly logical and self-conscious moralist.

Throughout the preceding chapter I have undoubtedly attributed to the scribe several revisions that some readers might attribute to compositors. One group of scholars, championed by Alice Walker, believes that compositors automatically edited their copy: not only correcting obvious spelling, typographical, and even grammatical errors, but also making corrections for sense and revising to regularize meter. My study thus far leads me to concur with Shaaber: "I think of a compositor as a workman whose job is to make a typographical copy of the manuscript put in his hands. He is not responsible for the accuracy or the sufficiency of that manuscript and he has little or no incentive to give himself any trouble about it. . . . he is no more responsible for the meter, grammar, and diction of his copy than he is for its style and thought."[16] I would qualify this only by adding that control reprints show alert compositors correcting typographical and spelling errors and altering punctuation as a matter of routine.

Indirect support for Shaaber's position is found in Charlton Hinman's conclusion that the Folio proofreaders were "largely indifferent" to the accuracy of the text.[17] The fact that the very few press corrections were almost entirely concerned with typographical blemishes may suggest the prevailing attitude of all those concerned with setting the Folio. We find further support in Joseph Moxon's statement of the compositor's responsibility. Though written over a half century after completion of the Folio, it probably reflects long-established principles. A good compositor, says Moxon, needs to have a natural gift, but other than that he need only know the letters and characters that he will meet in his copy, know how to punctuate a sentence properly, know when to begin a word with a capital letter, and know traditional spelling (which, of course, was far more stabilized in 1683 than in Shakespeare's day). As we have noted, Moxon believes that such a man may in fact be a better compositor than a highly trained scholar:

For by the Laws of Printing, *a* Compositor *is strictly to follow his* Copy, *viz, to observe and do just so much and no more than his* Copy *will bear him out for; so that his* Copy *is to be his Rule and Authority: But the carelessness of some good Authors, and the ignorance of other Authors, has forc'd* Printers

TEXTUAL CHANGES BY THE SCRIBE 161

to introduce a Custom, which among them is look'd upon as a task and duty incumbent on the Compositor, viz. to discern and amend the bad Spelling and Pointing of his Copy....[18]

Clearly, for Moxon, the compositor is not to attend to matters of grammar, idiom, diction, and metrics. By implication, he suggests that a trained scholar might do exactly what a good compositor should not do: take it on himself to edit his copy.

That Compositor A followed Moxon's injunction, there is little doubt. His dogged faithfulness to his copy has long been recognized. Compositor B, however, was scarcely a good compositor according to the rules laid down by Moxon. John Andrews' detailed comparison of the first quarto of *King Lear* with Compositor B's resetting for the Pavier quarto of 1619 indicates that B did, unquestionably, take it upon himself at times to make corrections for sense, although it is often difficult to tell which of his substitutions were conscious corrections and which were unconscious substitutions of the kind we see throughout his work. For this reason, his conscious attempts to improve his copy may be far fewer than the number of intelligent substitutions might indicate. Andrews' argument that B intentionally made corrections to regularize meter is open to more serious question. His evidence makes it clear that B often clipped non-syllabic *-ed* forms. Other than that, however, the few lines that B improved metrically in the Pavier quarto of *King Lear* are more than outweighed by the many good lines that he either damaged or revised when no revision was needed: for example, by adding words to turn a good pentameter line into an alexandrine. With only four exceptions out of approximately thirty instances cited by Andrews, I find B's modifications of meter by omission, addition, or substitution of words to be attributable to his attempts to make sense of a doubtful passage or to his well-known lack of attention to the exact wording of his copy.[19]

Despite these qualifications, I would agree that—under other circumstances—we might suspect B's hand in such spelling "corrections" as *Whitson* for *Wheeson*, in such diction revisions as *anything that tends to laughter* for *anything that intends*, and perhaps in such modernizations as *leather* for *letherne*, just as we might give him sole credit for clipping those non-syllabic *-ed* forms that are spelled out in the Quarto. However, the extensive, consistent, and highly distinctive kinds of revisions found throughout the entire text of *2 Henry IV* make it probable that the very few types of corrections B might have seen fit to make on his own authority had already been made before the transcript was placed in his hands. If Compositor B were responsible for automatically changing prepositions to conform to current idiom, for example, we should have to readjust rather radically our assumptions about A's faithfulness to his copy, for the same changes appear in his work. Similarly, B might change *I will inset you* to *I will set you*, but A would not be guilty of changing *loe* to *Looke* (2.4.32) or *thrust* to *truss'd* (3.2.325).

In short, it is my belief that none of the revisions noted in this chapter can be attributed to either of the compositors. The transcriber-editor's job was so painstakingly thorough that probably very few errors slipped by him, and those few—such as *hole* for *hold* (ln. 25)—probably remain.

CHAPTER V

Conclusion

⬥⬥⬥⬥

When a Folio text derives from a good quarto but consultation of an additional manuscript is suspected, a key question must be asked if one is to determine the nature of the Folio copy. Is there anything that cannot be explained without recourse to the theory of an independent manuscript? Because the major additions to the Folio text of *2 Henry IV* required some manuscript to supplement the Quarto, the question must be rephrased. Is there anything in the Folio that cannot be explained without recourse to the theory of a corrected manuscript that was subsequent to the copy for the Quarto, Shakespeare's foul papers?

In the preceding analysis of the problems faced by the Folio compositors and their solutions and of the scribe's type of mind and probable method of working, I have limited the discussion to typical examples only. In the course of my study, however, I have considered all Folio variants and can find only three improvements that cannot be readily attributed to the scribe or, in the case of "No more of that," to Compositor B. The first occurs at 1.2.171–73:

Q: all the other giftes appertinent to man, as the malice of his age shapes the one not worth a goosbery....
F: all the other gifts appertinent to man (as the malice of this Age shapes them) are not woorth a Gooseberry.

Conceivably, the scribe might have puzzled this out by logic, but such an argument would credit him with truly uncommon ingenuity. In this first part of the play, the scribe had to consult his supplementary manuscript for several additions. One added passage he had completed transcribing approximately 176 lines before this passage, at 1.1.209; another he would begin 95 lines later, at 2.3.21. This, then, may be one time when he looked at his manuscript, although it is impossible even to guess what Shakespeare had written that the Quarto compositor could so seriously have misread.

For the other two improvements, the scribe would have had no reason to consult his manuscript. In neither case does the Quarto reading present a problem. One improvement is the Folio's substitution of *continuantly* for the Quarto's *continually* (2.1.26). *Continuantly* seems characteristic of Mistress Quickly. Since the scribe elsewhere removed so many of her errors, he cannot be responsible for creating one here. A possible explanation for the variant occurs to me, though it may seem an argument from desperation. Quickly's characteristic blunders—such as *Wheeson* for *Whitsun* and *familiarity* for *familiar*—strike not only the eye but the ear. *Continuantly* looks comic to a reader but in the rapid speech of production would an audience hear the subtle difference in word ending? As Shakespeare would know, in order to make the joke clear the actor playing Quickly would need to pronounce the word with a clarity unnatural to the character. (As bad productions of *The Rivals* attest, Mrs. Malaprop ceases to be comic when the actress works to get laughs by focusing on her confused diction.) Is it, then, possible that Shakespeare actually wrote *continually* and that this apparent improvement may be the fortuitous result of one of Compositor B's many errors? The word is divided at the end of a line: *continu- / antly*. If B were momentarily distracted at the end of line 637 and not thinking—and substitutions such as *Imperiall* for *impartiall* (5.2.36) show that sometimes he was not—might he have returned to 638 and added a common adverbial ending?

The third improvement, and the most difficult to account for, is an addition that follows a deletion. For 2.2.21–27, the Quarto reads:

CONCLUSION 165

because the rest of the low Countries haue eate vp thy holland: and God knows whether those that bal out the ruines of thy linnen shal inherite his kingdom: but the Midwiues say, the children are not in the fault wherevpon the world increases, and kinreds are mightily strengthened.

For this the Folio substitutes

because the rest of thy Low Countries, haue made a shift to eate vp thy Holland.

The deletion need not concern us here, but the addition presents a serious problem. *Haue made a shift to* sounds like a distinctly Shakespearean pun. Did it require access to genuine Shakespearean material supplementing that available to the Quarto? The fact that the addition occurs immediately before a cut may be significant. Without the deleted passage, the Prince's speech ends rather weakly. Is it possible that the scribe suddenly had a stroke of genius? Not very, but it is at least conceivable.

That these three readings are superior, there is no doubt. In the light, however, of all the other evidence, can these three alone bear the burden of proving that the scribe had access to a corrected manuscript? Indeed, these three exceptions recede in importance when we consider a second question in our attempt to determine the nature of the Folio copy. Is there anything to indicate that the scribe did *not*, in fact, consult a corrected manuscript? It is one thing to conclude that he probably had no need of such a manuscript; it would be quite another if we could determine that he actually did not consult one.

Let us dismiss as irrelevant the scribe's introduction of error when no correction was needed, as is the case in his substitution of *Fates* for *faters* or *Scoggan's* for *Skoggins*. Given his predisposition to "improve" the play, he would have made this kind of revision even if he were transcribing Shakespeare's fair copy. Strikingly relevant, however, are the many Quarto readings that require correction. Too often the scribe's revisions are manifestly wrong.

When he supplies missing stage directions, he often places them incorrectly, revealing no understanding of the dramatic situation. When he moves stage directions, he often puts them too late, revealing no understanding of acting requirements. He compounds a minor Quarto error of omission by pointedly assigning the reading of Falstaff's letter to Poins. Because of a minor but easily resolvable error in the Quarto he becomes totally confused by Falstaff's page, turning him into "Bardolph's boy"—and not once, but twice. Whatever corrections he made in speech prefixes and stage directions were amenable to reason alone. His errors show that he could not have been collating the Quarto with a corrected manuscript, least of all one corrected with an eye to production.

Equally pertinent is the scribe's treatment of faulty verbal readings in the Quarto. Some of his corrections are flatly wrong. For 2.4.335–36, the Quarto reads, "for the boy there is a good angel about him, but the diuel blinds him too." The Folio substitutes "but the Deuill outbids him too." Many emendations have been offered: *the devil attends, the devil's behind, the devil bloats, the devil blinds him to't,* and—the most recent and perhaps the best suggestion—*the devil binds.** Only one reading seems impossible: the Folio's *outbids.* By logic, the scribe could have supplied *outbids,* but he forgot to cut the tell-tale *too,* the sign that he was attempting his own revision of the Quarto error.

Another faulty correction is found in the Prince's report of how he "upbraided the crown" (4.5.160–61):

Q: Therefore thou best of gold, art worse then gold,
    Other lesse fine, in karrat more precious. . . .
F: Therefore, thou best of Gold, art worst of Gold.
    Other, lesse fine in Charract, is more precious. . . .

---

* Davison suggests that the Quarto compositor found *binds* in his copy and made a characteristic error by adding an extraneous letter. His emendation is recommended by the context, by the specific religious meaning of *bind,* and by the known tendency of Simmes' Compositor A to make this kind of error. If, as seems likely, the error was not Shakespeare's, we have further evidence of the Folio's direct dependence on the Quarto.

CONCLUSION 167

Two Folio corrections in these lines were the product of logic. The Quarto compositor tended to omit small words, and the scribe replaced the obviously missing *is*. And how can gold be "worse" than itself? The substitution of *worst of Gold* is certainly preferable, though one hesitates to assert positively that Shakespeare might not have written the Quarto line. The substitution of *Charract*, however, introduces an error. The scribe was probably confused by the extraneous comma after *fine* in the Quarto passage. How could gold "lesse fine" than that in the crown weigh more carats? Medicinal gold might be said to be of greater worth to man because of its healing power, but it certainly is not "more precious in carat" than that of the crown. The scribe thus removed the misleading comma after *fine* and then implied a figurative meaning by substituting *Charract*—a spelling that arose by confusing *carat* with *caract*, meaning "mark" or "sign." The Prince, however, means *karrat* in its technical, not its figurative, sense, as the use of *fine* indicates. An accurate correction of the Quarto line would merely remove the comma after *fine* and replace the missing verb.[1]

A series of Folio attempts at correction cannot be unequivocally dubbed errors but they are so unsatisfying that it seems impossible they could derive from a corrected manuscript. Falstaff's mistaking of Silence for one "maister Soccard" makes no sense (at least to us today), but the Folio's substitution of *Sure-card* does not fully convince (3.2.86). It seems doubtful that Falstaff could take one glance at Silence and make up a name meaning "safe-bet" to convey his ironic estimation of a man he does not know. Other unsatisfying corrections include the following:

Q: Canst thou, ô partiall sleepe, giue them repose,
    To the wet season in an howre so rude. . . .
F: *thy Repose*
    wet Sea-Boy   (3.1.26–27)
Q: Will Fortune neuer come with both hands full,
    But wet her faire words stil in foulest terms?
F: *But write . . . in foulest Letters*[2]   (4.4.104)

CONCLUSION

Q: He hath a teare for pittie, and a hand,
   Open as day for meeting charitie. . . .
F: *melting Charity* (4.4.32)

Until Evans' emendation in the Riverside edition of *meting* for *meeting*, editors have been content with the Folio's *melting Charity*, but I find this variant as suspicious as those just noted. According to other Shakespearean uses, a man's heart might be "melting," but not charity itself. The King's commendation of Prince Henry lies in the fact that his hand is "open as day" for the doing of something. *Melting Charity* makes no sense.

In addition to ostensible corrections that are either manifestly wrong or, at the very least, unconvincing, one type of evidence even more strongly suggests that the scribe did not have access to a corrected manuscript of any kind. When faced with a problem that he could not figure out logically, his solution was simple: he cut the confusing passage. Several instances have already been noted: his cutting of the line assigned to Umphrevile in 1.1, his elimination of the misplaced entrance of Will and of the "Dispatch" line that is probably Will's entering speech at the opening of 2.2, and his deletion of the groom's "dispatch, dispatch" together with the first coronation procession at the opening of 5.5. Another instance baffles most editors too. What, exactly, should be the wording of Falstaff's boast when he delivers Colevile to Prince John? According to the Quarto, "he sawe me, and yeelded, that I may iustly say with the hooke-nosde fellow of Rome, there cosin, I came, saw, and ouercame" (4.3.40–42). "There cosin"? The total lack of agreement on emendation suggests the quandry in which the scribe found himself. Editors have suggested everything from *their Caesar* to *thrice their consul* to *three words*. The scribe, understandably, gave up and deleted *there cosin*. All of these problems would have been solved in a corrected manuscript. The fact that the scribe avoided them by the simple expedient of cutting is persuasive evidence that he could not, in fact, have had access to such a manuscript.

CONCLUSION

A related instance is found at the end of 2.4. Following Falstaff's exit, Bardolph calls for Doll to come join his master. For a literary man, the Hostess's response is thoroughly puzzling: "O runne Doll, runne, runne good Doll, come, she comes blubberd, yea! will you come Doll?" Some editors have been as confused by the passage as was the scribe. Kittredge, for example, treated "she comes blubberd" as a stage direction; Wilson assigned "come" and "yea! will you come Doll?" to Bardolph. The speech, however, may well be accurate, depending on stage action to clarify the sudden transitions. Doll is drunk in the scene and weeping after Falstaff's farewell. She is certainly in no condition to move with dispatch. The Hostess must urge her on with "O runne Doll, runne, runne good Doll." As Doll, still sobbing, begins to move erratically—perhaps weaving drunkenly—the Hostess must urge her more firmly with "come." Then the Hostess apologizes to Bardolph for the delay with "she comes blubberd." But Doll's progress is still fitful. Perhaps she totters into the Hostess's arms; perhaps she collapses against the door. Whatever the reason, the Hostess must urge further, "yea! will you come Doll?" as she helps her friend to exit. Unless one has an eye to production, the passage makes no sense on paper, and the scribe admitted defeat. He cut all but "Oh runne *Dol*, runne: runne, good *Dol*." A corrected manuscript might not have clarified this particular speech, but the scribe's deletion again shows his characteristic way of solving problems.

What, then, was the nature of the copy used to supply the eight major additions and 3.1? Throughout the preceding discussion, I have offered Shakespeare's foul papers as the hypothetical candidate, and primarily on the grounds that I see no logical challenger. With only the three minor exceptions noted, I believe that the text of Qa, revisions by the scribe, and copy adjustments by Compositor B can account for the Folio version of all but the added passages. If the scribe's supplementary manuscript were indeed a corrected one, would he not have consulted it when he encountered the many cruxes we have noted? The fact that so often he either introduced a new error or cut an insoluble problem suggests that he had no resource other than that available to the Quarto compositor: Shakespeare's foul papers.

Thus far the current study has been concerned only with the question of how the Folio text evolved. Based on an analysis of internal evidence—the types of changes made by the compositors to solve certain printing house problems and the types of changes made by the scribe to refine the script according to his own literary standards—that question can, I believe, be answered. A highly qualified scribe was commissioned to prepare a transcript of the complete play. Using Qa as his copy, he consulted a supplementary manuscript, probably Shakespeare's foul papers, primarily to obtain copy for passages that are omitted in the Quarto. On rare occasions, when he encountered unintelligible passages in his Quarto copy and when he could quickly locate the passage on the sheets of foolscap waiting in readiness to one side, he may have consulted the manuscript, but he did not keep his eye on both the manuscript and his printed copy concurrently as a matter of course. He worked slowly and with considerable care, making corrections according to his own principles of logic and decorum and refining the text for a sophisticated reader whose interests were purely literary. The result of his work was a thoughtful and workmanlike transcript that corrected many errors in the Quarto but also introduced much corruption. Further corruption was introduced by Compositor B. Faced with a unique problem in setting the copy for *2 Henry IV*, he deleted and added words, phrases, and even lines in order to accommodate the amount of copy assigned to the given number of pages.

The question of why the Folio text evolved in this particular way is quite another matter. One major question remains unanswered and, indeed, it probably can never be answered without the discovery of some new external evidence. Why did Heminges and Condell present Jaggard with a transcript rather than with a copy of the Quarto and the company's promptbook to supply copy for the omitted passages? On this question, we can but speculate, and I offer the following only as further speculation on a very perplexing problem.

To begin, let me raise still another question that can probably never be answered definitively. Why was there only one edition of *2 Henry IV*? One theory holds that the copy for Qa had been officially censored and allowed for printing but that when the omission of 3.1 was detected after printing had already begun, the new scene was not submitted for censorship before running off the corrected issue, Qb. Because 3.1 contains the same kind of material on Richard II deemed censorable elsewhere in the play, the argument goes, a total ban was placed on reissuing the play in any form. There are far too many arguments against this theory for it to be convincing. A printer who proceeded to incorporate material that he knew in advance would be disallowed would be very foolhardy indeed. Moreover, if the authorities discovered the insertion in Qb, their expected response would have been not only to ban future publication but to suppress the offending issue. The fact that eleven copies of Qb are extant, over and above the ten extant copies of Qa, suggests that the second issue was not, in fact, suppressed. Most damaging to this theory is the fact that after the accession of James, the passages in question would no longer have been deemed inflammatory. In 1608, Q4 of *Richard II* restored the abdication scene that had been omitted in 1597 and 1598. No political considerations can satisfactorily explain the failure to reprint *2 Henry IV*.[3]

A second theory, proposed by A. R. Humphreys, is that the popularity of *1 Henry IV*, which had been printed three times between 1598–99, led the printers to expect a large sale and thus prompted an unusually large printing. Thus no reprints were required. As Humphreys himself notes, however, without a special license the Stationers' Company permitted only 1500 copies to be printed from one setting of type, and there is no record that such a license was granted for *2 Henry IV*.[4]

One consideration has not, to my knowledge, been mentioned, but it seems to me worth pursuing. Was the play sufficiently popular on the stage to create a continuing demand by the reading public? I believe it safe to say that few today consider *2 Henry IV* a good play in its own right.* The Prologue of Rumour seriously undercuts the first scene, forewarning the audience that all the contradictory reports are irrelevant to any serious issue. The first scene itself is one of Shakespeare's poorest, with Northumberland more interested in finding apt similes than in learning the fate of his son. The Prince and Falstaff have only one scene together before the rejection, and that is but a pallid echo of the great foolery in Part 1. The rebels are a cold lot. There is no Hotspur to excite our imagination and inspire our sympathy, no dramatic issue among the rebels to compare with the Hotspur–Glendower tension, no intrigue to compare with Worcester's toying with Hotspur. On the whole, the poetry is uninspired. We analyze the play endlessly, but primarily as a postscript to Part 1. Our interest is largely thematic, not dramatic or literary. Witness the many productions that combine both parts, retaining little of Part 2 other than a shortened version of the reconciliation scene and the rejection of Falstaff. What do we really savor in it other than the encounter between Falstaff and the Chief Justice, the brief Falstaff-Doll interlude, the scenes in Gloucestershire and some rich moments with the Hostess? One senses that Shakespeare set out to repeat a success but that his inspiration as well as his best source material was expended in Part 1. May Shakespeare's audience have felt the same?

It has often been stated that contemporary allusions, especially to Pistol, indicate the popularity of the play. In point of fact, *The Shakespeare Allusion-Book* cites only three relevant quotations: two echoes of Pistol's "Have we not Hyren here" in *Eastward Hoe* (1605) and *Law Tricks* (1604–7) and a possible echo in "Die men like dogs" in *Ram-Alley* (1607–8). If one counts the number of allusions as a guide to popularity, Justice Shallow may have made

---

* For an eloquent defense of the play, see Peter Davison's introduction to his New Penguin edition, In comparison with *1 Henry IV*, he finds it to be "the more interesting and, in some ways, the greater play" (p. 8).

a greater impression, since we find four uses of his name between 1599 and 1605 (once coupled with the name of Justice Silence). None of them refers specifically to the play, however, and the allegorical name may have become popular as a type-name. The only other relevant allusions prior to the publication of the Folio are Robert Armin's echo in "I have seen the stars at midnight" in the Epistle-dedicatory to *A Nest of Ninnies* (1608), an echo of "I'll tickle your catastrophe" in *The Merry Devil of Edmonton* (1599–1604), and Jonson's reference to "Dol Teare-sheet or Kate Common" in *Epicoene* (1609). In several of these cases, it is difficult to know whether Shakespeare was the first to use the name or the expression, or whether he was putting common lore to good use. On the basis of allusions, then, little can be determined, other than the probability that Pistol and Justice Shallow made a vivid impression on audiences around the turn of the century.[5]

Stage history—or, in this case, the lack of it—may provide more pertinent evidence than do allusions. There is no certain evidence that there was any demand for revivals after the first performance. In fact, prior to 1720 (when a radically revised adaptation entered the repertory in response to the success of Part 1), there is only one possible reference to production. In the winter of 1612–13, a list of plays put on by the King's Men for the marriage festivities of Princess Elizabeth to the Elector Palatine includes *the Hotspur* and *Sir John Falstaff*, titles that may represent the two parts of *Henry IV*. A few other references, such as that to a play called *Ould Castel* in Cockpit in Court in 1638, tell us nothing.[6] Such popularity as the play enjoyed in the eighteenth and nineteenth centuries can be largely attributed to the famous actors who wanted to capitalize on their successes as Falstaff in Part 1, to comedians like Colley Cibber who made a star role of Shallow, and, especially in the nineteenth century, to the spectacular pageantry of the coronation procession. Today, the play is staged almost exclusively by Shakespearean companies that are faithfully devoted to producing the entire canon. If there were no Part 1, would we ever have a production of Part 2?

Moreover, in the badly mutilated form in which we find the text in Qa and Qb, would the play have found a wide reading market? Qb is bad enough, with the omission of the eight passages creating several serious gaps in dramatic continuity, but those unfortunate enough to have purchased Qa did not have even the redeeming feature of the King's apostrophe to sleep, one of the very few scenes with poetry that is worth rereading. A clue that may be of considerable significance is found in the Crichton Stuart copy of the Quarto at the National Library of Scotland. On the title page, a contemporary hand has written "31 Dec̃ber 1610. price vd."[7] If copies of the play were still available for public sale over ten years after publication, the reason for the failure to reprint seems self-evident.

May there, then, have been only one edition because the play passed out of the repertory and there was simply no demand for reading texts? The witness of the number of extant copies of different quartos seems to bear out this hypothesis. *Richard III* was issued in six quartos, with thirty-eight copies and a fragment extant; *Richard II* in five quartos, with thirty-two copies extant; *Henry V*, in three quartos, with thirty-two copies extant. Of the extremely popular *1 Henry IV*, there were seven quartos before the Folio, of which forty-one copies and a fragment are extant. Of *2 Henry IV*, there are only twenty copies and a fragment. To be sure, there was only one edition of the play, but if only one edition was available—and if the play was indeed as popular as *1 Henry IV*—one would expect more copies of it to have been preserved.

These considerations may throw light on the vexed question as to why Heminges and Condell, fellow members of Shakespeare's company and co-editors of the Folio, presented Jaggard with a transcript, rather than a copy of the Quarto together with a supplementary manuscript. It is quite possible that no copy of the Quarto was available. Why would the company have kept such a useless edition? Moreover, it is quite possible that no manuscript —whether company promptbook or foul papers—remained in the editors' possession.

CONCLUSION 175

The irregularity in the order of printing *Richard II* and the two parts of *Henry IV* would seem to confirm this possibility. Hinman argues persuasively that copyright difficulties caused the delay in completing *Richard II* and setting *1 Henry IV*, but *2 Henry IV* presented no such problem. John Smethwick and William Aspley held the title to six plays including *2 Henry IV*, and it is undoubtedly for this reason that the two men were included in the syndicate that published the Folio. Since there were no copyright difficulties with the play, why, then, did work not proceed immediately from *The Winter's Tale* to *2 Henry IV*, rather than to *Henry V*? Similar delays had occurred in setting *Twelfth Night* and *The Winter's Tale*, to both of which the publishers held clear title. Those delays, Hinman suggests, probably arose because copy for the two plays was temporarily unavailable.[8] The title for *2 Henry IV* was also clear and its setting too was delayed. It would thus seem to follow that copy was, again, temporarily unavailable. In short, an atypical literary transcript of the play may have been used solely because better copy was not available.[9]

Of one thing we can be fairly certain. The transcript was not commissioned specifically to serve as copy for the Folio. If the required Quarto and supplementary manuscript had been available, they would have sufficed for Jaggard's compositors. If any transcribing at all had been necessary—if, for example, the supplementary manuscript had decayed to such an extent that it would have been too difficult for the compositors to decipher—a transcript of the passages to be added would have sufficed. Moreover, a transcript commissioned specifically for the Folio would not reflect the intensive process of literary sophistication that we have noted throughout the Folio text.

Why, then, was such a transcript prepared? We can probably never know. The simplest answer may be that a private collector was dissatisfied with the mutilated Quarto text and wanted a copy of the full play. Though not a man of the theater, a fact made manifest by the types of revisions made by the scribe, he (or the scribe) was probably acquainted with someone from Shakespeare's company in order to borrow the full manuscript to supplement the Quarto. Moreover, he was probably known to Heminges and Condell for them to remember the transcript in his possession when they were searching for copy for the Folio.

A recent theory by George Walton Williams has much to recommend it. Concurring with Alice Walker's proposal that the 1598 quarto of *1 Henry IV* reflects the same kind of literary sophistication as the Folio text of Part 2, and thus that the two texts derive from manuscripts that were "companion pieces," Williams suggests that a "fair copy of both parts might have been prepared to prove to Oldcastle's angry posterity that their ancestor had been removed from both plays."[10] It is clear from traces of revision in both plays that Falstaff was originally named Oldcastle and that the influential Cobham family had vigorously protested the insult to their eminently respectable ancestor. Before the publication of Part 1 in 1598 and after most, if not all, of Part 2 had been written, both plays were revised to transform Oldcastle into Falstaff, and Harvey and Russell (also influential names at court) into Bardolph and Peto.[11] Thus, Williams suggests, both plays may have been transcribed from Shakespeare's revised foul papers specifically to mollify the "irate, influential, and puritanical" Cobhams.[12] His theory is particularly attractive in that it provides the kind of reader for whom the meticulously edited manuscript underlying the Folio text of Part 2 must have been prepared.

Williams' hypothesis, however, raises several questions. If, as his theory requires, the Cobhams returned the transcript of Part 1 in time for it to serve as copy for the 1598 quarto, why did they retain Part 2? That is, why was the first quarto of Part 1 set from fair copy but the 1600 quarto of Part 2 set from foul papers? Moreover (and Williams acknowledges this problem), the Cobham family line died out shortly after the controversy. Where, then, was the manuscript of Part 2 between 1598 and 1623?

And were the manuscripts underlying these two texts really, as Alice Walker argued, "companion pieces," prepared by the same scribe? The only evidence that she offered to support this

CONCLUSION 177

conclusion is the presence in Part 1 of some unelided forms (such as *is it not* and *vpon it* rather than *is't* and *vpon't*). Such "pedantry in language," she felt, was the same as that found in the Folio text of Part 2.[13] My own comparison of the two texts, however, reveals marked dissimilarity. Part 1 has far more elided forms (such as *whats, thats, weel, shees,* and *twas*) than expanded forms and many colloquial contractions (such as *nere* for *neuer* and *mo* for *more*)—all routinely expanded in the Folio Part 2. Part 1 has much profanity (*what a diuell, O Iesu, before God,* and the like)—all zealously deleted in Part 2. Stage directions in Part 1 are not simplified as they are in Part 2. Where Part 1 gives *Enter prince of Wales, and Sir Iohn Falstaffe,* the scribe of Part 2 would reduce to *Enter Prince Henry and Falstaffe.* Part 1 also has descriptive directions (*Enter a Carrier with a lanterne in his hand*) and directions for sound effects, both eliminated in the Folio Part 2. Finally, there are some dialectal spellings in Part 1 such as *Yedward* and *Ebrew* that the scribe of Part 2 would undoubtedly have regularized, and we consistently find *vile* rather than the scribe's *vilde*. For these reasons, I find no relationship between the two texts, and thus a major premise of Williams' hypothesis is shaky.[14]

But might his theory be valid for the Folio copy of Part 2 alone? The answer to this question largely depends on whether or not one believes that all of the Folio's copy except for the additions and 3.1 was transcribed directly from the Quarto. Williams finds the arguments of Walker, Greg, and Humphreys unconvincing, and his hypothesis requires preparation of the manuscript for the Cobhams at the time of the controversy, well before the printing of the Quarto in 1600. In addition to the evidence discussed in the introductory chapter, I feel that certain unsatisfactory revisions apparently based on Quarto errors make the Folio's dependence on the Quarto highly probable, but the issue is by no means settled.*

* Particularly strong evidence for the Folio's reliance on the Quarto is found, I believe, in the scribe's confusion about the reading of Prince Henry's letter and about "Bardolfes boy," in his treatment of the Drawers scene, and in his faulty revisions of "Other less fine, in karrat" and "the diuel blinds him too." See above, pp. 37–38, 49–50, 42–45, and 166–67.

CONCLUSION

Though the intriguing questions we have considered in this chapter can be given no final answer—questions as to why there was only one quarto, why Heminges and Condell gave Jaggard a transcript, and, indeed, why a transcript should have been made at all—they present no obstacle to an editor in his pursuit of the authoritative text itself. The unresolved questions are really tangential. Of far greater significance are the questions that are raised by a comparison of the Quarto and Folio texts. And most of these, as I have proposed, can be plausibly answered. If the conclusions of the present study are valid, eighty-six readings that have been universally or widely adopted should be rejected. Of these, fifty-nine are sophistications by the scribe, nineteen are corruptions introduced by Compositor B, one is an unnecessary emendation, and seven are Quarto readings that undoubtedly represent characteristic errors by the Quarto compositor and were properly corrected by the scribe.* Some of the proposed new readings would make little difference in the text (for example, *he is* for *he's* and *in* for *into*), but the restoration of Quarto readings that reflect speech patterns, the omission of half-lines introduced by the scribe to regularize verse, and the return to the Quarto staging of three scenes could have considerable impact on production, if not on interpretation.[15]

In the two texts of *2 Henry IV* we are fortunate in having what may be a unique opportunity. On the one hand, we have witness to Shakespeare's foul papers in the Quarto. On the other, in the Folio we have a text that is distinctive in two ways. We know that it was prepared by a transcriber-editor with certain habits and concerns that can be rather precisely defined. We also know that Jaggard's compositors faced special problems leading them to make certain types of revisions that can be rather precisely isolated. By carefully analyzing and classifying all variants, we can

---

* The last seven are discussed in Appendix A. For a detailed summary of readings recommended by the present study and of recent editorial adoptions, see Appendix C. From a survey of twelve influential and/or widely available editions, I classify as "widely adopted" any reading that has been adopted by four or more editors.

learn much: not only about the authority of certain Folio variants in *2 Henry IV*, but also about the types of compositorial corruption to which we must be alert. It is also possible that analysis of the scribe's work on this particular play may raise pertinent questions about other Folio texts thought to be based on transcripts.

One major implication of the present study is already clear. Editors must pay close attention to the specific problems that compositors faced in setting a given play. When dealing with Folio texts that derive from good quartos, they should be especially alert to the possibility that Folio additions, deletions, and even revisions may represent solutions to compositorial problems. In particular, they should be wary of relying on Dover Wilson's principle that compositors are more prone to omission than they are to addition and thus that longer variants should be preferred "when the merits are otherwise fairly evenly balanced." I have found almost no evidence in *2 Henry IV* that Compositor A added words, but Compositor B most certainly did.[16] Until Hinman's breakthrough, Wilson's principle seemed eminently reasonable, and as a result editors have not subjected Folio additions to the intense scrutiny that they now appear to require, especially when they occur in the work of Compositor B. It is a sobering thought to realize that the major burden of setting those Folio texts for which we have no good quartos fell on his shoulders.

APPENDIX A

The Nature of the Copy Underlying Folio Additions

———◆••◆———

Because of the scribe's extensive editing, it is difficult to determine the type of copy underlying the added passages. In the eight additions other than 3.1, we find only one unmistakable error: "Or what hath this bold enterprize bring forth" (1.1.178). The scribe may have substituted his characteristic *hath* (perhaps for *does*, on the grounds that the action was in the past) and then failed to complete his revision. On the other hand, when one is dealing with Compositor B, one hesitates to attribute an error such as *bring* for *brought* or *hath* for *doth* to his copy. Another probable error is found at 4.1.137:

> all their prayers, and loue,
> Were set on *Herford*, whom they doted on,
> And bless'd, and grac'd, and did more then the King.

A few editors accept the Folio's *and did* on the grounds that the structure is elliptical ("and they did so more than for the King"), but Theobald's emendation of *indeed* seems preferable. Here the setting is by Compositor A, so the source of the error is unclear.

One other error in the additions has been widely assumed: Mowbray's insistence that Richard "was forc'd, perforce compell'd to banish" Norfolk (4.1.114). Theobald's emendation of *force* for *forc'd* has been generally adopted. If the scribe misread *force* as *forcd*, we would have yet another instance of Shakespeare's final *e* being misread as a *d*, but is the Folio reading necessarily wrong? It is true that Shakespeare uses *force perforce* adverbially elsewhere, but he uses *perforce* alone far more often. Note, for example, the following:

APPENDIX A

But she, perforce, withholds the loved boy
(*A Midsummer Night's Dream*, 2.1.26)
And made him to resign his crown perforce
(*3 Henry VI*, 1.1.142)
Rain added to a river that is rank
Perforce will force it overflow the bank.
(*Venus and Adonis*, 71-72)

The Folio reading is probably accurate. The comma after *forc'd* indicates, if not Shakespeare's own punctuation, at least the scribe's understanding of the line. Mowbray is being doubly emphatic: Richard "was forced—perforce compelled—to banish him." Neither the one definite nor the two possible errors tell us anything about the nature of the scribe's copy. Only in 3.1, for which we have the independent witness of Qb, can we hope to detect any traces of the elusive supplementary manuscript.

In the Folio version of 3.1, we find familiar evidence of the scribe's sophistications: the substitution of *vilde* for *vile* (15) and of *which* for *who* (84). We also find several corrections of Qb's errors that could derive from logic alone if the errors were indeed in the scribe's manuscript. More probably the Folio's corrections reflect his superior ability to read and reproduce his copy accurately: *Mast* for *masse* (18), *Billowes* for *pillowes* (22), *nature of* for *natures or* (81), and *of* for *or* (87). In addition, the scribe correctly punctuates "When *Richard*, with his Eye, brim-full of Teares," whereas Qb reads "his eye-brimme full of teares"(67). That the Qb compositor confused a comma for a hyphen seems doubtful in light of the clarity of Shakespeare's commas in the addition in Hand D to *Sir Thomas More*. In the foul papers the line probably had no punctuation. The scribe was merely better equipped to interpret the line. None of the above changes helps to identify the scribe's manuscript because it is impossible to determine which of Qb's many errors were the compositor's and which, if any, were found in his copy. It is equally impossible to determine whether the scribe's corrections were his own or whether he found the correct readings in his manuscript.

There are, however, a few clues suggesting that the scribe's manuscript for 3.1—and thus the supplementary manuscript we are seeking to identify—was not corrected. One has already been cited at lines 26-27:

Q: Canst thou, ô partiall sleepe, giue them repose,
    To the wet season in an howre so rude. . . .
F: *thy repose*
    wet Sea-Boy

Neither of these revisions in the Folio satisfies; both are probably the result of the scribe's characteristic logic. He rejected *them* on grammatical grounds and did his best to invent a word beginning with *sea* that could represent someone to whom sleep can give repose. Probably the line he saw before him was exactly what the Quarto compositor saw. A comparison of the two versions of line 11 may be even more telling:

Qb: And husht with buzzing night-flies to thy slumber
F: And huisht with bussing Night, flyes to thy slumber

Huisht and *bussing* both suggest Shakespeare's foul papers: *huisht*, because of its occurrence in Q1 of *Richard II* (1.1.53), and *bussing*, because of Shakespeare's known habit of substituting *s* for *z*, as in *mussel* for *muzzel* at 4.5.131 (also in Q1 of *Much Ado* at 1.3.33). It should be noted that 3.1 was set by Compositor A, a man who methodically adhered to his copy. Such curious spellings as *huisht* and *bussing*, as well as *Pallads* in line 10, cannot be dismissed as typographical errors. Nor can they be explained as A's misreadings. A professional scribe could not be so grossly illegible. He may himself have misread *pallats* to give *Pallads*, but *huisht* and *bussing* were probably in his manuscript.* *Huisht* was an obsolete spelling of *hushed* still found in the last quarter of the sixteenth century, and the scribe may have assumed that *bussing* was accu-

* The retention of these three irregular spellings suggests an interesting possibility. Was the scribe more faithful to his copy when he was working with the author's manuscript than when he was working with printed copy, which he knew could be corrupted by printing-house errors?

rate. The image of night gently kissing a man to sleep does have a certain appeal, though the context requires *buzzing*.

One other possible clue deserves at least brief mention. At 3.1.71, we find the scribe reproducing the known Shakespearean spelling of *Bullingbrooke* where the Qb compositor uses the historically accurate *Bolingbroke*. All other instances of the name occur in passages that were added in the Folio, and all are spelled *Bullingbrooke*. The influence of Shakespeare's autograph may again be suggested.

If the Folio's version of 3.1 is accepted as an independent witness to Shakespeare's foul papers, I believe that three, and possibly four, Folio readings that have been widely rejected should now be adopted. Simmes' Compositor A, the man who set both Qa and the new pages for Qb, was prone to several types of error. He had a marked tendency to add a terminal *s* and to substitute connectives, a fact that gives warrant to the Folio's reading of line 81: "Figuring the nature of the Times deceas'd" (Qb: *natures or*). He had an even stronger tendency to drop the terminal letters of words. In his setting of *2 Henry IV*, the following are typical examples: *you* for *your* (1.1.164), *tapestrie* for *tapestries* (2.1.147), *master* for *masters* (2.4.266), and *accommodate* for *accommodated* (3.2.66). Apparently this particular error was characteristic of all his work. In setting Q2 of *Richard II*, he dropped a terminal *s* ten times.* The same kind of error is found in 3.1. At line 59, he set *in two yeare after*, although the context confirms the Folio's reading: "Tis not tenne yeeres gone . . . in two yeeres after. . . . It is but eight yeeres since . . ." (lines 57–60). In line 2, the King orders that Surrey and Warwick read "these letters" before consulting with him, but at line 36 in Qb we find reference to "the letter."

These errors are so flagrant that most editors have adopted the Folio's corrections, but on the assumption that Qb is the only witness to Shakespeare's foul papers in 3.1 they have rejected the

---

* See Alan E. Craven's list of his literal errors in "Simmes' Compositor A and Five Shakespeare Quartos," *Studies in Bibliography*, 26 (1973), 53.

Folio's addition of -s to *beginning, sound,* and *clamour.* Shakespeare often failed to resolve agreement in lines such as the following (82–85):

Q: a man may prophecie,
With a neere ayme of the main chance of things,
As yet not come to life, who in their seedes,
And weake beginning lie intreasured.
F: *weake beginnings*

It is conceivable that the singular *beginning* is Shakespeare's error and that the scribe's attention to such logical details (different "things" have different "seedes" and thus different "beginnings") led to the correction. But what reason could the scribe have had for adding *s*'s in lines 14 and 24 of 3.1 unless they were in his copy?

Qb: And lulld with sound of sweetest melody?
F: *sounds*
Qb: With deaffing clamour in the slippery clouds
F: *Clamors*

One consideration points to the authority of the Folio's "sounds of sweetest Melodie." In similar contexts, Shakespeare uses the plural: "sounds of woe" (*Much Ado About Nothing,* 2.3.68) and "sounds of music" (*Merchant of Venice,* 5.1.55). He uses the singular for the sound of a voice (*Measure for Measure,* 5.1.327), of a tongue (*Merchant of Venice,* 1.1.109; *Coriolanus,* 1.6.26), and of words (*King John,* 3.1.230, 3.3.51). *Sounds* is probably authorial. No such evidence supports the Folio's reading of *Clamors,* but nowhere does the scribe show a tendency to make changes without a purpose. In light of the tendency of Simmes' Compositor A to drop the terminal *s,* I would recommend adoption of all three of these plurals.*

   * These typical errors of Simmes' Compositor A raise questions about several Quarto readings elsewhere in the play: for example, "By which his grace must mete the liues of other [F: *others*]" (4.4.77); "From enemies, heauens [F: *Heauen*] keep your maiesty" (4.4.94); "tis merry in hal when beards wags [F: *wagge*] all" (5.3.34); and "How ill white heires becomes [F: *become*] a foole and iester" (5.5.48). In recent years, conservative editing has led to the increasing adoption of

A fourth adoption from the Folio that should be given serious consideration is the substitution of *deaff'ning* for *deaffing* (24). The only occurrence of related forms is *deafning* in *Pericles* (3.1.5) and *deaffing* in *Two Noble Kinsmen* (5.3.9), and such evidence is insufficient. Possibly relevant are the many occurrences of an analogous word. We find *threatning* and *threatening* throughout the canon, but never *threating*. The Quarto compositor's habits of dropping final letters, omitting minor words, changing single letters, and dropping medial letters (*pince* for *prince*, 2.2.174, and *snepe* for *sneape*, 2.1.122) make his omission of the *n* possible. If one accepts the hypothesis that the Folio version of 3.1 is an independent witness to Shakespeare's foul papers, the superior skill of the scribe in reading his copy as compared to the inaccuracy of the Quarto compositor, together with Folio Compositor A's recognized faithfulness to his copy, should shift the weight of authority to the Folio readings in this scene unless identifiable scribal corruption is detected.

---

such awkward Quarto readings, but Craven's study of Simmes' Compositor A requires that, in each instance, the possibility of compositor error be considered. For example, in the first two lines quoted above, the context recommends the Folio variants: *others* and *Heauen*. (I doubt that an experienced actor would write such an ugly mouthful as "From enemies, heavens keep you majesty.") The second two Quarto readings—*beards wags* and *heires becomes*—are more problematical. The first seems quite fitting for the drunken Silence, but the second fits neither the character of the new King nor the sound of the line. Undoubtedly Simmes' Compositor A added a terminal *s*—but to *heire* or *become*? Bibliographical evidence may be of some help here. Elsewhere in the Quarto he consistently spelled *haire* (1.2.24, 160, 242, and 2.4.254). Note, then, his setting of the King's first two lines addressed to Falstaff:

> I know thee not old man, fall to thy praiers,
> How ill white heires becomes a foole and iester. . . .

Was the spelling *heires* influenced by his copy, and did Shakespeare himself echo *praiers* with *heires*?

APPENDIX B

The Placement of Stage Directions in Elizabethan Manuscripts

When W. W. Greg published his important study of *Dramatic Documents from the Elizabethan Playhouses* in 1931, his concern with the exact placement of stage directions was necessarily minimal, and to my knowledge his conclusions have not been carefully reviewed. The present study suggests that further work is needed, not only to correct possible misconceptions but, more importantly, to throw light on the type of copy that may underlie certain published plays. The following brief notes merely offer some preliminary observations and suggest questions that deserve further investigation.

The two extant manuscripts by Anthony Munday are of particular significance because they offer the only extensive evidence of the authorial habits of playwrights at the end of the sixteenth century. Greg's treatment of Munday's placement of stage directions can be easily misunderstood if one does not consult the documents in question. Of the manuscript of *John a Kent* (c. 1590), Greg says, "Entrances are centered with few exceptions: exits as usual are on the right; other directions appear indifferently in either margin, rarely in the center" (I, 240). The statement is true, but it is an inaccurate reflection of Munday's practice. Munday wrote a large hand, so that verse lines take approximately four inches, leaving no more than one and one-half inches in the right margin free for directions. In *John a Kent*, most stage directions are very long because they are descriptive. As a result, almost all directions are the length of a line of verse or longer and thus are centered. There are only three short internal entries in the play. One on fol. 5^a is set to the right. Another on 5^a is centered because there was no space to the right of the line preceding, and Munday was always careful to have a directed entry precede the sign of entry in the dialogue. One on 8^b is centered at the top of a page because he had no space to place it to the right of the preceding line at the bottom of the previous page. Two longer internal entrances are staggered on two lines to the right (fols. 5^b and 8^b) and one on three lines to the left (fol. 4^b) when no space was available to the right. In short, Greg is right in saying that "entrances are centered with few exceptions," but the exceptions indicate that Munday might normally have preferred to place internal entrances laterally if he had had the space.

A better guide to Munday's practice is his work in *Sir Thomas More* (1590–93 ?), because there we find almost twenty internal entries shorter than a line of verse. Of this manuscript, Greg says, "Normally the longer entrances are centered but shorter ones are often noted on the right" (I. 247). The important distinction in *Sir Thomas More* is not, however, between long and short directions but between opening scene directions and internal entries. The former are invariably centered. The latter, however, are, with only one exception, set to the right. Though Greg's brief conclusions about both plays are factually accurate, they imply that Munday "normally" centered all directions unless they were short. On the contrary, he normally set internal entrances laterally unless they were too long or no space was available. Again, as in *John a Kent*, we find some longer internal entries staggered to the right and left (fols. 10^b, 20^b, and 21^a). Munday, then, preferred to set internal entrances laterally.

Greg's statement about Hand C's placement of directions in *Sir Thomas More* is similarly misleading. "Hand C's usage," he states, "is the same as Munday's" (I. 247). If Munday's usage was to center all directions unless they were short, as Greg has implied, the conclusion is wrong. We have few directions by Hand C in his added passages, but those few reflect Munday's actual practice we have just noted. Hand C centers opening scene directions but

THE PLACEMENT OF STAGE DIRECTIONS   189

sets internal entrances laterally, staggering even such a long direction as "*Enter The Shreiue w*th / *Fawkner a ruffin* / *and officers*" (fol. 12ᵃ).

The only other authorial manuscript contemporaneous with Shakespeare is probably *Charlemagne* (c. 1600), of which Greg says, "entrance directions are centered. ... All other entrances, which are numerous, are marked in the right margin" (I. 262). Here Greg maintains the necessary distinction between opening directions and internal directions, and his conclusion is accurate. The practice of this author, then, was the same as that of Munday and of Hand C in *Sir Thomas More*.

Our greatest help in determining the kind of copy underlying a Shakespeare play would, of course, be Shakespeare's own practice. Unfortunately, the addition to *Sir Thomas More* in Hand D contains only one internal entrance and it is too long to set to the right of the preceding lines. Given the size of Shakespeare's capital letters, the direction would have had to be staggered on three lines, but the preceding dialogue did not allow the necessary room. It is impossible to know how Shakespeare would have placed shorter internal entries, though one notes that most of his verse lines do allow adequate space for brief or staggered directions.

This preliminary study, brief as it is, indicates need for close attention to the types of directions (whether opening entrances, internal entrances, or incidental directions) as well as to the spacing problems the author or scribe faced at the point of a given direction. One should be especially wary of Greg's reference to the treatment of "main" or "important" entrances. Thus far, I cannot see that treatment varied according to the dramatic importance of the characters entering. For example, Greg states that the scribe who wrote *Richard II or Thomas of Woodstock* (c. 1591–95) "wrote central directions between rules for the main entrances, whether or not a new scene was intended. Entrances requiring only a short direction are normally marked in the left margin, very rarely in the right" (I. 253). "Main entrances" is confusing. Opening directions and long internal entrances are centered, but many dramatically important entrances are set to the left. (They are not set to the right because of lack of space.)

Thus far, then, my study suggests that the normal practice for authors and scribes was to treat opening directions and internal directions differently: centering opening scene directions but setting all internal directions, including even important entrances, to the right when space permitted.

APPENDIX C

Recommended Adoptions

The following lists offer a summary of recommended readings that have been rejected by four or more editions in current use. Editions consulted, together with identifying abbreviations, are as follows:

K   George Lyman Kittredge, *The Complete Works* (Boston, 1936)
W   John Dover Wilson, New Cambridge edition (Cambridge, 1946)
A   Peter Alexander, *The Complete Works* (London, 1951)
C   Hardin Craig, *The Complete Works* (Chicago, 1951)
P   Allen Chester, Pelican edition (Baltimore, 1957)
M   John Munro, *The London Shakespeare*, Vol. IV (New York, 1957)
S   Norman N. Holland, Signet Classics edition (New York, 1965)
H   A. R. Humphreys, Arden edition (London, 1966)
R   Irving Ribner and George Lyman Kittredge, *The Complete Works*, (Waltham, Mass., 1971)
B   David Bevington and Hardin Craig, *The Complete Works* (Glenview, Ill., 1973)
E   G. Blakemore Evans, *The Riverside Shakespeare* (Boston, 1974)
D   P. H. Davison, New Penguin edition (Harmondsworth, 1977)

The summary is of readings discussed in the present study only, a study that does not pretend to be exhaustive. Its purpose has been to establish the principles governing an edition of *2 Henry IV*, not to establish a definitive text. Similarly, the survey of adoptions is not comprehensive. The twelve editions have been selected because they provide a representative sample of influential and/or widely available tests.

An index to my discussions of the readings is provided by page numbers in the right column.

Appendix C

Recommended Adoptions Based on the Quarto

Line no.	Recommended Reading Based on Q	Rejected Reading Based on F	F Adoptions	See Pages
1.1.28	who I sent	whom I sent	All but E,M,S	122
96	slain	slain, say so	All but D	152
126	So soon	Too soon	All but D,E,M,S	138–39
1.2.36	rascal—yea forsooth, knave!—	rascally yea— forsooth knave	All but A,S	140
38	smoothy-pates	smooth-pates	All but D,E	123
47–49	it—where's Bardolph?—and yet	light him. Where's Bardolph?	All	130
50	in Smithfield	into Smithfield	All but D	119
98	of an ague	of age	All but E	80–81
98–99	of time in you	of time	All but E,M,P,S	80–81
143	my waist slender	my waist slenderer	All but S	125
160	in your face	on your face	B,C,K,R,W	123
169	bear'ad*	bearherd	All but A,E,K,S,W	122
170	and his quick	and hath his quick	B,C,P,S	125–26
203	severed you	severed you and Prince Harry	All but A,E,M,W	126
1.3.26	Hotspur's cause	Hotspur's case	All but D,E,W	139
28	air and promise	air on promise	All but A,D,E,H,S	139–40
78	need not to be	need not be	All but E,S	148–49
84	against the French	'gainst the French	All but A,E,M,S	141
2.1.14	most beastly	and that most beastly	A,B,C,P,R,S	130–31
22	view	vice	All	140–41
45	arrest you	arrest you, Sir John	All but D,E	128
68	hang'st thou upon	hang'st upon	B,K,P,R,W	141
2.2.15–16	with these	viz. these	All	139
82	petticoat	new petticoat	All but D,E,S	102
94	this blossom	this good blossom	B,C,K,P,R	102
118	but the letter	but to the letter	B,C,K,P	125
2.4.42	diseases make	diseases make them	All but E,M,S	126
116	shall not hardly†	shall hardly	B,C,K,P	122

* A,K,S: *berod* (as in the Quarto). E: *berrord* (as in 2.1.40 of *Much Ado*). W: *bear'ard* (on the basis of *Berard* and *Bearard* in *2 Henry VI*, 5.1.149 and 210). Only in *Shrew* do we find *Beare-heard* (Ind. 2.20). In the other four occurrences, the endings of *-od*, *-ord*, and *-ard* suggest that Falstaff is using a clipped pronunciation of *bearward*, rather than *bearherd*. An accurate modern spelling for *berod—bear'a'd—*would be misleading to an actor. Thus I suggest *bear'ad* as an accurate guide to pronunciation.

† S: *not hardily* (from the Quarto's *hardely*).

RECOMMENDED ADOPTIONS

Line no.	Recommended Reading Based on Q	Rejected Reading Based on F	F Adoptions	See Pages
167	Trojant*	Trojan	B,C,K,P,R,S	133
174	Men like dogs	Die men like dogs	All	134–35
184	no things†	nothing	B,C,K,P	133
301	of me now	of me even now	All but D,S	139
321	with thee	with him	B,C,K,P	129
346	vict'lers	victuallers	B,C,D,P,S,W	131
3.1.84	who in their seeds	which in their seeds	B,C,K,P	122
3.2.8	woosel	ousel	All but D,E,H,K,M	132
30	Scoggin's	Skogan's	B,C,K,P,R	133
38	Samforth	Stamford	All	132–33
40, 52	Dooble	Double	All but K	133
86	Soccard	Surecard	All	167
134	shadows fill	shadows to fill	B,C,K,P,R,W	99
175–76	prick Bullcalf	prick me Bullcalf	All but D,E,S	102
196	Shallow	Shallow. No more of that.	All but D,S	108–9
4.2.8	iron man talking	iron man	All but E,S,W	141
48	hold his quarrel	hold this quarrel	All but E	126–27
117	rebellion	rebellion and such acts as yours.	All	152–53
4.3.2	place?	place, I pray?	A,B,C,K,P,R	128
86	had the wit	had but the wit	All but D,E,S	123
4.4.32	[meting] charity‡	melting charity	All but E,S	168
33	he is flint	he's flint	All but A,B,D,E	141
39	time and scope	line and scope	All but D,E,H,P,S	127
52	accompanied?	accompanied? Canst thou tell that?	All	154–55
120	through.	through and will break out.	All	155–56
132	chamber.	chamber. Softly pray.	All	153–54
4.5.49	Majesty?	Majesty? How fares your Grace?	All but D	154–55
74	tolling	culling	M,R,S,W	159
75	om.	The virtuous sweets,	All but D	156–58

* A,E: *Troiant*. D,H: *Troyant*. I am puzzled by these four adoptions in modern spelling editions. Neither Alexander nor Evans adopts the Renaissance *Aiax* in *Troilus and Cressida*.

† A,D,H,M,R,W: *nothings*.

‡ S: *meeting* (as in the Quarto). This is probably an error, for Holland does not annotate the unique adoption.

APPENDIX C

Line no.	Recommended Reading Based on Q	Rejected Reading Based on F	F Adoptions	See Pages
81	sickness [have]	sickness hath	All but D,E,H,M,W	208n14
107	thoughts, / Whom	thoughts, / Which	All but E,M,W	122
177	om.	O my son,	All but D	105–8
220	om.	My gracious Liege,	All but D	105–8
5.1.24	lost at	lost the other day at	All but D,E	98
24	Hunkly	Hinckley	All	131
49	have little	have but a very little	All but D,E	98
51	I beseech you	I beseech your worship	B,C,H,M,W	98
66	observing him	observing of him	All but D,E,M,P,S	125
5.2.16	of he	of him	B,C,K,P,R	122
5.3.34	beards wags	beards wag	All but D,E,H	185n
5.4.5	whipping cheer	whipping cheer enough	All but D,E,S	101
6	or two killed	or two lately killed	All but D,E,S	101
9	child I go with	child I now go with	A,B,C,K,P,R	101
11–12	I would make	He would make	All but D,E,S	129
5.5.5	Master Shallow	Master Robert Shallow	All but D,E,S	101–2
28	'tis in every	'tis all in every	All	134
5.5.81	cannot perceive	cannot well perceive	B,C,K,P,R	103
81	you give	you should give	B,C,K,P,R	103
96	*spero contenta*	*spero me contenta**	A,D,H,W	133–34
Ep. 24	seen in	seen before in	All but D,E,S	111

Recommended Adoptions Based on the Folio

Line no.	Recommended Reading Based on F	Rejected Reading Based on Q	Q Adoptions	See Pages
3.1.14	sounds	sound	All	184–85
24	deaf'ning†	deafing	All but B,C,K,P	186
24	clamors	clamor	All	184–85
81	nature of	natures [of]‡	A,D,E,W	184
85	beginnings	beginning	A,D,E,M,S	184–85
4.1.114	forced—perforce compelled—	om.	(None adopts F)§	181–82
4.4.77	lives of others	lives of other	A,D,E,H,R,W	185n
5.5.48	hairs become	hairs becomes	D,E,H,M,S	185n

* No one adopts the Folio's *spera* and *contento*.
† B,C,P: *deafening*.
‡ W: *natures or* (as in the Quarto).
§ All editors adopt Theobald's emendation *force perforce*.

Notes

Chapter I

1. Line references are to the Riverside edition of G. Blakemore Evans (Boston, 1974).
2. *The Second Part of the History of Henry IV*, corr. ed. (1953; rpt. Cambridge, 1968), p. 116.
3. The ensuing discussion of textual matters is based largely on the following: W. W. Greg's *The Shakespeare First Folio* (Oxford, 1955), pp. 266–76; Matthias A. Shaaber's detailed discussion of the text appended to the New Variorum edition of the play (Philadelphia, 1940), pp. 463–515, and his paper on "The Folio Text of *2 Henry IV*," *Shakespeare Quarterly*, 6 (1955), 135–44; Alice Walker's *Textual Problems of the First Folio* (Cambridge, 1953), pp. 94–120; J. Dover Wilson's textual note to his Cambridge edition of the play as corrected in 1953, pp. 115–23; and the excellent summary of A. R. Humphreys in his introduction to the New Arden edition (London, 1966), pp. lxviii–lxxxiv.
4. "*2 Henry IV* ought to have been an Elizabethan 'best-seller'" (Alfred Hart, *Shakespeare and the Homilies* [Melbourne, 1934], p. 176). See also Shaaber, New Variorum edition, p. 497, and Humphreys, New Arden edition, p. xiii.
5. A. W. Pollard, "Variant Settings in *II Henry IV*," *Times Literary Supplement*, 21 Oct. 1920, p. 680. John Hazel Smith believes that the leaf was misplaced among the leaves of *Much Ado About Nothing*, which was printed immediately after *2 Henry IV* in the same shop and by the same compositor. See "The Cancel in the Quarto of *2 Henry IV* Revisited," *Shakespeare Quarterly*, 15 (1964), 173–78.
6. For a full discussion, see Hart, *Shakespeare and the Homilies*, pp. 154–218. Greg's rejoinder should also be consulted (*First Folio*, pp. 273–75).
7. "Sincklo" is, in fact, the name of an actor in Shakespeare's company. Shakespeare probably envisaged Sincklo in the role of the unnamed beadle as he wrote the scene. From the epithets hurled at the beadle in 5.4—"thou damnd tripe visagde rascall," "thou paper-facde villaine," "you starude blood-hounde," "you thinne thing" (8, 10, 27, 30)—one gathers that Sincklo was a pale skeleton of a man, ideal for many comic parts.
8. In addition to setting most of Q1 of *Richard II*, Simmes' Compositor A set all of Q2, which was a straight reprint of Q1. By collating the two editions, Alan E. Craven has demonstrated that 155 substantive variants are introduced

in Q2, only 6 of which are corrections of Q1 errors. On the basis of his study, Craven classifies the types of errors to which Simmes' A was prone. When we turn to Qb of *2 Henry IV* we find exactly the same types of errors in the same compositor's resetting of the material cancelled in Qa. See "Simmes' Compositor A and Five Shakespeare Quartos," *Studies in Bibliography*, 26 (1973), 37–60.

9. Matthias A. Shaaber, discussed below. Shaaber's detailed lists of Folio variants remain useful, though the bases of his classification are open to question (New Variorum, pp. 499–507).

10. Moreover, punctuation is totally revised. Throughout the following, however, I shall largely ignore questions of punctuation. There is too much evidence that punctuation was at the mercy of compositors to use it as evidence in determining textual questions. Joseph Moxon, our principal authority for matters pertaining to English printing-houses in the seventeenth century, specifies that it is "*a task and duty incumbent on the* Compositor . . . *to discern and amend the bad* Spelling *and* Pointing *of his Copy* . . ." (*Mechanick Exercises* [1683–84], ed. Herbert Davis and Harry Carter [London, 1958], p. 192). There is abundant evidence that Elizabethan compositors obeyed the same injunction.

11. New Variorum edition, p. 511.

12. Dover Wilson endorsed Shaaber's position in the 1946 New Cambridge edition of the play, but even he recognized a minimum of nine common verbal errors, errors he attributed largely to coincidental misreadings by the Quarto compositor and the scribe (p. 117). In *The Shakespeare First Folio*, Greg responded to Wilson's argument, explaining why the common errors could not be dismissed (pp. 270–71).

13. In addition, Walker cites the shift from *sawcines* to *sawciness* at 2.1.113, 123, but the Folio compositor's need to justify his lines may explain this particular coincidence. She also makes a case on the basis of the spelling *maner* at 2.1.110 in both texts (*Textual Problems*, p. 103). In the Quarto, the compositor used the shortened spelling to fit this last word in at the end of a line, whereas, as she notes, the word appears in the Folio at the beginning of a line. This is true, but the Folio compositor at this point was, as we shall see, under even greater pressure to compress his copy. Line 111 is jammed. In order to squeeze in the final word (*not*), he may have removed one *n* in *manner*, the only place in the line where he could gain needed space. For further discussion, see George Walton Williams, "The Text of *2 Henry IV*: Facts and Problems," *Shakespeare Studies* 9 (1976), 182n.

14. Common errors in the attribution of speeches at 2.2.126, 3.2.149, and 5.5.17 and 19 are also frequently cited as signs of the Folio's dependence on the Quarto, but they could result from dependence on a common source.

15. In private correspondence, T. H. Howard-Hill has suggested that *Amurah* could have been a spelling variant for *Amurath*, as *Goliah* was for *Goliath* (see *Merry Wives*, 5.1.22). The possibility should be considered, but the common *Goliah* variant is well documented, whereas *Amurah* is not. Moreover,

pronunciation suggests that the *Goliah* variant has more justification than would *Amurah*. *Goliath* is accented on the second syllable, so that the vowel of the final syllable easily slurs into the schwa. The final syllable of *Amurath* is given secondary stress, suggesting that the *-th* would normally have been articulated.

16. The three errors are not, however, typical of Compositor B's work. His substitutions are usually logical and bear at least some relation to the word in his copy: e.g., *head* for *hard*, *able* for *armed*, *the* for *that*, or *knolling* for *tolling* *2 Henry IV*, 1.1.36, 44, 55, 103). *Ioyne* for *win* is uncharacteristic of him. Typographical error probably cannot account for the repeated error of *Amurah*, nor can either typographical or memorial error account for *Couitha*.

17. I began studying the play by collating the two texts and attempting to enter all Folio variants in my facsimile of the Quarto, but quickly gave up. My annotated text omits all changes in punctuation, all substitutions to replace expurgated profanity, and all repeated revisions of colloquialisms such as the spelling out of contractions and the substituting of *he* for *a*. Even so, the copy is almost illegible in places. (And the Elizabethan annotator would not have been blessed with a fine-line ball-point pen.)

18. "A Definitive Text of Shakespeare: Problems and Methods," in *Studies in Shakespeare*, ed. Arthur D. Matthews and Clark M. Emery (Coral Gables, Fla., 1953), p. 26.

19. Pp. lxxxi–lxxxii. Humphreys' conclusions have been countered by two recent theories. The more attractive, that of George Walton Williams, is reserved for discussion in the concluding chapter (pp. 176–77). The second theory is proposed by Peter Davison in the New Penguin edition of the play (Harmondsworth, 1977), pp. 287–96. Other theories do not, he believes, account for "the crux of the problem": "the excision, wholly or in part, of some twenty-five Quarto stage directions that are superior to those remaining in the Folio" (p. 290). He thus proposes that the Folio copy was an "assembled text," reconstructed from actors' parts and transcribed specifically for printing in the Folio. As Davison notes, an actor's part gave both his speeches and his cues, but it did not name the speakers of cues. Therefore, he suggests, the scribe preparing the transcript also used a copy of the Quarto, but primarily as a guide to the order of speeches. Under these circumstances, he believes, it would be fairly easy for the scribe to miss entries and instructions for sound effects that are in the Quarto.

I find the theory unconvincing for several reasons. In the first place, the theory of "assembled texts" is, in itself, highly improbable. I shall not repeat here the arguments of Chambers and Greg (*William Shakespeare* [Oxford, 1930], I, 153–55; *First Folio*, pp. 156–58) but turn to the specific improbability that, in the absence of better copy, the Folio text of *2 Henry IV* was so assembled as a last resort. If, as Davison's theory requires, Jaggard had a copy of the Quarto, the only supplementary material needed would be copy for 3.1 (omitted in Qa) and for the eight passages added in the Folio. Why would a scribe be commissioned to undertake the long and arduous task of reconstructing the entire play from actors' parts? A transcript of the additions and 3.1—less than three hundred lines—would have sufficed. And if the transcript was made solely to serve as copy for the Folio, why does the Folio text give evidence of extensive revision to expurgate profanity and to meet sophisticated literary standards? Any theory about Jaggard's copy for *2 Henry IV* must account for this curious phenomenon, but Davison offers no explanation.

The basic assumption on which Davison bases his theory—the omission of "some twenty-five" essential stage directions that are in the Quarto—is also open to question. As I shall argue in Chapter II, the scribe was interested only in the literary aspects of the play. He routinely cut mutes, descriptive stage directions, and instructions for sound effects, and he eliminated other stage directions in the process of revising two scenes. Given his method of working, I find only three omissions of essential Quarto stage directions that need explaining: two exits (at 2.1.162 and 4.1.180) and the entrance of Davy at the opening of 5.3. In a text in which so many directions are missing, incomplete, or inaccurate, I doubt that these three omissions are significant.

Davison's theory that some Folio additions may be actors' interpolations is also problematic. The few additions that he cites may sound like actors' interpolations, but there are many more additions that cannot be so explained. Moreover, it is doubtful that actors would have written interpolations into their parts. As we all know from having seen productions of Shakespeare's plays, self-indulgent and careless actors often slip unauthorized words into their speeches, but I have never known one to write them into his copy of the script. In light of Shakespeare's annoyance at the "villainous" license of clowns who spoke more than was "set down for them" (*Hamlet*, 3.2.38–45), would his actors have had the temerity to commit their folly to paper, and to an official company document at that?

20. (1935; rpt. Oxford, 1970), pp. 57, 49. Simpson himself provides an interesting bit of evidence indicating that copy was not "always" returned. When Ralph Brooke charged that Jaggard alone was responsible for the many errors in the 1619 printing of his *Catalogue and Succession of the Kings* ..., Jaggard responded in the preliminary pages of another work published three years later. It was true, he said, that Brooke had been unable to come to the printing house because of illness, but proofs and "reviews" were regularly sent to him for correction. Thus any errors remaining in the book were the author's, not the printer's. And, Jaggard crowed, he still retained the original manuscript and could prove it (pp. 6–7). At least this one manuscript was neither returned nor destroyed.

21. The name of Ralph Crane, originally proposed by Quincy Adams, keeps recurring in discussions of the unknown scribe. In *Ralph Crane and Some Shakespeare First Folio Comedies* (Charlottesville, Va., 1972), T. H. Howard-Hill analyzes Crane's work in his extant manuscripts and in the five Folio comedies

that were based on his transcripts. Some of Crane's characteristics are, indeed, reflected in the Folio setting of *2 Henry IV*: for example, his lavish use of hyphens and parentheses and his use of apostrophes to indicate the omission of words as in *'saue* for *God saue* and *'pray* for *I pray*. In view of all current evidence, however, I doubt the attribution. The erratic and inaccurate "massed entrances" of the Folio *2 Henry IV* are totally unlike those in *The Two Gentlemen of Verona*, *The Merry Wives of Windsor*, and *The Winter's Tale*. As I shall argue in the next chapter, I believe that most of the massed entrances in *2 Henry IV* are merely scribal errors, resulting from the scribe's misunderstanding of the action, rather than a Crane-like attempt to follow the model of the Jonson Folio. Moreover, the Folio comedies based on Crane transcripts retain the same types of colloquialisms and contractions that are rigorously eliminated in *2 Henry IV*: *moe*, *nere*, *for't*, *Ile*, *i'th*, and the like. If Crane was responsible for this transcript, he must have been given instructions at odds with his usual practices. For further discussion, see Walker, *Textual Problems*, pp. 107–8.

Chapter II

1. For example, see Greg, *First Folio*, p. 269.
2. In the addition to *Sir Thomas More* thought to be in Shakespeare's hand, a directed entry for the Lord Mayor, Surrey, and Shrewsbury omits the most important entrant: More himself.
3. Unless otherwise noted, quotations in this chapter are from the Quarto. Obvious typographical errors have been silently corrected when they do not affect the argument.
4. For similar instances in which a scribe seriously misunderstood staging, see Fredson Bowers' discussion of Edward Knight's errors in transcribing the promptbook of *Beggars Bush* ("*Beggars Bush*: A Reconstructed Prompt-Book and Its Copy," *Studies in Bibliography*, 27 [1974], 122–23).
5. An early theory that massed entrances were taken from backstage "plots" has been convincingly refuted by E. K. Chambers (*William Shakespeare*, I, 154; also see Greg, *First Folio*, p. 157). Massed entrances, moreover, are not the same as the anticipatory stage directions we find in some promptbooks: warnings to an actor, only a few lines before his entrance, that he be ready backstage. In short, they do not derive from the playhouse, nor could they serve a purpose backstage. Howard-Hill believes that Crane introduced them for "no conceivable reason other than his choice to follow the model of Jonson's Folio" (*Ralph Crane*, p. 80).
6. Humphreys, New Arden edition, p. 95.
7. Greg's analysis of the placement of stage directions in *Dramatic Documents from the Elizabethan Playhouse* (2 vols. [London, 1931]) is brief and at times misleading. Greg can give the impression that central placement of entrances was more common than lateral. For further discussion, see Appendix B, "The

Placement of Stage Directions in Elizabethan Manuscripts." In his Jacobean transcripts, Ralph Crane wrote all internal entrances to the right of the dialogue after he had finished writing the main text. See Howard-Hill, *Ralph Crane*, pp. 25–26.

8. The long prose lines of Hand D in *Sir Thomas More* suggest that Shakespeare's prose dialogue left little room in the right margin for stage directions.

9. In *Dramatic Documents*, Greg stated that "naturally an author will place a direction exactly at the point where it belongs," space permitting, but that the bookkeeper often moved the entrance a few lines earlier to warn actors backstage (I, 216–17). There is some evidence that authors themselves often wrote anticipatory entrances. On fol. 5^a of *Sir Thomas More*, for example, Munday placed the entrance of a messenger two lines before he is addressed. When space allowed, he usually placed a direction at least one line before the dialogue gives sign of entry. In *Thomas of Woodstock* the scribe may have reflected authorial practice in setting several anticipatory entrances. For example, a two-line entrance is staggered beside lines 1706–7 although the "here comes" line is 1709.

10. Shakespeare was typically inconsistent in his speech prefixes in *2 Henry IV*. Eighteen uses of the prefix *Iohn* for Falstaff survive in the Quarto.

11. *Textual Problems*, pp. 104–5.

12. *Textual Problems*, pp. 115–16.

13. Kempe would not be wasted in so small a part. He could double in other comic roles, most notably the role of Shallow. Dover Wilson suggests that the stage direction refers to Will Kempe as Falstaff, who passes over the rear stage at that moment hastening to the "jordan," but few have found the explanation convincing (New Cambridge edition, p. 157).

Chapter III

1. *Textual Problems*, pp. 119–20.

2. See "Cast-off Copy for the First Folio of Shakespeare," *Shakespeare Quarterly*, 6 (1955), 259–73, and *The Printing and Proof-Reading of the First Folio of Shakespeare*, 2 vols. (Oxford, 1963).

3. For the methods of composing and printing the Folio, see Philip Gaskell, *A New Introduction to Bibliography* (Oxford, 1972), pp. 5–141.

4. In *Printing and Proof-Reading* in 1963, Hinman was unsure whether B's co-worker in the histories was A or C, but in the introduction to the Norton Facsimile of the Folio he notes his subsequent conviction that it was A (*The First Folio of Shakespeare* [New York, 1968], p. xviii). The identification is confirmed by Howard-Hill's study of the different habits of compositors in regard to the spacing of punctuation, the arranging of turn-overs, and other new evidence that will prove useful in identifying compositors. See "The Compositors of Shakespeare's Folio Comedies," *Studies in Bibliography*, 26 (1973), 61–106.

NOTES TO PAGES 54-59 201

5. "Cast-off Copy," pp. 268, 269n. The response to his ground-breaking study of 1955 was such that in *Printing and Proof-Reading* he cautioned that the difficulty of casting off had been overestimated (I, 72n). The present study suggests the contrary.

6. The following discussion in large part supplements that of Hinman. He deals with the problems briefly in "Cast-off Copy" (pp. 263-69), and touches on them in *Printing and Proof-Reading* (II, 505-9).

7. For example, eight long verse lines on q1^v (*3 Henry VI*) had to be either overrun or divided, but Compositor A had to compensate for only two of them, sacrificing two blank lines that would otherwise have framed the entrance in the lower right column. In contrast, casting off did not anticipate three long lines on m3^v (*2 Henry VI*). One (298-99) had to be overrun; one required setting an exit on a separate line (272); one, as I will suggest (below, p. 118) required Compositor B to cut a word. Although general practice in the Henry VI plays was to space all internal entrances, two on m3^v are unspaced and one, in the lower right column, is set to the right.

8. Through line numbers from the Norton facsimile of the Folio, rather than Riverside line numbers, will be cited when the interest is purely typographical: that is, when generally adopted readings are not affected.

9. *Mechanick Exercises*, p. 217.

10. John Hazel Smith has noted the same concern for aesthetics in one of the Shakespearean quartos. See "The Composition of the Quarto of *Much Ado About Nothing*," *Studies in Bibliography*, 16 (1963), 21. In three instances—on A3^v, B4^v, and C2^v—the compositor avoided a break-line of one word at the top of a page by adding an extra line at the bottom of the preceding page.

11. The other three long columns are on L1, Bb3, and t2. On L1 and Bb3, compositors were conserving space. On t2, Compositor B was probably careless or in a hurry. *Alarums* is on the sixty-seventh line in the right-hand column. If casting off did allot it to t2 rather than t2^v, one wonders why B divided a line of verse needlessly only seven lines before the end of the column. Perhaps he did not notice the marginal *Alarums* until he reached the end of the page and then could not take time to make the necessary adjustment.

12. The only columns in the Folio that end after the opening stage direction of a new scene are on T4 and v2. No column ends with a scene box alone.

13. Short columns are found on the following pages (listed in the order of setting): C2, F3^v, L3, a2, a4^v, a6, b1, c5, Aa4, and v2.

14. For two speakers on one line, see H3, R2^v, T3, Y3, Bb3, b3, h3, and n5. Entrances are found to the right on F1^v (twice), L1, N4^v, Y1, Y3^v, Aa2^v, Aa5, Bb2^v, Bb6^v (twice), b2, c5^v, e1, i2, i3^v, i5^v, m3^v, n3, and n6^v. In many of these cases, compositors had little or no choice. Thus far my study of typesetting practices has been limited largely to plays set in the first half of the Folio, because my primary concern has been to determine the usual practices of Compositors A and B at the time they set *2 Henry IV*. B almost invariably

gives each speaker his own line and centers internal entries unless compensating for casting off. By the time of *2 Henry IV*, A had set no speeches to the right, but he shows a far greater tendency than B to set entries to the right even when under no pressure. Ten of the twenty instances cited above were set by him.

15. In 1955, Hinman's original study of "Cast-Off Copy" pointed the direction for future study. Noting that pressures of space probably account for the realignment of verse in several plays and for the omission of a part-line in *Othello*, he issued what scholars should have seen as a stimulating challenge: "Whether compositors, when pressed for space, often solved their problems by tampering with the text in these or other 'more drastic' ways I do not know" (p. 268). In 1963 he briefly touched on further evidence of tampering in the Folio (in *Printing and Proof-Reading*, II, 508–9), and in 1965 noted similar tampering by the compositor in Q1 of *Richard II* ("Shakespeare's Text—Then, Now and Tomorrow," *Shakespeare Survey* 18 [1965], 29–30). To date, few scholars have followed his lead.

16. The term "white line" is Moxon's (*Mechanick Exercises*, p. 213). To create a white line, the compositor set a line of quadrats, special types that did not take ink. The modern term is, of course, "blank line."

17. *Mechanick Exercises*, p. 217.

18. For further examples from the Folio, see Hinman, "Cast-Off Copy," pp. 265–69.

19. "There were almost certainly copyright difficulties over *Richard II* and the two parts of *Henry IV*" (Hinman, *Printing and Proof-Reading*, II, 98). We shall return to this question.

20. "The Printing of the Folio Edition of *2 Henry IV*," *The Library*, 32 (1977), 258.

21. Note, for example, the lavish use of blank space on e6 and e6^v, where even incidental directions such as *The Lady speakes in Welsh* and *The Musicke playes* are framed by blank lines. Similarly set off are three entrances that occur in the middle of another character's speech: 883 on e3, 1282 on e4^v, and 1982 on f1. According to normal practice, one would expect them to be centered but unspaced. On f2, B divided two prose speeches into pseudo-verse (2177–88) and, against normal practice, set an exit on a separate line (2183) when there was ample space to the right of the one preceding. On the whole, space seems to have been allotted generously during casting off. B's anticipation of a potentially long final page explains his sudden cramping on the two penultimate pages of the play. He shortened four stage directions to hold them to one line each (2905, 2947, 3036, and 3093) and even cut one entirely (at 3066). At 2937 he omitted two words, *yet* and *I*, perhaps to avoid an overrun. At 3052, the Q5's "Fare thee well great heart" is shortened to "Farewell great heart," probably for the same reason.

22. This supplementary quire is normally distinguished from regular quire gg, which completes *Romeo and Juliet* and begins *Timon of Athens*, by identifying

it as "ˣgg." Because the present discussion is concerned only with the supplementary quire, I shall use the Folio signature of "gg." For Hinman's full discussion of the problems faced in setting *2 Henry IV*, see *Printing and Proof-Reading*, II, 96–100.

23. As early as 1953, a decade before Hinman's discovery that the Folio was cast off by formes, Alice Walker noted that several of B's omissions and revisions on g2 and g3 enabled him to accommodate an abnormal amount of copy on these pages and thus "suggest a deliberate effort to compress, which may have affected the Folio readings. . . . B may have been as intent on saving space during his first stint as he was on stretching the matter out by split lines in his second stint. Whatever the cause, it is fortunate, stylistically and textually, that the Folio text of the play is of secondary importance" (*Textual Problems*, p. 120). As the widespread adoption of several questionable Folio variants indicates, editors have not heeded her warning.

24. Hinman suggests that the lower rule of the box "has been sacrificed" because of the need to crowd text ("Cast-off Copy," p. 265). Elsewhere in the Folio, however, B used the rule with even shallower boxes. For example, note the shallow two-line box with rules on Aa1.

25. S. W. Reid's statement that B used the ampersand only in long lines should be slightly qualified. By chance, I have noticed one instance in a short line (651 on g3), but there, as we shall see, B was concentrating on a difficult task of compressing a long speech and had used & eight lines earlier. He may have varied from his customary practice as a kind of reflex, simply because he was intent on compressing at the time. See Reid's article, "Justification and Spelling in Jaggard's Compositor B," *Studies in Bibliography*, 27 (1974), 93.

26. In determining B's preferred spellings, I have followed the guidelines laid down by S. W. Reid in the study just cited (see note 25) and in "Some Spellings of Compositor B in the Shakespeare First Folio," *Studies in Bibliography*, 29 (1976), 102–38. Beginning with the history plays and moving on when necessary, I have examined B's spelling of a given word, and often of analogous words, in unjustified lines and in justified lines that could have tolerated variant spellings.

27. B's cavalier treatment of the text should come as no surprise to us. In his study of B's work in the Pavier Quartos, John Andrews cites abundant evidence that Compositor B omitted words, phrases, and even whole lines when he was under pressure to compress. He also on occasion substituted shorter words, as we have seen him do on g2, and sometimes changed verse to prose. For the evidence see "The Pavier Quartos of 1619, Evidence for Two Compositors," Diss. Vanderbilt University, 1971, especially pp. 83–86, 135, 139, and 154. In several instances, Andrews feels that Compositor B made changes only to justify a line or to avoid a turn-over.

28. *Printing and Proof-Reading*, II, 92–93.

29. Howard-Hill first suggested to me that A is an "expansive" compositor.

This trait is most noticeable in one-line verse speeches. Even in stints that were not cast off, Compositor B tried to hold a line of verse to one type-line by using short spellings, close spacing, abbreviations, and substitutions such as y^t and the ampersand. (For example, see 2575 on d4, 2077 on l4^v, and 2155 on l5.) Compositor A, on the other hand, freely used overruns rather than deviate from his normal practices. On p4, for example, A set nineteen overruns, at least seven of which he could easily have avoided had he used some of the standard methods of compression. In the first half of quire gg, we find the same avoidable overruns on gg4 and gg4^v.

30. I have made a preliminary study, but with inconclusive results. The practice of a given compositor in regard to the use of blank lines—for scene boxes, opening entrances, and internal directions—varies widely from play to play (sometimes from page to page) and often without discernible reason. If we are to detect signs that a compositor was working under pressure, we need to know his preferences in regard to such matters. Further work is needed.

31. The four are on Bb1, e2^v, k5, and mm5. In B's eighteen boxes at the top of a column, he used five-line boxes only three times: on k5, Aa4, and this page. Often scene boxes were left standing in type and reused as occasion required. Prior to the setting of gg7, only one *Scena Quinta* box of similar size had been set, on b5. Comparison of the type and the box rules shows that the box on gg7 is not the same one.

32. B prefers to spell with terminal -*y*, rather than with -*ie*. See Howard-Hill, "A Reassessment of Compositors B and E in the First Folio Tragedies," privately circulated, 1977.

33. *Had'st* is not the work of the scribe. His grammatical corrections reveal too sensitive an ear for him to be responsible for *thou had'st . . . thou had'st*. He apparently found nothing objectionable in *thou wert better*, which B set (as *wer't*) at 1.2.89.

34. For another suspicious *good* in B's settings, see below, p. 108. A fifth *good* not found in the Quarto is set by Compositor A: "Oh, the Lord preserue thy good Grace" (1317; 2.4.291).

35. Dover Wilson suggests that the Quarto compositor omitted *me* because he was pressed for space, citing the fact that he turned up *roare again* at the end of the line (New Cambridge edition, p. 176). This explanation would be persuasive if the context did not support the Quarto reading.

36. For an example from another play, see the opening stage direction to 4.1 of *1 Henry IV* on f2. We know that Compositor B was under pressure to expand on this page because he set two lines of prose as three lines of verse at the top of the right column and divided two lines of verse at the bottom of the column. In light of these adjustments, the expanded stage direction in the lower right column seems deliberate. The entrance of Hotspur, Worcester, and Douglas would normally have been set on one line, but B added Hotspur's first name to expand the direction and then divided it into two lines. Nowhere else in the play do we find *Harrie Hotspurre* in a stage direction.

37. A seemingly quixotic setting on q5^v of *Richard III* probably reflects the same concern: "*Bra*. With this (my Lord) my selfe haue nought to / doo" (101–2). The freak spelling of *doo* cannot be explained by mere carelessness. A compositor might pick up a wrong letter by mistake, but he would not reach out in error to pick up a third letter for such a simple two-letter word as *do* (B's normal spelling). B probably chose to extend the word. He could have set *doe*, an acceptable alternative, but he may have worked in haste, picking up two *o*'s in one movement.

38. The following summarizes the total of fifty type-lines (including three on gg7^v) set by B that were not required by his copy. On gg1: 1699 and 1707 by setting wide; 1678 and 1684 by dividing lines; 1670 and 1732 by adding words. On gg5: 2672, 2699, 2731, and 2749 by dividing lines; 2763 by expanding and dividing a stage direction; 2712 and 2757 by adding words. On gg5^v: 2825, 2831, 2874, 2877, and 2882 by setting wide; 2779, 2794, 2806, 2816, 2821, 2828, 2845, 2849, and 2885 by dividing lines; 2880 by expanding and dividing a stage direction; 2812 and 2841 by adding words. On gg6: 2898 by expanding a stage direction. On gg6^v: 3117 by setting wide; 3104 by adding a blank line; 3129 and 3136 by dividing lines. On gg7: 3164 by setting wide; 3147, 3151, 3198, and 3203 by dividing lines; using two additional lines at the scene box top right; 3170 and 3249 by expanding and dividing stage directions; 3177, 3182, and 3215 by adding words. On gg7^v: 3316 by dividing the line; 3284 by expanding the stage direction to excuse setting it on a new line; 3295 by adding words. All of the preceding have been discussed.

39. Walker, *Textual Problems*, pp. 11–12.

40. *Printing and Proof-Reading*, I, 235–39. Hinman suggests that Isaac Jaggard himself did the proof-reading.

41. Without B's expanding, *Othello* would, at best, have ended with parallel columns of only one line each. He probably also wrote the "Names of the Actors" to help balance the page. Four of the seven such lists in the Folio are appended to plays set from transcripts by Ralph Crane. The other three—for *Othello*, *Timon of Athens*, and *2 Henry IV*—were all set by B and all were solutions to typographic problems. In Crane's lists, decorum required naming the character of highest rank first. For *Othello*, the play's chief character is named first, with the Duke of Venice relegated to sixth place, his position of dramatic importance. The cast list for *2 Henry IV* shows some care in classifying characters, but one doubts that either Shakespeare or the scribe would rank Sir John Falstaff second in a list of "Irregular humorists." The list for *Timon* is chaotic. Among other errors, Sempronius is named twice and Phrynia and Timandra are omitted. I suspect B's hand in all three of these lists.

42. Moxon, of course, would disagree with my assessment of Compositor B, but he did not cast off copy by formes. As a result, his compositors did not face many of the problems that challenged Jaggard's staff. A clue to the different pressures in Jaggard's and Moxson's shops may be seen in the fact that many apparently acceptable expedients used by Jaggard's compositors were later to

be called "botches" by Moxon: "viz. *Pidgeon-holes* [abnormally thick spaces], *Thin-Spaces*, no *Space* before a *Capital, Short* &s, *Abbreviations* or *Titled Letters* [for example, õ standing for *om* as in *cõpose*], *Abbreviate Words*, &c" (*Mechanick Exercises*, p. 237).

43. For additional examples, see gg (2177–81), e6 (1696–1701), l2 (1484–86), p4^v (1741–44), and q1^v (2452–55). On m5^v alone, there are at least four instances: 761–63, 819–21, 822–26, and 827–29. Elsewhere on this page, faulty lineation may reflect errors in the copy (e.g., 740–44).

44. New Arden edition (London, 1957), pp. xxxii–xxxix, 19n.

Chapter IV

1. The most detailed treatment is by Shaaber, New Variorum edition, pp. 499–507. For a useful summary, see Humphreys' New Arden edition, pp. lxxiv–lxxix.

2. New Cambridge edition, p. 192. The compositor in question is A; thus *line* is not the type of careless substitution associated with B.

3. As noted above in Chapter III, the substitution of *him* for *his father* should probably be attributed to Compositor B. The substitution of *lik'ning* for *liking* is not, however, characteristic of him. As Andrews' study of his work in the Pavier Quartos reveals, Compositor B was quite sensitive to dialect and sometimes even introduced colloquial spellings. (See, especially, Andrews' chapter on *Oldcastle* and *Lear*.) Here, *lik'ning* seems a deliberate correction.

4. The line occurs on g3, one of Compositor B's very tight pages. The spelling of *rescu* and the use of tight spacing show B's attempt to compress the line, but I doubt that the deletion of *or two* is his. Even with *or two*, the speech could have been held to its present two lines had B abbreviated the speech prefix to *Ho.* and omitted the space after it (as he often did).

5. None of these deletions can be attributed to compositors. On gg1, a page on which B was pushing to spread copy, the deleted three *so*'s would not have required another line, but his attention was on expanding. Since he elsewhere seems to have added words unnecessarily when he was concentrating on spreading copy, it is doubtful that he would have carelessly omitted words here. The other two passages are on gg5^v, another page on which B was spreading.

6. *Dooble* for *Double* could be explained as a graphic error, but have we tended to assume too easily that the possibility of a compositor's error in reading necessarily proves that such an error has, in fact, been made?

7. In setting Q2 of *Richard II*, Simmes' Compositor A omitted words twenty-seven times, but none of the omissions occurs at the beginning of a line and only one is a verb. At 4.1.26, he omitted *I say* in "That makes thee out for hell, I say thou liest" (Craven, p. 52).

8. Unless—and this is highly speculative—Shakespeare used an abbreviation here, as he probably did for *Warwicke* (3.1.1) and *knighthood* (5.3.126), set as *War* and *Knight* in the Quarto. The form that the abbreviation might take cannot be

determined, but the common initial letter and the medial -*ings*-, together with the ease of mistaking Shakespeare's terminal *k* for a *t*, make a misreading of *Billingsgate* for *Basingstoke* at least within the realm of possibility. The passage in Hand D of *Sir Thomas More* uses many abbreviations: the familiar w^t, w^{ch}, and yor, as well as the *p* with a stroke through its tail to stand for *par-*, *per-*, and even *pro-*. The use of *L* for *Lord* is scarcely noteworthy, but the repeated use of *matie* for *maiestie* may show a significant tendency to abbreviate.

9. The *OED* has confused the meaning of *fist* in this passage. It cites Fang's use under the definition "to strike with the fist." Shakespeare, however, never uses *fist* to mean "hit." Only one word in his work seems relevant, a word the *OED* properly cites under the definition "to grasp or seize with the fist"; in *Coriolanus*, Aufidius recalls the days when he and his enemy joyed in "unbuckling helms, [and] fisting each other's throat" (4.5.125). By "fist," Fang thus means "grasp"—exactly what the scribe seems to mean by "vice," a word Shakespeare never used in this sense. The Folio variant has been universally adopted on the formidable authority of Dover Wilson, who posited that the Quarto compositor misread *vice* as *vue* (New Cambridge edition, p. 145; see also *The Manuscript of Shakespeare's Hamlet* [Cambridge, 1934], pp. 106–8). Graphic error should be invoked only when a reading is clearly wrong.

10. A third seven-foot line, 5.5.94–95, may have been divided by the compositor because of the width of the Folio column. There the verse is not regularized; a dimeter line is created.

11. Most editors follow the Folio in the belief that Shakespeare originally wrote *talking*, then reconsidered and wrote *cheering*, but forgot to cancel *talking*. If he did, in fact, mean to cancel *talking*, we should find it before *cheering* at the beginning of the next line, not at the end of this one. The major argument against *talking*—that it is "extra-metrical"—is invalid. Shakespeare sometimes uses *iron* as a monosyllable: for example, "Put in their hands thy bruising irons of wrath" (*Richard III*, 5.3.110) and "As iron to adamant, as earth to th' centre" (*Troilus and Cressida*, 3.2.179).

12. The following revisions are characteristic. "Euermore thanke's the exchequer of the poore" (F: *thankes, th'Exchequer*; 2.3.65). "And I challenge law, Atturnies are denied me" (F: om. *I*; 2.3.134). "I wil not peace, what is the matter Aumerle?" (F: *matter Sonne*; 5.2.81). "I cannot do it: yet Ile hammer it out" (F: *hammer't*; 5.5.5). "To threed the posterne of a small needles eie" (F: om. *small*; 5.5.17). "While I stand fooling heere his iacke of the clocke" (F: *iacke o'th'Clocke*; 5.5.60).

13. The realignment to this point in the speech could be the work of Compositor A. If the seven-foot line remained in his copy, he would have had to divide it, and we have noted his tendency to realign in such cases. Given, however, the scribe's attention to metrics, I find it doubtful that he would have allowed this seven-foot line to stand. He did so at 4.4.12–13, but there it was in a sequence of irregular lines.

14. *Hath* is a sign of the scribe, a literary nicety he has often substituted for

has. Here he was facing *hands* in his Quarto copy, a nonsense word. Logic demanded a singular verb for the singular subject *sicknesse* and *hath* is the result. The Quarto's *hands* was probably a misreading for *haue*, which, if he checked the foul papers, the scribe would have rejected as a solecism.

15. In his study of A's setting of the second quarto of *Richard II*, Craven lists twenty-seven omissions of words, but twenty-five are of one word only (pp. 52–53). The other two are of two minor words each: "the death [or fall] of Kings" and "hell, [I say] thou." In his resetting of the cancelled pages of Qa of *2 Henry IV*, Simmes' A once deleted three words—*let me see*—but Shallow repeats the phrase three times and the omission is a relatively easy error to make. None of his omissions suggests that he would overlook an entire "waist line."

16. "The Folio Text of *2 Henry IV*," pp. 143–44.
17. *Printing and Proof-reading*, I, 227.
18. *Mechanick Exercises*, p. 192.
19. For the relevant evidence see Andrews, "The Pavier Quartos," pp. 136–224.

Chapter V

1. The Folio substitution of *Charract* is universally rejected, but it has led to misleading annotation of *carat*. The OED confuses the meaning by quoting the Folio version under sense 4 of *carat*: "*fig*. Worth, value; estimate. *Obs*." The Quarto's *karrat* should be cited under sense 3, the technical sense, illustrated by a passage from 1575–76 *Act* 18 Eliz. XV: "No . . . Golde lesse in fynesse than that of xxij Carrottes."
2. No matter how this passage has been emended, the line makes no sense for what the King is saying: that Fortune gives a good but, at the same time, an evil that makes it impossible to enjoy the good. Most editors uneasily adopt the Folio reading, combine the Quarto and the Folio (using *write* and *terms*), or adopt Walker's *mete* for *wet* (*Textual Problems*, pp. 117–18). If one can push the argument of foul case this far, might a possible reading be *set* for *wet*, or even, perhaps, *weigh* (from *wey*)?
3. See Greg's discussion in *The Shakespeare First Folio*, pp. 273–75.
4. New Arden edition, pp. xiii–xiv.
5. Allusions to *1 Henry IV* are more numerous and occur over a longer span of time. Among the several allusions to Falstaff, five pointing to his role in Part 1 date from 1600–1618.
6. In a list of plays for c. 1619–20, we find the following entry:
[Seco] part of Falstaff
[not p]laid theis 7. yeres.
(Chambers, *William Shakespeare*, II, 346). The list is on a slip of what appears to be waste paper from the Revels Office, but it may give plays only considered

for performance. Moreover, we cannot be sure that the entry refers to Shakespeare's play.

7. Wilson, New Cambridge edition, p. 123.

8. Hinman, *Printing and Proof-Reading*, I, 27–28, 521–23.

9. These facts may explain the miscalculations in estimating the length of *2 Henry IV*. Jaggard may not have had the copy in hand until work on Part I was well under weigh or even until it was completed. Davison agrees that the delay in printing the play was occasioned by the absence of copy, but he offers an alternate theory for the miscalculations. See "The Printing of the Folio Edition of *2 Henry IV*," *The Library*, 32 (1977), 257–59.

10. Walker, *Textual Problems*, 109–11; Williams, "The Text of *2 Henry IV*," p. 179.

11. For a summary of the Cobham controversy and the evidence of revision in both plays, see A. R. Humphreys' New Arden edition of *1 Henry IV* (London, 1960), pp. xii–xviii.

12. "The Text of *2 Henry IV*," p. 179.

13. Walker, *Textual Problems*, p. 109.

14. Conceivably, transcripts of the two plays might have been made for the Cobhams by different scribes, but if so the scribe preparing Part 1 was remarkably insensitive to his intended audience; witness not only the profanity but also the remaining reference to "my old lad of the castle" at 1.2.42.

15. The three scenes are 2.1, 2.4, and 3.2. For discussion, see above, pp. 25–26, 42–45, and 24–25.

16. Either A or the scribe added one *good* at 1317.

Index

All's Well That Ends Well, 73–74. See also under Miscalculation in casting off
Andrews, John, 161, 203, 206
Archaic forms, 122–23
Armin, Robert, 173
Aspley, William, 175

Bank, 114
Bank man, 115
"Bardolph's boy," 12n, 37, 49–50, 166, 177
Blank lines: and setting of stage directions, 31–32, 59, 61, 67, 73, 78, 90, 202; and casting off, 53; and adjustments in setting, 58, 65, 91–95 *passim*, 98n, 99, 201, 205; method of setting of, 202; in practice of different compositors, 204
Bookkeeper, 5f, 20, 25, 32, 45, 50, 55
Bowers, Fredson, 14, 199
Break-line, 57f, 109, 201

Cairncross, Andrew S., 118
Casting off: required by order of setting Folio, 52–53; process of, 53; difficulty of, underestimated, 53–59; adjustments for miscalculation in, 61–73 *passim*. See also Miscalculation in casting off; *and under 2 Henry IV*
Cast lists, 92–93, 205
Censor, official, 5–6
Chambers, E. K., 199
Characters, comic, 24–25, 42–44 *passim*, 128, 131, 195
Characters, ghost, 7

Characters, silent, see Mutes
Charlemagne, 189
Cibber, Colley, 173
Cobham family, 176f, 209
Cockpit in Court, 173
Colloquialisms, 122–23, 197, 199
Comedy of Errors, The, 65
Compositor A: and setting of quire e, 53; division of lines by, 70, 116–17, 146–47, 201, 207; realignment by, 70, 116–17, 206f; and setting of quire g, 91ff; and setting of various scenes in *2 Henry IV*, 127, 181, 183; faithfulness of, to copy, 161f, 179, 186; identified as Compositor B's partner in setting the histories, 200; setting of entrances by, 201–2; identified as an "expansive" compositor, 203–4. See also under Short lines; Turn-overs
Compositor A (Simmes'), see Simmes' Compositor A
Compositor B: spelling of 12, 83, 89, 93, 99, 101, 203ff; setting of stage directions by, 28–52 *passim*, 90, 103, 110, 201–4 *passim*; omissions and deletions by, 51, 102, 118, 201; and setting of quire e, 53; setting of songs by, 61; use of pseudo-verse by, 67, 70, 96–97, 202; adjustments by, to compress copy, 75–93, 203f; use of ampersand by, 82, 88, 93, 203; gratuitous additions by, 88, 102–3, 204, 206; adjustments by, to expand copy, 93–113, 119–20, 179; division of verse lines by, to expand copy, 96, 105, 119, 143; and habit of holding too much copy

212   INDEX

in his head, 102f, 113; and aesthetic considerations, 109–13, 205; careless substitutions by, 113, 124, 161, 197, 206; defense of, 113–15; received difficult stints in several plays, 114; scope of job of, 115; typical changes by, 117, 129, 161–62, 197, 203; Folio variants attributable to, 120, 163f, 169f; efficiency of, in regularizing meter, 142; and attributing error in the setting of the Folio, 181; setting of long column by, 201; compression of copy by, in Pavier Quarto, 203; tendency of, to hold a line of verse to one type line, 204; summary of type set by, not required by his copy, 205; supplying of "names of Actors" by, 205; sensitivity of, to dialect, 206. *See also under* Short lines; Speech prefixes; Turn-overs; *and entries for individual scenes*

Compositor C, 59, 65, 67, 142, 200

Compositor D, 132

Compositor E, 114

Compositors: and Dover Wilson's principle of editing, 3; problems facing, 4, 51, 61, 179; adjustments by, 9, 59, 65–70 *passim*, 78, 160, 162, 202; spellings of, 11; setting of stage directions by, 12, 27, 58–59; effect of, on comparison between Quarto and Folio, 28; methods of working, 51–54; and casting off, 53, 59; line divisions by, 55, 67, 70, 73, 146; treatment of break-lines by, 57f; responsibility of, for editing, 160–61; identification of, 200; concern of, for aesthetics, 201. *See also* Casting off; *and entries for individual compositors*

Condell, Henry, 170, 174, 176

Coriolanus, 185, 207

Counting, *see* Casting off

Crane, Ralph, 23, 55, 198–99, 200, 205

Craven, Alan E., 184n, 185n, 195–96, 206, 208

Crichton-Stuart copy of *2 Henry IV*, 174

Davison, Peter, 24n, 74, 166n, 172, 197–98, 209

Drawers' scene, *see* Scene 2.4

Driving, 65, 67, 93, 99, 103

Eastward Hoe, 172

Elizabethan stage, entrances on, 29

Elizabeth I, 5–6

Entrances: semimassed, 12; added or omitted in Folio, 20ff; massed, 22f, 40, 49, 199; added by scribe, 25f; placement of, 27, 67, 187, 189, 201–2; detected from dialogue, 29; anticipatory, 29, 199f; opening, 90. *See also* Entrances, internal; Stage directions

Entrances, internal: in Folio, 12f; placement of, in Elizabethan manuscripts, 27, 187–90 *passim*; setting of, 61, 75n, 90f, 201f; and compression of copy, 73, 78, 85; treatment of, by Ralph Crane, 200

Epicoene, 173

Epilogue, 92–93, 111, 136

Evans, G. Blakemore, 168

Exeunt, 41

Exit, 41

Exits, 20, 33, 187, 202

Extrametrical lines, 141, 149n, 207

Fair copy, 6, 10, 165

Final page of the play, 61–65, 111, 113, 205

First Part of the Contention, The, 118

Folio column: width of, and effect on line length, 55, 96, 117, 146f, 156, 207; length of, in page layout, 57, 201; width of, and need to use abbreviations, 61; ending of, after opening stage direction, 201

INDEX 213

Folio compositors: method of working, 51ff; use of heavy punctuation and capital letters by, in relation to line length, 56; and page length, 57; problems of, 109, 114; and regularizing meter, 142; spellings of, influenced by need to justify lines, 196. *See also* Compositor A; Compositor B; Jaggard's compositors

Folio edition of 1623: evidence of editing in, 1; variants in, general discussion of, 1–17 *passim*, 120, 138–40, 163–65, 169; meter regularized in, 1, 141–43, 149n, 152–55; question of use of an independent, corrected manuscript in setting of, 2f, 20, 39, 48, 98, 120–21, 124, 135, 144, 163–70 *passim*; literary sophistication in, 2, 19, 125; short lines in, 2, 144–59; realigning of lines in, 3; method of setting, 4, 51ff; nature of printer's copy for, 4, 8–18, 169–71, 175–77; question of dependence on Quarto of, 10–15 *passim*, 177, 196; spellings in, 11, 142; stage directions in, 12–15 *passim*, 19–42, 48–49; argument that stage practice reflected in text of, 15–23 *passim*, 28–32 *passim*, 42–50 *passim*; speech prefixes in, 15, 20, 32–39 *passim*; elimination of supernumeraries and silent characters in, 48; typographical features of, 51; problems in casting off, 53ff, 59; page layout in, 57; "corrections" by scribe in, 135–40; argument that set from an "assembled text" of actors' parts, 197. *See also* Compositors; Entrances, Metrics, regularizing of; Scribe, of transcript used for Folio text of *2 Henry IV*; Short lines; Speech prefixes; Stage directions; *and entries under individual scenes and quires*

Folio line, 56f

Folio proofreaders, 160

Forme, 4, 52, 205

Foul papers: as copy for Quarto, 6–8, 44, 163, 178; as copy for Folio, 10, 15–17, 34–35, 149, 169f, 181–86 *passim*; placement of internal entrances in, 13; permissive stage directions in, 26; and casting off, 55; served as basis for transcripts, 176. *See also under entries for individual scenes*

Frame, 52

Galleys, 114f
Gaskell, Philip, 200
Gaultree sequence, *see* Scene 4.1; Scene 4.2; Scene 4.3
Ghost characters, 7
Globe Theatre, 4
Greg, W. W., 122, 187–90, 195, 199f

Hamlet, 8, 113, 139–40
Hand C, *see under Sir Thomas More*
Hand D, *see under Sir Thomas More*
Hart, Alfred, 195
Heminge, John, 170, 174, 176
Henry IV, 89n
1 Henry IV: quarto editions of, 4, 174; Francis in, 44; setting of quire e of, 52; Folio variants in, 70, 102–3, 204; order of printing of, 73, 175; miscalculation in allotting pages for, 73–75; Hotspur's use of *forsooth* in, 140; metrics regularized in, 143; popularity of, 171f, 208; literary sophistication in, 176–77. *See also under* Miscalculation in casting off
2 Henry IV: partial lines added in Folio edition of, 1–3, 105–19, 152; only one Quarto edition of, 4, 171–74; two issues of Quarto edition of, 4–5; copy for Quarto of, 5–8; copy for Folio text of, 8–18, 163–70, 174–79 *passim*, 181–86; Folio copy of, not reflecting stage practice, 19–50;

routine problems in casting off Folio copy of, 51–73; special problems in setting of, 73–75, 76n, 84, 91–93, 175, 209; adjustments in setting title page of, 76f; signs of compression in quire g of, 78–92 *passim*; compositor's setting adjustments and revisions to compress copy in, 80–92, 117–18, 120; signs of expansion in quire gg of, 92–103 *passim*; compositor's setting adjustments and revisions to expand copy in, 93–109 *passim*, 205; compositor's additions in, for aesthetic reasons, 109–13; literary sophistications and assumed corrections by scribe in, 122–41; metrical revisions by scribe in, 141–42; treatment of short lines by scribe in, 143–59; popularity of, 171–74; contemporary allusions to, 172–73; stage history of, 173. *See also* Folio edition of 1623; Scribe, of transcript used for Folio text of *2 Henry IV*; *and entries for individual scenes*
Henry V, 73–74, 76, 78, 174f. *See also under* Miscalculation in casting off
1, 2, 3 Henry VI, see under Miscalculation in casting off
Henry VIII, 76
Hinman, Charlton: on Folio compositors, 4, 200, 202; on the manner of setting Folio, 4, 51–54; on miscalculations in casting off, 54, 73, 84–85, 201, 203; on type and order of setting quire g, 91; on Jaggard's lack of concern with purity of texts, 114; on Folio proofreaders, 160; on copyright difficulties, 175
Hotspur, the, 173
Howard-Hill, T. H., 196–97, 198–99, 203
Humphreys, A. R., 14–15, 15In, 171, 195, 197

Independent manuscript, *see under* Folio edition of 1623
Induction, 7, 10, 162
Internal entrances, *see* Entrances, internal

Jaggard's compositors, 51, 57f, 76n, 175, 178, 205–6. *See also* Folio compositors; *and entries for individual compositors*
Jaggard's shop, 58, 115
Jaggard, William, 13–14, 114, 121, 125, 170, 174, 198, 205, 209
James I, 171
John a Kent, 187f
John Magdalene, 89n
Jonson, Ben, 173
Julius Caesar, 149n
Justification, 83, 89, 101, 123n, 196, 203

Kempe, Will, 44, 200
King John, 73, 113, 159, 185
King Lear, 114. *See also* Pavier Quartos
Kittredge, George Lyman, 169

Law Tricks, 172
Lines, extrametrical, 141, 149n
Lines, short, *see* Short lines
Lines, waist, *see* Waist lines
Linotype, 114f
Love's Labour's Lost, 134n, 143

Macbeth, 117
Massed entries, *see under* Entrances
Measure for Measure, 65, 74, 151n, 185. *See also under* Miscalculation in casting off
Merchant of Venice, The, 142f, 185
Merry Devil of Edmonton, 173
Merry Wives of Windsor, The, see under Miscalculation in casting off
Metrics, regularizing of, 1, 141–58. *See also* Short lines; *and under* Folio edition of 1623; Scribe, of transcript used for Folio text of *2 Henry IV*

INDEX 215

Midsummer Night's Dream, A, 132, 142f. See also under Miscalculation in casting off
Miscalculation in casting off, signs of: in Henry V, 59; in 1 Henry VI, 59, 61; in A Midsummer Night's Dream, 59, 65–67 (N2); in Measure for Measure, 61 (f1^v); in Much Ado About Nothing, 61, 65; in The Winter's Tale, 61 (Bb3); in All's Well That Ends Well, 67 (V2, X1^v); in Richard II, 67 (c3), 73 (d1^v), 119–20; in 1 Henry IV, 70 (f2, f3^v), 73 (e1, f2), 116–17 (f3^v); in 2 Henry VI, 73 (m3), 118–19, 201; in Richard III, 73 (r1), in The Merry Wives of Windsor, 75; in 3 Henry VI, 201. See also under 2 Henry IV
Moxon, Joseph: describes casting off, 53–55; on break-lines, 57; on "setting wide," 65; on compositors, 114, 160–61, 196; use of "white line" by, 202; on expedients acceptable in Jaggard's shop, 205–6
Much Ado About Nothing, 8, 56, 142f, 183, 185. See also under Miscalculation in casting off
Munday, Anthony, 188–89
Mutes, 19–26 passim, 39, 44, 48ff

Nest of Ninnies, A, 173

Othello, 65, 114, 202, 205
Ould Castel, 173

Page layout, 57
Pavier Quartos, 161, 203
Pericles, 186
Phototypesetting, 115n
Profanity, 9, 87, 124, 151, 177, 197f
Prologue heading, 76
Promptbook, 5–9 passim, 14f, 19
Proscenium stage, 29
Pseudo-verse, 67, 70, 99, 202

Qa: mutilated form of 2 Henry IV in, 4–5, 174; number of extant copies of, 5; as copy for Folio, 15ff, 169f; relation of, to possible censorship, 171; spellings in, 184; omissions in, 208. See also Quarto edition of 1600; Scene 3.1; Scene 3.2
Qb: identified, 4f; resetting of, 15; Scene 3.1 in, 151n, 171, 182; mutilated form of 2 Henry IV in, 174; spellings in, 184; typical errors in, 196. See also Quarto edition of 1600; Scene 3.1
Quadrats, 202
Quarto column, 141, 146
Quarto compositor, see Simmes' Compositor A
Quarto edition of 1600: compared with Folio, 1, 139ff, 149n; only edition of 2 Henry IV before Folio, 4; nature of printer's copy for, 4–7 passim; passages omitted in, 5–6, 143; stage directions in, 6–7, 20–33 passim; errors in, 15, 44, 165; faulty speech prefixes in, 33f; closer to a Shakespearean production than Folio, 50; short lines in, 142–59 passim; spellings in, 142, 196. See also Qa; Qb; Speech prefixes; and entries for individual scenes
Quarto line, 56
Quire, 51ff, 73–74. See also entries for individual quires
Quire g, 73–92 passim
Quire gg, 74, 76, 91–111, 202–3
Quires, individual, see Quire g; Quire gg; and entries for individual plays

Ram-Alley, 172
Rape of Lucrece, The, 139
Reconciliation scene, see Scene 4.5
Recruiting scene, see Scene 3.2
Reid, S. W., 203
Richard II, 6, 89n, 171
Richard II, 1, 142f, 158, 171, 174f, 183, 207. See also under Miscalculation in casting off; Simmes' Compositor A

INDEX

Richard II or Thomas of Woodstock, see Thomas of Woodstock
Richard III, 8, 174, 205, 207. See also under Miscalculation in casting off
Rivals, The, 164
Romeo and Juliet, 114, 143, 202
Rules, irregular, 51
Rustic forms, see Archaic forms; Colloquialisms

Scene 1.1: short lines in, 2, 152; in Quarto, 5, 139; speech prefixes in, 7–8, 36; stage directions in, 13, 21, 25, 29–30; setting of scene divisions in, 76; spellings in, 122, 184; substitutions by Compositor B in, 129; changes by scribe in, 135, 164, 168; meter regularized in, 141; error in Folio version of, 181
Scene 1.2: stage directions in, 7, 19f; speech prefixes in, 8; changes by Compositor B in, 80–84 passim; changes by scribe in, 122–30 passim; Quarto readings for, preferable to Folio changes, 140; variant in, difficult to account for, 163; setting of, by Quarto compositor, 164
Scene 1.3: Quarto omissions in, 5, 143; ghost characters in, 7; spellings in, 11; assignment of speech prefixes in, 34; changes by scribe in, 123, 135, 139; meter regularized in, 141; short lines in, 148; setting of, by Quarto compositor, 148–49
Scene 2.1: stage directions in, 6, 19, 26–28, 49; placement of entrance in, in foul papers, 28; Quarto setting of, 28, 184, 186, 198; mutes eliminated in, 48; "Bardolph's boy" in, 49; changes by Compositor B in, 85–91, 129; Folio variants in, general discussion of, 102, 140, 164; changes by scribe in, 122–31 passim, 135, 138; meter regularized in, 141

Scene 2.2: ghost character in, 7; questionable reading in, 10n; spelling in, 11; entrances in, 12, 22; speech prefixes in, 37–38; in foul papers, 38; setting of, by Quarto compositor, 38, 139, 186; "Bardolph's boy" in, 49; Folio additions in, 102, 164–65; changes by scribe in, 123ff, 129, 131, 137, 168; substitutions by Compositor B in, 129; Quarto readings in, compared with Folio, 139
Scene 2.3: 5, 124, 126, 135, 164
Scene 2.4: reset in Qb, 5, 15; speech prefixes for Doll Tearsheet in, 6f; stage directions in, 7, 20f, 41, 44; Folio variants in, general discussion of, 10n, 11, 12n, 162; offstage sound effects eliminated in, 19; drawers in, 42–45; and Quarto compositor, 45; speech prefixes in, in foul papers, 45; "Bardolph's boy" in, 49; spellings in, 122f, 184; changes by scribe in, 124–29 passim, 137–38, 166, 169; Falstaff's dialogue in, 130; Pistol's speeches in, corrected by scribe, 133–35; Quarto readings in, compared with Folio, 139; short lines in, 144
Scene 3.1: omitted in Qa, 4–5; source for, in Folio, 8, 169, 197–98; reset in Qb, 15; spellings in, 122; short lines in, 145; Folio changes in, 151, 167; addition of, in Folio, 171, 177; and foul papers, 182, 186; setting of, by Quarto compositor, 183f; comparison of Qb and Folio settings of, 183–86
Scene 3.2: Folio changes in, 3, 10, 102, 162, 167; reset in Qb, 5, 15; stage directions in, 6, 29, 35, 49; entrance of recruits in, 24–25; Falstaff's soliloquy in, 33; and Quarto compositor, 33, 35; stage directions in, in foul papers, 35; in Qa, 36f; speech prefixes in, 36–38; "Bardolph's boy" in, 50;

INDEX   217

changes by Compositor B in, 99,
108, 110; changes by scribe in, 122ff,
130–36 passim; spellings in Quarto
setting of, 184
Scene 4.1: Quarto omissions in, 5;
ghost character in, 7; stage
directions in, 7, 9, 23, 29, 39–42, 49,
198; questionable Folio readings in,
10, 181; division of, 40; changes by
scribe in, 136–37; meter regularized
in, 141; short line in, 144
Scene 4.2: short lines in, 2, 145, 149–
53 passim; questionable readings in,
10; stage directions in, 19f, 30, 33;
division of, 40; changes by scribe
in, 127, 136; meter regularized in,
141
Scene 4.3: stage directions in, 6, 20,
41, 44, 50n; sound effects in,
eliminated, 19; and Colevile, 39;
division of, 40; changes by scribe
in, 123–28 passim; meter regularized
in, 141; short lines in, 144;
confusion over wording in, 168
Scene 4.4: short lines in, 2, 144–45,
153–55; ghost character in, 7;
Folio changes in, 11, 167–68;
changes by scribe in, 127; meter
regularized in, 141; readings in, and
errors of Simmes' Compositor A,
185n, 186n
Scene 4.5: metrics of, 2, 141, 145–47;
short lines in, 2, 150, 153–59;
questionable readings in, 10;
spellings in, 11f, 122f; Folio revision
in, 12n; stage directions in, 21, 30,
41; changes by Compositor B in,
105–8, 129; changes by scribe in,
136, 166–67; and Quarto compositor, 159; in foul papers, 159
Scene 5.1: stage directions in, 22f, 44;
changes by Compositor B in, 95–
98; changes by scribe in, 125, 131;
scribe corrects Shallow's speeches
in, 132
Scene 5.2: spellings in, 12, 122f; stage
directions in, 30, 97; changes by

Compositor B in, 129; meter
regularized in, 141; short lines in,
144, 148; readings in, and errors
of Simmes' Compositor A, 185n,
186n
Scene 5.3: spellings in, 12, 122; stage
directions in, 21, 23, 198; entrance
of Pistol in, 31–32; placement of
entrances in, in foul papers, 31;
changes by scribe in, 125, 136;
scribe corrects Shallow's speeches
in, 132; setting of, by Quarto
compositor, 136
Scene 5.4: stage directions in, 6, 21,
44, 109; speech prefixes in, 7;
spellings in, 11; Folio additions in,
possibly due to Compositor B, 99,
101; changes by scribe in, 129
Scene 5.5: stage directions in, 20, 33f,
41; speech prefixes in, 39; strewers/
grooms in, 46–47; and Quarto
Compositor, 47; processions in,
48, 168; setting of scene division in, by Compositor B, 99;
additions in, as a result of expansion
by compositor, 101–3; changes by
scribe in, 122, 126, 132, 134;
metrics of, 145–48; readings in,
and errors of Simmes' Compositor
A, 185n, 186n
Scene boxes: setting of, 53, 58–61,
204; and compositor adjustments,
75, 78n; in quire g, 78, 91f; in
quire gg, 95, 99; and aesthetic
problems of compositors, 109
Scene headings, see Scene boxes
Scogan, Henry, court poet to Henry
IV, 133
Scoggin, 133
Scoggin, John, jester to Edward IV,
133
Scribe, of transcript used for Folio
text of 2 Henry IV: and metrics, 2,
141–47, 152–57; and dialogue, 9,
17; Shaaber on, 10f; methods of,
17, 25, 32–34, 39, 41, 137, 170,
183n; and stage directions, 17,

INDEX

21–26 *passim*, 32, 40f, 49f, 97, 110; and speech prefixes, 17, 19, 32–33, 37–38; interested only in lines of play, 19–20; and consulting of supplementary manuscript, 35–38 *passim*, 149, 163–64; deletions by, 36, 81–82, 168; logical mind of, 43, 45, 126–27, 135–40 *passim*, 157; and errors relating to production, 48; lack of interest in minor characters, 48; and possibility of a corrected, independent manuscript, 48, 50; created "Bardolph's boy," 49–50; corrected grammar, 82, 122–23; possible substitutions by, compared with those of Compositor B, 88–89; literary sophistication of, 122f, 130, 198, 208; typical changes by, 122–24, 131, 165–69, 178; eliminated profanity, 124; concerned about propriety in syntax, 125; sense of decorum of, 128–30; lack of dramatic sense of, 129; deaf to speech patterns and rhythms, 130; methodical thought of, 138–39; incorrect changes by, 165–66; commissioned to do transcript, 170; editing by, and Folio additions, 181–85; more accurate than Quarto compositor, 186. *See also* Short lines; Speech prefixes; Stage directions; *and entries for individual scenes*

Setting wide, 65, 67

Shaaber, M. A., 10–14 *passim*, 122, 151, 160, 195f

Shakespeare's autograph, *see* Foul papers; *and under* Sir Thomas More

Shakespeare, William: and stage directions, 6–7, 22, 33, 44, 50n, 189; and ghost characters, 7; spelling of, 8, 139, 184; and clearing of stage at end of scenes, 20; preparing of drafts by, 44; and speech prefixes, 45, 200; possible error of, in Scene 5.5, 47; and "Bardolph's boy," 49n; use of short lines by, 118, 150f, 152n, 156; use of imagery by, 127, 156; use of speech patterns for characterization by, 130ff; use of additional light syllables by, 149n; failure of, to resolve agreement, 158, 185; and actors' failure to stick to text, 198; use of abbreviations by, 206–7

Short columns, 58

Short lines: completed in Folio, 1–2; added in Folio, 2–3, 55, 142–59; and internal entrances, 61; in expanding prose, 67; created by Compositor A, 116–17, 146–47; created by Compositor B, 118–20; and scribe, 143ff. *See also* Metrics, regularizing of

Signature, 52

Simmes' Compositor A: prone to error, 8, 159, 166n, 184, 208; resetting by, to accommodate Scene 3.1, 14–15; errors by, in setting Quarto of *2 Henry IV*, 49n, 138, 141, 166, 178, 184ff, 204; errors by, in setting Q2 of *Richard II*, 184, 195–96, 206, 208

Simpson, Percy, 16, 198

Sincklo, 7, 25, 195

"Singing-Man of Windsor," 89n

Sir John Falstaff, 173

Sir Thomas More: Shakespeare's hand in (Hand D), 5, 49n, 182, 189, 199, 200, 207; Munday's hand in, 188–89; Hand C in, 188–89

Smethwick, John, 175

Smith, John Hazel, 195–201

Songs, 61, 75n

Sound effects, offstage, 19

Spanish Tragedy, The, 48

Speech prefixes: in Quarto 6–8; in Folio, 9, 15, 20, 32–36; and Folio column, 55; spelled out to expand copy, 65, 67, 101–2, 108; setting of, 80; treatment of, by Compositor B, 95, 111, 117–18; treatment of, by scribe, 166; inconsistent, in *2 Henry IV*, 200

INDEX

Stage directions: in Quarto, 6–7 20, 29–32, 197f; in Folio, 9–15 *passim*, 19f, 29–32, 91; supplied by scribe, 21ff, 165–66; omitted, 24; permissive, 26, 44; placement of, in manuscripts, 27, 58, 188–90, 199–200; setting of, 31, 58, 67, 75, 78, 107, 204; and casting off, 53; setting of, by Compositor B, 90, 95, 98n, 103, 202; and aesthetic considerations, 109f; and Hand D, 200. *See also* Blank lines; Entrances; Exits; *and under* Compositors; Folio edition of 1623; Quarto edition of 1600; Scribe, of transcript used for Folio text of *2 Henry IV*, *and entries for individual compositors and scenes*

Staging, *see* Entrances; Stage Directions; *and entries for individual scenes*

Stationers' Company, 171

Stationers' Register, 4

Supernumeraries, 19, 48

Taming of the Shrew, The, 44

Tempest, The, 27, 58–59, 61, 75, 85, 114, 152n

Theobald, Lewis, 181

Thomas of Woodstock, 189–90, 200

Timon of Athens, 202, 205

Tiring-house, 29, 44

Title page, display, 76

Titus Andronicus, 114, 143, 151n

Troilus and Cressida, 207

Turn-down, *see* Turn-overs

Turn-overs: used to compress copy, 61, 80f; treatment of, by Compositor B, 75, 118; treatment of, by Compositor A, 117; in *2 Henry VI*, 118; and identifying compositors, 200; and changes in copy, 203

Turn-up, *see* Turn-overs

Twelfth Night, 113, 175

Two Noble Kinsmen, 186

Types, distinctive, 51

Waist lines, 105, 107, 151–54

Walker, Alice, 10–12, 14, 37f, 51, 160, 176–77, 195, 196, 203, 208

White lines, *see* Blank lines

Whore's son, *see* Break-line; Widow

Widow, 57, 115. *See also* Break-line

Williams, George Walton, 15n, 176–77

Wilson, Dover, 45n, 127, 169, 195f, 200, 204, 207; principle of, for editing, 3f, 15, 179

Winter's Tale, The, 58, 73–74, 151n, 175. *See also under* Miscalculation in casting off

OHIO UNIVERSITY LIBRARY

Please return this book